Persecution and Cosmic Conflict

Persecution and Cosmic Conflict

The Biblical-Theological Reading of Genesis in Galatians

JOSHUA CALEB HUTCHENS

Foreword by Thomas R. Schreiner

WIPF & STOCK · Eugene, Oregon

PERSECUTION AND COSMIC CONFLICT
The Biblical-Theological Reading of Genesis in Galatians

Copyright © 2024 Joshua Caleb Hutchens. All rights reserved. Except for brief quotations in critical publications or reviews, no part of this book may be reproduced in any manner without prior written permission from the publisher. Write: Permissions, Wipf and Stock Publishers, 199 W. 8th Ave., Suite 3, Eugene, OR 97401.

Wipf & Stock
An Imprint of Wipf and Stock Publishers
199 W. 8th Ave., Suite 3
Eugene, OR 97401

www.wipfandstock.com

PAPERBACK ISBN: 979-8-3852-0347-5
HARDCOVER ISBN: 979-8-3852-0348-2
EBOOK ISBN: 979-8-3852-0349-9

Unless otherwise noted, all translations of Scripture are the author's translations. The Christian Standard Bible. Copyright © 2017 by Holman Bible Publishers. Used by permission. Christian Standard Bible®, and CSB® are federally registered trademarks of Holman Bible Publishers, all rights reserved.

To Stacy Leigh, my bride

If there is anything in us, it is not our own; it is a gift of God.... Thus my learning is not my own; it belongs to the unlearned and is the debt I owe them.

—Martin Luther, *Lectures on Galatians (1519)*

Table of Contents

List of Tables ix
Foreword by Thomas R. Schreiner xi
Acknowledgments xiii
Abbreviations xv

1. Introduction 1
2. Cosmic Conflict in Galatians 29
3. Cosmic Conflict in Earlier Scripture 54
4. Cosmic Conflict in Early Judaism 80
5. Persecution in Galatians 112
6. Cosmic Conflict Manifested as Persecution in Galatians 143
7. Conclusion 176

Bibliography 183
Ancient Documents Index 211

List of Tables

1. צחק in the MT 157
2. שׂחק in the MT 157
3. Παίζω in the LXX 158
4. Παίζω + μετά in Greek Literature 159

Foreword

THE LETTER TO THE Galatians has been studied, meditated upon, and even fought over in the history of interpretation. Since the time of Martin Luther in particular, division over the proper interpretation of the letter ensued. In the early days of historical critical study, some hoped that questions would be settled through objective interpretation. From our perspective, such confidence seems amusing and amazingly naïve. Historical critical interpreters haven't succeeded in bringing unanimity in terms of the meaning of the letter. This isn't to say that we haven't learned from historical critical study. Fascinating interpretations have been offered that have opened new windows into the world and meaning of Galatians. The project hasn't been entirely in vain. At the same time, evangelical interpreters are justified in saying that interpretation also reflects one's worldview, and too many interpreters have come to New Testament documents with an atheological or even atheistic stance that doesn't accord with the intention of the New Testament writings.

It is exciting to see, then, interpreters like Joshua Caleb Hutchens who have engaged in careful historical and exegetical study of Galatians. Along with this, however, Hutchens shares the presuppositions and the worldview of the biblical writers. Galatians isn't merely a historical artefact reflecting the culture and thought of the first century AD. It is, of course, a historical artefact, but it is more than that. The letter is also God's word and message to the church of Jesus Christ both in the first century and in every era until the end of time.

One might think that interpreters who see Galatians as a transcendent word might be destined to merely repeat the wisdom of previous generations, and such interpretations should not be scorned. C. S. Lewis warned us about the danger of chronological snobbery, and we are prone to fall into the error of the snobbish Athenians who were only content to hear and learn about something new (Acts 17:20–21). Still, Hutchens spies a theme in Galatians that has too often been ignored. The church suffered from persecution, from suffering. Remarkably, this theme hasn't been excavated sufficiently in Galatians, and I think readers will see from Hutchens's astute work that suffering plays an important role in our understanding of the letter. Hutchens also creatively and faithfully shows us that the suffering in Galatia took place on the canvas of cosmic conflict. A great battle was being waged since God had intervened in the world apocalyptically in Jesus Christ. The suffering the believers experienced represents the battle between cosmic forces.

Hutchens's work provides many fresh insights, and they come from asking new questions. But these questions don't mean that Hutchens has read his interpretation into Galatians. Rather, his questions provided him with a platform to understand the letter at a deeper level, and thus this study doesn't only represent thoughtful scholarship but also a message for the church, which is engaged in the same cosmic conflict experienced by the earliest Christians.

Thomas R. Schreiner
James Buchanan Harrison Professor of New Testament Interpretation
The Southern Baptist Theological Seminary

Acknowledgments

WHEN I WAS FOURTEEN years old, my youth pastor, Trad York, gave me a cassette tape that contained the sermon, "Doing Missions When Dying Is Gain" by John Piper. The message challenged my assumptions about the Christian life. Suffering, Piper proclaimed, is both the price of missions and the means of missionary advance. A few years later, I would read Piper's book, *Let the Nations Be Glad! The Supremacy of God in Missions* and be impacted again by his words in the chapter, "The Supremacy of God in Missions through Suffering."

This monograph began its life as my doctoral dissertation at The Southern Baptist Theological Seminary. My *doktorvater*, Tom Schreiner, has been an example of a scholar with a pastoral heart. His continued encouragement, even after graduation, enabled me to bring this work to publication. Alongside him, I thank God for the faculty of The Southern Baptist Theological Seminary who have been vital in shaping me as a person as well as a biblical theologian. I especially owe thanks to Robert Plummer and Jarvis Williams, who offered early feedback on this project. Jarvis Williams, in particular, encouraged me to continue my work on Galatians after I took a course with him on early Judaism. Daniel Gurtner helped me refine my thesis and my thinking about my chapter on early Judaism at a critical point. Michael Bird's external review of the project as a dissertation also gave me great confidence to pursue publication.

Several of my peers also contributed significantly to the development of this project, including Richard Blaylock, Mitch Chase, Trey Moss, Jones Ndzi, Johnson Pang, Aubrey Sequeira, Paul Sanchez, Chase Sears, and Andres Vera. Fellow Galatians enthusiast Chris Wehrle used his expertise to proofread and improve each chapter as I finished them, and by doing so he often saved me the embarrassment of making weak arguments or forgetting significant research.

Finally, I thank God for my family. My mom and dad encouraged both education and the pursuit of my calling into the gospel ministry. I am thankful for their loving example and the countless sacrifices they have made for my sister, Jessi, and me. My bride, Stacy Leigh, has endured much during the course of my studies and pursuit of God's calling on my life, but she has always encouraged me to press on, believing (wrongly, since love is blind) that I possess exceptional brilliance. God gave me the perfect helper for the work to which he has called us. She always serves as my first editor, but more importantly she serves as my partner and fellow soldier in God's mission. I pray that the sacrifices we have made as a family will only serve to magnify the glories of the gospel in the eyes of our children: Haylee, Jude, Taylah, J. J., and Abraham.

Most importantly, I thank the Lord Jesus Christ for the innumerable and immense gifts that he has given me. *Soli Deo gloria.*

Joshua Caleb Hutchens
Zomba, Malawi
December 2023

Abbreviations

AB	Anchor Bible
ABD	*Anchor Bible Dictionary*. Edited by David Noel Freedman. 6 vols. New York: Doubleday, 1992.
ABRL	Anchor Bible Reference Library
AcBib	Academia Biblica
AGJU	Arbeiten zur Geschichte des antiken Judentums und des Urchristentums
ANTC	Abingdon New Testament Commentaries
ApOTC	Apollos Old Testament Commentary
ATANT	Abhandlungen zur Theologie des Alten und Neuen Testaments
BECNT	Baker Exegetical Commentary on the New Testament
BEHEH	Bibliothèque de l'École des hautes études: Sciences historiques et philologiques
BBR	*Bulletin for Biblical Research*
BDAG	Bauer, Walter, et al., eds. *Greek-English Lexicon of the New Testament and Other Early Christian Literature*. 3rd ed. Chicago: University of Chicago Press, 2000.
BDF	Blass, Friedrich, et al. *A Greek Grammar of the New Testament and Other Early Christian Literature*. Chicago: University of Chicago Press, 1961.
BHGNT	Baylor Handbook on the Greek New Testament
BibInt	*Biblical Interpretation*
BJRL	*Bulletin of the John Rylands University Library of Manchester*
BN	*Biblische Notizen*
BZ	*Biblische Zeitschrift*

BZAW		Beihefte zur Zeitschrift für die alttestamentliche Wissenschaft
BZNW		Beihefte zur Zeitschrift für die neutestamentliche Wissenschaft
CBC		Cambridge Bible Commentary
CBQ		*Catholic Biblical Quarterly*
CBR		*Currents in Biblical Research*
CEJL		Commentaries on Early Jewish Literature
ConBOT		Coniectanea Biblica: Old Testament Series
CSCO		Corpus scriptorium christianorum orientalium
CTJ		*Calvin Theological Journal*
DSD		*Dead Sea Discoveries*
EBib		Etudes bibliques
EJL		Early Judaism and Its Literature
ETL		*Ephemerides Theologicae Lovanienses*
ETR		*Études théologiques et religieuse*
EvQ		*Evangelical Quarterly*
ExAud		*Ex Auditu*
FAT		Forschungen zum Alten Testament
FRLANT		Forschungen zur Religion und Literatur des Alten und Neuen Testaments
FO		*Folia Orientalia*
FoiVie		*Foi et Vie*
FOTL		Forms of Old Testament Literature
GTJ		*Grace Theological Journal*
HALOT		Koehler, Ludwig, et al. *The Hebrew and Aramaic Lexicon of the Old Testament*. Translated and edited under the supervision of Mervyn E. J. Richardson. 4 vols. Leiden: Brill, 1994–99.
HBM		Hebrew Bible Monographs
HBS		Herders biblischen Studien
HSM		Harvard Semitic Monographs
HThKAT		Herders Theologischer Kommentar zum Alten Testament
HThKNT		Herders Theologischer Kommentar zum Neuen Testament
HTR		*Harvard Theological Review*
HUCA		*Hebrew Union College Annual*

ICC	International Critical Commentary
IDBSup	*The Interpreter's Dictionary of the Bible: Supplementary Volume*. Edited by Keith Crim. Nashville: Abingdon, 1976.
Int	*Interpretation*
IOS	*Israel Oriental Society*
JAAR	*Journal of the American Academy of Religion*
JBL	*Journal of Biblical Literature*
JBQ	*Jewish Bible Quarterly*
JECS	*Journal of Early Christian Studies*
JETS	*Journal of the Evangelical Theological Society*
JJS	*Journal of Jewish Studies*
JR	*Journal of Religion*
JRS	*Journal of Roman Studies*
JSHRZ	Jüdische Schriften aus hellenistisch-römischer Zeit
JSJ	*Journal for the Study of Judaism in the Persian, Hellenistic and Roman Period*
JSJSup	Journal for the Study of Judaism in the Persian, Hellenistic and Roman Period Supplement Series
JSNT	*Journal for the Study of the New Testament*
JSNTSup	Journal for the Study of the New Testament Supplement Series
JSOT	*Journal for the Study of the Old Testament*
JSOTSup	Journal for the Study of the Old Testament Supplement Series
JSP	*Journal for the Study of the Pseudepigrapha*
JSPSup	Journal for the Study of the Pseudepigrapha Supplement Series
JTC	*Journal for Theology and the Church*
JTI	*Journal of Theological Interpretation*
JTS	*Journal of Theological Studies*
KEK	Kritisch-exegetischer Kommentar über das Neue Testament
L&N	Louw, Johannes P., and Eugene A. Nida, eds. *Greek-English Lexicon of the New Testament: Based on Semantic Domains*. 2nd ed. New York: United Bible Societies, 1989.
LEH	Lust, Johan, et al., eds. *Greek-English Lexicon of the Septuagint*. Rev. ed. Stuttgart: Deutsche Bibelgesellschaft, 2003.

LNTS	Library of New Testament Studies
LS	Lewis, Charleton T., and Charles Short, eds. *A Latin Dictionary*. Oxford: Clarendon, 1879.
LSJ	Liddell, Henry George, et al. *A Greek-English Lexicon*. 9th ed. Oxford: Clarendon, 1996.
LSTS	Library of Second Temple Studies
MNTC	Moffat New Testament Commentary
ModTh	*Modern Theology*
NA28	*Novum Testamentum Graece*, Nestle-Aland, 28th ed.
NAC	New American Commentary
NCBC	New Cambridge Bible Commentary
NEchtB	Neue Echter Bibel
Neot	*Neotestamentica*
NIBC	New International Biblical Commentary
NICNT	New International Commentary on the New Testament
NICOT	New International Commentary on the Old Testament
NIGTC	New International Greek Testament Commentary
NIVAC	NIV Application Commentary
NovT	*Novum Testamentum*
NovTSup	Supplements to Novum Testamentum
NSBT	New Studies in Biblical Theology
NTL	New Testament Library
NTS	*New Testament Studies*
OBT	Overtures to Biblical Theology
OTL	Old Testament Library
OtSt	Oudtestamentische Studiën
PNTC	Pillar New Testament Commentary
PRSt	*Perspectives in Religious Studies*
RB	*Revue biblique*
RevQ	*Revue de Qumran*
RGG	*Die Religion in Geschichte und Gegenwart*
RHPR	*Revue d'histoire et de philosophie religieuses*
RTR	*The Reformed Theological Review*
SBJT	*Southern Baptist Journal of Theology*
SBLDS	Society of Biblical Literature Dissertation Series

SBT	Studies in Biblical Theology
ScEs	*Science et esprit*
SEÅ	*Svensk exegetisk årsbok*
SJLA	Studies in Judaism in Late Antiquity
SJOT	*Scandinavian Journal of Theology*
SJT	*Scottish Journal of Theology*
SNTSMS	Society of New Testament Studies Monograph Series
SSN	Studia semitica neerlandica
ST	*Studia theologica*
StBibLit	Studies in Biblical Literature
STDJ	Studies on the Texts of the Desert of Judah
StudOr	Studia Orientalia
SUNT	Studien zum Umwelt des Neuen Testaments
SVTP	Studia in veteris testamenti pseudepigrapha
SymS	Symposium Series
TDNT	*Theological Dictionary of the New Testament*. Edited by Gerhard Kittel and Gerhard Friedrich. Translated by Geoffrey W. Bromiley. 10 vols. Grand Rapids: Eerdmans, 1964–76.
THKNT	Theologischer Handkommentar zum Neuen Testament
TJ	*Trinity Journal*
TNTC	Tyndale New Testament Commentaries
TOTC	Tyndale Old Testament Commentaries
TynBul	*Tyndale Bulletin*
USQR	*Union Seminary Quarterly Review*
VT	*Vetus Testamentum*
VTSup	Supplements to Vetus Testamentum
WBC	Word Biblical Commentary
WTJ	*Westminster Theological Journal*
WUNT	Wissenschaftliche Untersuchungen zum Neuen Testament
ZAW	*Zeitschrift für die alttestamentliche Wissenschaft*
ZECNT	Zondervan Exegetical Commentary on the New Testament
ZNW	*Zeitschrift für die neutestamentliche Wissenschaft*
ZTK	*Zeitschrift für Theologie und Kirche*

1

Introduction

IN 1984, NORWEGIAN SCHOLAR Ernst Baasland pointed to persecution as a "neglected feature" in Galatians.[1] Since the publication of Baasland's article, there has been some movement toward recovering the theme as a vital part of the letter. The central question concerning persecution in Galatians is this: how does that theme fit within the book's theology? This monograph argues that persecution manifests the cosmic conflict between God and the present evil age. By contrast, Baasland himself contends that Paul is challenging the traditional Jewish concept of the "cursed man."[2] Baasland claims that Paul's opponents would have pointed to his suffering as evidence that he was under the curse of the law, but Paul turns this traditional understanding on its head.[3] The monographs of Basil S. Davis and Todd A. Wilson have sought to build on Baasland's explanation by further examining the curse theme in Galatians.[4] A second perspective on the theme comes from John Muddiman, who focuses less on theology and more on group conflict from a sociological point of view.[5] The most recent perspective on the theme comes from John Anthony Dunne in his published doctoral thesis.[6] Dunne builds on

---

1. Baasland, "Persecution," 135–50.
2. Baasland, "Persecution," 135.
3. Baasland, "Persecution."
4. Davis, *Christ as Devotio*; Wilson, *Curse of the Law*. For a third examination of curse that focuses less on the connection to persecution, see Morland, *The Rhetoric of Curse*.
5. Muddiman, "Anatomy of Galatians," 257–70.
6. Dunne, *Persecution and Participation*

the earlier work of Mathew S. Harmon on Isaianic echoes in Galatians.[7] Dunne claims that Paul presents Jesus as the Isaianic servant from Isa 53, presents himself as the Isaianic servant from Isa 49, and calls the Galatian churches to imitate him as suffering servants.[8] To summarize, besides the position of minimizing or neglecting the theme altogether, three perspectives of the persecution theme in Galatians have been proposed: (1) Paul is confronting the cursed man tradition. (2) Paul is participating in group power dynamics. (3) Paul is echoing the Isaianic suffering servant.

Despite the increase of attention since Baasland's article, several questions remain about the theme of persecution in Galatians: Are these perspectives sufficient to explain all the data in Galatians? Furthermore, even if these three perspectives possess a certain amount of exegetical merit, could there be a different category that has greater explanatory power of the evidence while possibly encompassing many other perspectives? Finally, since all three of these perspectives rely either on mirror-reading or the identification of echoes, could there be a simpler explanation that emerges from a close reading of the text of Galatians itself? This monograph will address these questions.

COSMIC CONFLICT AND GALATIANS

Paul Middleton has argued that Christians in the second and third centuries exhibited the phenomenon of "radical martyrdom" or enthusiasm for a martyr's death. Radical martyrdom made sense theologically because they saw their death as contributing to the final outcome of a cosmic conflict between God and Satan.[9] He finds the roots of this martyrology in the Israelite holy war tradition that was then transformed by apocalyptic literature, especially Daniel and 2 Maccabees.[10] Middleton demonstrates how the Pauline corpus, Mark, and Revelation developed the apocalyptic theme of cosmic conflict and connected it with Christian suffering.[11]

---

7. Harmon, *She Must and Shall Go Free*.
8. Dunne, *Persecution and Participation*, 128–92.
9. Middleton, *Radical Martyrdom*, 6.
10. Middleton, *Radical Martyrdom*, 128–34.
11. Middleton, *Radical Martyrdom*, 135–71.

While the term "cosmic conflict" has appeared in scholarship on both the Gospels[12] and Revelation,[13] Middleton seems to pioneer its use in Pauline studies.[14] Nonetheless, cosmic conflict as a concept has repeatedly been identified by apocalyptic interpreters of Paul. For example, J. Christiaan Beker calls dualism a basic component of the Jewish apocalyptic worldview.[15] According to Beker, Paul believes that the powers of the future and of life have invaded the present age, which is dominated by the forces of evil, and this apocalyptic invasion has instituted a battle between these opposing forces.[16] Since the church is at the center of God's redemptive plan, by necessity it experiences suffering due to the cosmic battle.[17]

J. Louis Martyn identifies this conflict in Gal 5:17 and labels it as warfare.[18] Elsewhere Martyn writes that in Galatians Paul shows that the crucifixion of Christ and the invasion of the Spirit instituted a "war of liberation from the powers of the present evil age."[19] Unlike Middleton who specifically sees cosmic conflict as a holy war between God and a personal being called Satan, Martyn and other apocalyptic interpreters of Galatians view the cosmic conflict more generally as between God and the powers of this age. This more generalized concept of cosmic conflict can be found throughout Galatians but is especially evident in the following key texts: 1:4; 4:3–5, 8–11; 5:17; 6:14–15. Rather than invalidating Middleton's argument that Paul related Christian suffering to a cosmic conflict, a more generalized understanding of the concept affirms his thesis on the development of early Christian martyrology. This monograph, then, will build on Middleton's work by arguing the following: In Galatians, persecution manifests the cosmic conflict between God and the present evil age.

12. Mackey, "Light Overcomes the Darkness."

13. Abir, *Cosmic Conflict of the Church*; Grabiner, *Revelation's Hymns*.

14. For one minor exception to this statement, see Fast, "Pauline Concept of Cosmic Conflict." Two Adventist scholars have also utilized the terminology: Fowler, *Kampf im Kosmos*; Magyarosi, *Holy War and Cosmic Conflict*. Beyond this, "cosmic conflict" often appears in non-scholarly works as a synonymn for spiritual warfare. It should be noted, however, that similar terms have been used by others, e.g., "cosmic battle" (Pobee, *Persecution and Martyrdom*, 45–46).

15. Beker, *Paul's Apocalyptic Gospel*, 30.

16. Beker, *Paul's Apocalyptic Gospel*, 41.

17. Beker, *Paul's Apocalyptic Gospel*.

18. Martyn, "Daily Life of the Church," 257–60.

19. Martyn, "Apocalyptic Gospel," 258.

A defense of this thesis will require answering three sets of questions: First, historical questions: What do Paul's references to persecution in Galatians indicate about the circumstances of these churches? Who was being persecuted or was vulnerable to persecution? Who were the persecutors? What types of persecution were occurring or were likely to occur?

Second, contextual questions: Does cosmic conflict in Galatians parallel a theme found in other Jewish texts—both Israel's Scriptures and texts from the Second Temple period?[20] To what degree do these texts speak as a unity about the theme? How do they differ? How does Paul operate within this intellectual context? How does Paul understand earlier Scripture as instructive in the Galatian situation?

Third, theological questions: How do the references to persecution in Galatians fit within the larger framework of cosmic conflict? How does Paul utilize this theological understanding of persecution to execute his goals in writing the letter? How does it relate to important themes in the letter such as gospel, cross, faith, law, etc.?

The second set of questions especially will be decisive in proving my thesis. Not only does Paul interpret Scripture for the Galatians in his letter, but even more importantly, Paul interprets the situation in Galatia *through Scripture*. Galatians 4:29 is at the center of Paul's biblical-theological reinterpretation of the conflict he has with his opponents, where he will identify his opponents with Ishmael in Gen 21:9. Paul's understanding of Genesis guides his understanding of Galatia.

Such an examination may contribute both to the study of Galatians and to the broader fields of Pauline and biblical theology. Galatians, along with Romans, has stood at the epicenter of the seismic shifts unleashed in the field of Pauline studies after the Holocaust, especially in relation to the work of E. P. Sanders.[21] Authors have suggested numerous approaches to Galatians based on divergent understandings of Paul's relation to Judaism as well as divergent reconstructions of a grand thematic narrative supposedly undergirding the text.[22] Because it involves the relation of Paul and his churches to their Jewish and Greco-Roman communities, the study of persecution can address the twin issues that

---

20. Harmon, *She Must and Shall Go Free*, 30. For an explanation of "thematic parallels," see below in the section titled "Methodology."

21. Sanders, *Paul and Palestinian Judaism*.

22. See Das, *Paul and the Stories of Israel*.

occupy so much of Pauline studies today: Paul's relation to Judaism and his relation to Rome.

VIEWPOINTS ON PERSECUTION IN GALATIANS

The topics of persecution and cosmic conflict in Galatians intersect with three important areas of research that will be examined below: (1) Persecution and Pauline Theology Generally, (2) The Apocalyptic Paul, and (3) Persecution in Galatians.

Persecution and Pauline Theology Generally

Several scholars have contributed significant monographs and articles that have sought to explain Paul's theology of suffering and persecution generally in Paul's letters.

Merrill Proudfoot (1964). Proudfoot outlines his understanding in two brief chapters of his 1964 work on Paul and suffering. Proudfoot claims, primarily on the basis of Romans and 2 Corinthians, that in the experiences of suffering and comfort believers participate in the death and resurrection of Christ and have fellowship with one another.[23] Suffering exists because of the fallen state of creation, but God in his love gives the believer security in suffering.[24] He then contrasts Paul's understanding of suffering with three competing views. First, citing Epictetus, he critiques those who reject suffering outright.[25] Second, turning to Rabbi Akiba, Proudfoot rejects those who would view suffering as divine retribution.[26] Finally, he argues against Ignatius's practice of relishing suffering.[27] In conclusion, Proudfoot cites Paul's main contribution to a Christian theology of persecution as his insight into "the community of suffering," that is the sharing of suffering between Christ, apostle, and believers.[28] Proudfoot offers an insightful observation on Paul's theology and helpfully

---

23. Proudfoot, *Suffering*, 15–28.
24. Proudfoot, *Suffering*, 29–40.
25. Proudfoot, *Suffering*, 43–82.
26. Proudfoot, *Suffering*, 83–123.
27. Proudfoot, *Suffering*, 123–73.
28. Proudfoot, *Suffering*, 175.

compares Paul with other important thinkers, but his representation of Paul's theology is somewhat one-dimensional. This shortcoming is due to his focus on Romans and 2 Corinthians, which causes him to downplay the contribution of other letters and, most relevant for this project, ignore Galatians completely.[29]

Robert Tannehill (1967). Tannehill, strongly influenced by Käsemann, discusses the death of Christ in three stages: (1) as a past event, (2) as a present experience, and (3) as a reference for the future resurrection.[30] In part one on Christ's death as a past event, Tannehill discusses several texts, including Gal 2:19-20; 5:24-25; and 6:14-15.[31] His survey of these texts demonstrates that the past event of Christ's death is related to two opposing "dominions or aeons" and "indicates release from one and transfer to another."[32] When Tannehill turns to the present experience of the cross in suffering, he examines texts from Romans, 2 Corinthians, Philippians, and 1 Thessalonians.[33] He concludes that Christians have been transferred from the old age into the new, but "the old world has not yet accepted God's judgment of it and claim upon it, and the Christian is still bound to this old world through his present body."[34] By dying with Christ in suffering, the Christian continually affirms his or her break with the old dominion so that "dying with Christ is not only the basis of the new dominion but remains a present reality within it."[35] Tannehill helpfully examines suffering within the context of Paul's eschatology, but while he examines Galatians for the past significance of Christ's death, he ignores the letter when he turns to the present suffering of the believer.

Morna D. Hooker (1981). Hooker works on the basis of her earlier articles about "interchange" and participation in redemption.[36] To examine the relationship between participation with Christ and suffering, Hooker

---

29. Proudfoot, *Suffering*, 26-27. He mentions Gal 4:13 and 6:17 only in passing.
30. Tannehill, *Dying and Rising with Christ*, 6.
31. Tannehill, *Dying and Rising with Christ*, 55-64.
32. Tannehill, *Dying and Rising with Christ*, 7.
33. Tannehill, *Dying and Rising with Christ*, 84-129.
34. Tannehill, *Dying and Rising with Christ*, 127.
35. Tannehill, *Dying and Rising with Christ*, 127.
36. Hooker, "Interchange in Christ," 349-61; Hooker, "Interchange and Atonement," 462-81.

explores passages from Romans, 2 Corinthians, Philippians, Colossians, and 1 Thessalonians.³⁷ In conclusion, she posits, "The tendency to stress the belief that Christ's death was a substitute for ours to the exclusion of the Pauline conviction that Christians must participate in the suffering of Christ is perhaps a very early one."³⁸ Paul insists that "the Christian life was a continuous process of self-identification with Christ."³⁹ Those who follow the path of faith in the cross "must be prepared to share the humiliation and suffering that it brings, if they wish to experience also the glory that God gives."⁴⁰ Hooker offers a strong defense of participation as an explanation for Christian suffering, but she does not examine Galatians.

Karl Theodor Kleinknecht (1984). Kleinknecht seeks to demonstrate that the theme of the suffering righteous forms the "*dominierenden* Hintergrund" of Paul's theology of suffering.⁴¹ He begins his work by surveying the theme in the OT and Jewish literature.⁴² The background of Paul's thought then is formed from Jewish thought generally as well as the Jesus traditions available to Paul.⁴³ When Kleinknecht turns toward Paul's reception of the tradition, he examines five Pauline letters: Romans, 1 Corinthians, 2 Corinthians, Philippians, and 1 Thessalonians.⁴⁴ Kleinknecht's study does demonstrate significant continuity between Paul's thought and the theme of the suffering righteous, but since he does not examine Galatians, work remains to be done.

John S. Pobee (1985). Pobee has written the only monograph dedicated to comprehensively reconstructing Paul's theology of persecution and martyrdom. Pobee's second chapter is vital to his approach. In it, he attempts to reconstruct a Jewish theology of martyrdom. According to Pobee, the main component for a Jewish theology of martyrdom was the Maccabean

---

37. Hooker, "Interchange and Suffering," 70–83.
38. Hooker, "Interchange and Suffering," 82.
39. Hooker, "Interchange and Suffering."
40. Hooker, "Interchange and Suffering," 83.
41. Kleinknecht, *Leidende Gerechtfertigte*, 365. Italics original.
42. Kleinknecht, *Leidende Gerechtfertigte*, 19–166.
43. Kleinknecht, *Leidende Gerechtfertigte*, 167–92.
44. Kleinknecht, *Leidende Gerechtfertigte*, 193–364.

martyr tradition, especially as found in 2 and 4 Maccabees.[45] Pobee outlines four theodicies of martyrdom found primarily in relation to the Maccabean martyrs but also in consultation with other Jewish texts: (1) Martyrdom was chastisement for the nation's sins (2 Macc 6:12–16). (2) Martyrdom atoned for the nation's sins (Isa 53:5, 10; Dan 11:35; 4 Macc 17:22). (3) Martyrdom was part of God's eschatological action, especially in preparation for the Messiah (Dan 8:23; 9:24). (4) Martyrdom was an earthly manifestation of cosmic battle between angelic creatures (Dan 3, 6; Ascen. Isa.).[46] Pobee then argues that Paul presents Jesus's death as the death of a martyr. Then through this martyr theology, Paul is able to transform the shame of the cross into "a thing of glory."[47] From here, Pobee moves toward an examination of Paul's apostolic suffering. Persecution demonstrated Paul's zeal and authenticated his apostolic ministry. It also showed his part in the cosmic battle between the forces of God and of Satan.[48] Paul's churches were to imitate Paul's zeal and endure persecution as a manifestation of the cosmic battle that precedes the return of Christ.[49] Pobee's work is the most extensive on the topic, but it possesses a methodological weakness. He identifies a Jewish martyr theology based on a limited number of Jewish texts, and then he looks for his reconstruction of martyr theology in Paul. Not surprisingly, he finds what he is looking for. Jewish martyr theology becomes for Pobee the central metaphor for atonement in Paul.[50] Because he sees such strong continuity between Paul and Jewish martyr theology, he fails to adequately contrast Christian persecution and martyrdom with the Maccabean martyrs. Finally, like others, Pobee's work largely ignores the contribution of Galatians to Paul's theology of martyrdom and persecution. Pobee briefly cites 1:4 and 2:20 as evidence of Christ's self-giving martyr's death.[51] Later, he mentions 6:17 in relation to Paul's apostolic suffering, observing that Paul's scars indicate his imitation of Christ, but he does not attempt to relate 6:17 to the larger message of the letter.[52]

---

45. Pobee, *Persecution and Martyrdom*, 24–33.
46. Pobee, *Persecution and Martyrdom*, 34–46.
47. Pobee, *Persecution and Martyrdom*, 72.
48. Pobee, *Persecution and Martyrdom*, 106.
49. Pobee, *Persecution and Martyrdom*, 107–18.
50. For a more nuanced position, see Williams, *Christ Died for Our Sins*.
51. Pobee, *Persecution and Martyrdom*, 49.
52. Pobee, *Persecution and Martyrdom*, 95–96.

Barry Smith (2002). Smith offers seven Pauline explanations for the suffering of the righteous: (1) persecution, (2) remedial discipline, (3) salvation-historical necessity, (4) probation or testing, (5) the effect of Adam's sin, (6) instruction, and (7) participation in Christ's suffering.[53] Smith investigates a Second Temple background for each of these explanations, and then he compares this background with passages from Paul. He briefly examines 3:3–4 to demonstrate that Paul did not consider reception of the Spirit incompatible with persecution, but otherwise he does not engage Galatians.[54]

Paul Middleton (2006). As has already been introduced, the innovation of Middleton is to view an apocalyptic cosmic conflict as the key element of early Christian martyrology that eventually led to the phenomenon of radical martyrdom in the second and third centuries. In making this argument, Middleton rejects the explanation that Christian martyrology arose from the Greco-Roman Noble Death tradition, and he modifies the theory that Christian martyrology arose from the Maccabean tradition in Judaism.[55] The biggest influence on later Christian martyrology was apocalyptic eschatology, which itself emerged from the holy war tradition of ancient Israel.[56] While Paul himself did not advocate radical martyrdom, Middleton argues that he did develop "many of the theological concepts that enabled radical martyrology to develop."[57] Middleton's brief eleven page examination of Paul focuses on 2 Corinthians, Philippians, Colossians, 1–2 Thessalonians, and 2 Timothy.[58] While Middleton references Gal 1:4; 2:19; 4:12–15; and 6:17, he nowhere significantly engages Galatians to see how the book might contribute to or modify his argument about Pauline theology.

L. Ann Jervis (2007). Attempting to offer a theological interpretation of Scripture, Jervis probes Paul's response to suffering in hopes that "Paul's

53. Smith, *Paul's Seven Explanations*.
54. Smith, *Paul's Seven Explanations*, 40.
55. Middleton, *Radical Martyrdom*, 110–23. In another short contribution on the subject, Middleton emphasizes imitation of Christ in Christian suffering ("'Dying We Live,'" 82–93).
56. Middleton, *Radical Martyrdom*, 128–34.
57. Middleton, *Radical Martyrdom*, 146.
58. Middleton, *Radical Martyrdom*, 136–46.

response might also be ours."[59] She does this by analyzing three of Paul's letters: 1 Thessalonians, Philippians, and Romans. For Jervis, each of these three letters makes a distinctive contribution to Paul's theology of suffering. Of 1 Thessalonians, she writes that Paul "understands suffering to be part of the warp and woof of the gospel, that acceptance of the gospel is at the same time acceptance of suffering."[60] While Paul accepts suffering in 1 Thessalonians, in Philippians he values suffering as participation in Christ's own suffering.[61] Finally, Romans does not neatly divide the suffering of believers and unbelievers but focuses on "the common tribulations all humanity knows" because of sin in the world.[62] Jervis examines suffering broadly and generally, and so she is unable to focus on the particular theological purpose of persecution. Furthermore, she does not choose to examine Galatians.[63]

James L. Kelhoffer (2010). Kelhoffer's study is broader than the previously cited ones. He goes beyond Paul to cover Matthew, Mark, Luke-Acts, John, 1 Peter, Hebrews, and Revelation. In examining persecution, Kelhoffer applies the work of sociologist Pierre Bourdieu on cultural, social, economic, and symbolic capital.[64] He argues that "in much of the NT withstanding persecution constitutes a form of cultural capital that can be translated into social capital, namely standing, or even a position of leadership, within the church community."[65] His work, therefore, focuses on the social effects of the theology of the NT. In his section on Paul, Kelhoffer discusses 1:13–14 and claims that Paul's former status as persecutor demonstrates "his independent apostolic status."[66] Then turning to Gal 4–6, Kelhoffer writes that Paul's "suffering renders unnecessary any questions about his authority."[67] In the course of his monograph, however, Kelhoffer only briefly mentions Galatians. Nonetheless, his focus

---

59. Jervis, *At the Heart*, 2–5.
60. Jervis, *At the Heart*, 15.
61. Jervis, *At the Heart*, 39, 42.
62. Jervis, *At the Heart*, 77, 130.
63. Jervis has written an earlier commentary on Galatians for general readership, but it does not give any significant focus on persecution (see Jervis, *Galatians*).
64. Kelhoffer, *Persecution, Persuasion, and Power*, 183–98.
65. Kelhoffer, *Persecution, Persuasion, and Power*, 11.
66. Kelhoffer, *Persecution, Persuasion, and Power*, 48.
67. Kelhoffer, *Persecution, Persuasion, and Power*, 50–51.

on the social function of persecution is complimentary to the theological focus of the present project.

Conclusion. These monographs and articles represent a variety of helpful perspectives on the issue of persecution in Paul's theology, but, in general, they fail to pay proper attention to the contribution of Galatians.

The Apocalyptic Paul

Since cosmic conflict is an element of an apocalyptic worldview, the present project is indebted to the apocalyptic reading of Paul. This section reviews the history of this school of interpretation and offers points of continuity and discontinuity between the present project and the apocalyptic Paul.

Ernst Käsemann (1969) and J. Christiaan Beker (1980-94). The present dispensation of the apocalyptic school of interpretation can be traced to two victims of Nazi tyranny—Käsemann and Beker.[68] Käsemann famously writes that apocalyptic is "the mother of Christian theology."[69] By doing so, he rejects the reconstructions of his teacher Bultmann who found the root of Christian origins in Gnosticism and reconstructed theology around individual existential categories.[70] Beker follows Käsemann's lead but gives a more comprehensive account of Paul and apocalyptic. Beker claims that while the apocalyptic genre did not necessarily influence Paul directly he nonetheless shared an apocalyptic worldview built from components vital to that genre.[71] Beker notes four components: (1) the hope of God's self-vindication, (2) the expectation of God's universal reign, (3) a dualistic struggle between good and evil, and (4)

---

68. Schweitzer preceded both in arguing for apocalyptic thought in Paul but did not develop the proposal to the same degree as those who followed him (*Quest of the Historical Jesus*, 368–71).

69. Käsemann, "Primitive Christian Apocalyptic," 137.

70. For more on the rejection of Bultmann and transition to apocalyptic, see Oswalt, "Recent Studies," 289–90.

71. Note the differentiation between the apocalyptic literary genre and apocalyptic worldview or eschatology as a worldview influenced by but not confined to the apocalyptic genre. Additionally, apocalypticism refers to the ideology of certain religious movements. See Hanson, "Apocalypticism," 29–30.

the imminence of God's triumph.[72] Beker, however, does not read Galatians apocalyptically since it lacks significant focus on the future and does not give proper emphasis to Christ's resurrection.[73] Nevertheless, Beker does significantly connect Paul's theology to the issue of suffering. He writes that "apocalyptic is born out of a deep existential concern and is in many respects a theology of martyrdom."[74] Elsewhere he explains, "The central question that occupies the apocalypticist is how to overcome the discrepancy between what is and what should be."[75] Thus, for Beker, apocalyptic functions as a theodicy, that is a way of explaining suffering and coping with it. In particular, the dualistic struggle between good and evil explains why suffering is necessary for the church as it pursues its mission in the world.[76] Beker also advises Christians today to embrace an apocalyptic theodicy.[77]

J. Louis Martyn (1997) and Martinus C. de Boer (2011). While Beker rejected Galatians as apocalyptic, two other scholars have offered apocalyptic readings of the letter—Martyn and de Boer. Martyn argued for an apocalyptic reading of Galatians on the basis of "apocalyptic antinomies" or pairs of opposites present in the text (e.g., slave/free, law/promise, flesh/Spirit, etc.).[78] In one sense, Martyn sees apocalyptic antinomies as continuing the theology of "the Two Ways" present in Deuteronomy and Wisdom Literature, but antinomies are more than mere choices.[79] They are "the fundamental building blocks of the cosmos."[80] This present age and the age to come possess different sets of antinomies, which explains why the ages are "locked in combat with one another."[81] Martyn based much of his work on the research of de Boer. De Boer contends that two

---

72. Beker, *Paul's Apocalyptic Gospel*, 30–45; Beker, *Triumph of God*, 21–36. These four components were an expansion of Beker's earlier "three basic ideas" in apocalyptic (*Paul the Apostle*, 136).
73. Beker, *Paul the Apostle*, 58.
74. Beker, *Paul the Apostle*, 136.
75. Beker, *Paul's Apocalyptic Gospel*, 30.
76. Beker, *Paul the Apostle*, 41.
77. Beker, *Suffering and Hope*.
78. Martyn derives the term "antinomies" from Aristotle's τὰναντια in *Metaph.* 5.1018a ("Apocalyptic Antinomies," 413).
79. Martyn, "Apocalyptic Gospel," 247.
80. Martyn, "Apocalyptic Antinomies," 413.
81. Martyn, "Apocalyptic Antinomies," 420. See also Martyn, *Galatians*, 100.

tracks of apocalyptic exist: (1) cosmological and (2) forensic. Cosmological apocalyptic sources emphasize God's action to deliver the world from evil forces (e.g., 1 En. 1–36). Forensic apocalyptic, by contrast, stresses the need for humans to take responsibility for their sin and prepare for the end by submitting to the law (e.g., 4 Ezra; 2 Baruch). Both Martyn and de Boer then build their interpretation of Galatians on the foundation of de Boer's two tracks.[82] Paul's opponents promote a forensic apocalyptic that requires a "human movement into blessedness" characteristic of religion. Paul, on the other hand, proclaims a cosmological apocalyptic of "God's liberating invasion of the cosmos" in Christ.[83] While de Boer correctly identifies a difference in emphasis between various apocalyptic texts, he does not prove that these different emphases constitute opposing theological tracks, and thus Martyn and de Boer's conception of Paul's opponents is also flawed. Nonetheless, the comparison between Paul and apocalyptic texts helpfully highlights how Paul understands the work of Christ and the Spirit as God's invasive liberating action.

Even though cosmic conflict lies at the center of Martyn and de Boer's conception of apocalyptic in Galatians, neither adequately incorporates the theme of persecution into their reading. On the historical questions, both Martyn and de Boer see the persecutors in 4:29 as Paul's opponents pressuring the Galatian Christians to undergo circumcision.[84] Theologically, Martyn suggests that persecutors actively oppose God's redemptive action by propagating religion.[85] Furthermore, persecution serves as "the present epiphany of the crucifixion" and thus a sign of God's redemptive action.[86] Similarly, de Boer explains that the message of the cross causes offense because it is the end of human religion.[87] For both of them, persecution is the friction between God's invasive revelation and human religious attempts.

---

82. De Boer, *Defeat of Death*; de Boer, "Paul and Jewish Apocalyptic," 169–90. See Martyn, *Galatians*, 97–105; de Boer, *Galatians*, 31–35.

83. Martyn, "Apocalyptic Gospel," 255. The division between religion and revelation demonstrates the influence of Barth on Martyn and de Boer. See Barth, *Church Dogmatics*, 280–361.

84. Martyn, *Galatians*, 445, 561–62; de Boer, *Galatians*, 307.

85. Martyn, *Galatians*, 163, 445, 477, 562.

86. Martyn, *Galatians*, 569.

87. De Boer, *Galatians*, 324, 398–99.

John M. G. Barclay (1988, 2015) and Michael J. Gorman (2009-16). In addition to the standard apocalyptic readings of Martyn and de Boer, one might identify a "softer apocalyptic" in the work of scholars like Barclay and Gorman.[88] In his recent work on "gift," Barclay emphasizes what he calls "Pauline polarities" in Galatians.[89] He writes, "Paul's letter to the Galatians thus remaps reality with a cartography capable of blurring traditional categories by means of newly minted distinctions."[90] Barclay, however, rejects the attempts of Martyn and de Boer to avoid a forensic understanding of righteousness as well as the sharp discontinuity they propose between the Christ-event and salvation history.[91] Barclay does not give particular emphasis to the theme of persecution, but his nuanced approach to Galatians remains significant. Similar to Barclay, Gorman gives a more eclectic reading of Paul that nonetheless features the influence of apocalyptic. For example, he describes the cross as "an apocalyptic act of liberation."[92] Gorman emphasizes themes that he variously labels participation, cruciformity, and, even, theosis—all of which stress the conformity of the believer to the character of Christ.[93] Thus, he primarily interprets persecution as a means of becoming like Christ.[94]

Summary and critique. In summary, this reading of Paul serves an important role in the present project for two reasons.[95] First, the apocalyptic

---

88. Blackwell et al. describe two approaches to apocalyptic: (1) Eschatological Invasion, (2) Unveiled Fulfillment. "Unveiled Fulfillment" seeks to unify apocalyptic and salvation history (Blackwell et al., "Introduction," 3-21). The categories are helpful but should not be seen as absolute. Rather, the two approaches represent positions on a continuum. The adjective "softer" signifies degrees of difference between interpreters.

89. Barclay, *Paul and the Gift*, 337-38. See also Barclay, *Obeying the Truth*, 217.

90. Barclay, *Paul and the Gift*, 338.

91. Barclay, *Paul and the Gift*, 414.

92. Gorman, *Cruciformity*, 102.

93. See Gorman, *Cruciformity*; Gorman, *Inhabiting the Cruciform God*; Gorman, *Becoming the Gospel*; Gorman, "Apocalyptic New Covenant," 317-37.

94. E.g., Gorman, *Cruciformity*, 25.

95. Three other significant representatives of this school are Susan G. Eastman, Beverly Roberts Gaventa, and Douglas A. Campbell. Eastman has contributed to the study of Galatians. See Eastman, "Evil Eye," 69-87; Eastman, "'Cast Out the Slave Woman,'" 309-36; Eastman, *Recovering Paul's Mother Tongue*; Eastman, "Israel and the Mercy of God," 367-95. Gaventa's work has primarily focused on Romans, but she has written on Galatians as well. On the present topic, however, her work does not depart significantly from that of Martyn and de Boer, and so I have not discussed her work in detail.

scholars rightly highlight the theme of cosmic conflict in Galatians. Paul certainly does reflect what Beker called an "apocalyptic worldview."[96] Even so, it is not clear what is uniquely apocalyptic about an apocalyptic worldview. As noted above, Käsemann, working within a history of religions framework, advocated apocalyptic as an alternative to Bultmann's proposal that Gnosticism formed the basis of early Christian theology,[97] but many of those themes claimed as apocalyptic in character predate the apocalyptic genre and can be found even in the Torah. Most notably for this project, a theme of cosmic conflict can be discerned as early as Gen 3:15. While Paul shares certain "conceptual affinities" with the apocalyptic genre,[98] that genre shares those affinities with earlier texts. Rather it is the form and the function of those texts that are unique. Apocalyptic literature shares a unique form by presenting theological themes through dramatic literary features (e.g., visions, symbols, etc.) and shares a unique function by seeking to apply OT theology to contemporary crises.[99] By not recognizing apocalyptic literature's significant continuity with earlier OT texts, many apocalyptic scholars have misattributed cosmic conflict to the apocalyptic genre rather than to the broader family of early Jewish thought.[100] Nonetheless, although perhaps mislabeled, the apocalyptic reading essentially understands Paul's thought in Galatians correctly. As

---

See Gaventa, *From Darkness to Light*; Gaventa, "Galatians 1 and 2," 309–26; Gaventa, "Maternity of Paul," 189–201; Gaventa, *Our Mother Saint Paul*; Gaventa, "Singularity of the Gospel Revisited," 187–99. Campbell also has focused primarily on Romans but has written one article relevant to the topic. See Campbell, "Galatians 5.11," 325–47.

96. Or "apocalyptic eschatology" as apocalyptic scholar Collins has termed the phenomenon (*Apocalyptic Imagination*, 2).

97. Käsemann, "Primitive Christian Apocalyptic." Wright critiques the school as a poor reconstruction in the tradition of the History of Religions approach (*Paul and His Recent Interpreters*, 145–47).

98. De Boer, "Paul and Jewish Apocalyptic," 173.

99. For an explanation of apocalyptic form and function, see Collins, *Handbook of Apocalyptic Literature*, 123–252. In his earlier work, Collins highlights these two aspects as the primary ways Christianity was influenced by apocalyptic. He writes that the apocalypses gave Christianity "the *expressive* language of poetry" (i.e., form) and "a pragmatic aspect" (i.e., function. Collins, *Apocalyptic Imagination*, 214–15).

100. This issue will be addressed in chs. 3–4. Wright makes a similar critique of apocalyptic scholars' view of two ages (*Paul and His Recent Interpreters*, 157–60). The issue may also be seen as an example of how apocalyptic interpreters generally claim too sharp a discontinuity between Paul and the OT. For a critique of this aspect of the apocalyptic school, see Hays, "Apocalyptic *Poiēsis*," 200–219. For a broad and appreciative critique of the movement, see Davies, *Paul among the Apocalypses?*.

many scholars have recognized, including the examples of Barclay and Gorman above, apocalyptic and salvation history are complementary.[101]

Second, while Galatians does not share the form of apocalyptic literature, it does share in that genre's function.[102] Beker identified the apocalyptic worldview as a theodicy.[103] The cosmic conflict, explicated and applied in the apocalypses and Galatians, explains why God's people suffer, and it gives God's people hope that their suffering will end with God's universal victory. In summary, the term "cosmic conflict," applied to Paul by Middleton, seeks to identify much of what is helpful about the apocalyptic reading while seeking to avoid some of the extremes to which Martyn and de Boer are especially prone.[104]

Persecution in Galatians

The following section examines significant studies on persecution in Galatians in order to demonstrate the necessity of the current thesis.

The curse: Baasland (1984), Davis (2002), and Wilson (2007). Baasland identified persecution as a neglected feature of Galatians in 1984. His article begins as an investigation of Gal 4:29. From there, he develops the thesis that Paul challenged a traditional Jewish concept of the "cursed man."[105] After surveying the occurrences of διώκω in Galatians, Baasland speculates that Paul's opponents would have pointed toward Paul's suffering as evidence that he was under the curse of the law. Paul therefore must turn "the whole thing upside down."[106] His sufferings do not indicate his status as a cursed man, but rather he is imitating the sufferings of

---

101. E.g., Bird writes, "On the one hand, there can be no muting of the apocalyptic chords that play in Paul's theological symphony in Galatians. . . . On the other hand, Paul's apocalypticism does not create a cacophony of noises altogether dissonant from the story of Israel's Scriptures and covenantal promises. The invasive action of God declared in the gospel still stands within a promise-fulfillment scheme that Paul frequently utilizes in his theological discourse" (*Anomalous Jew*, 115–16).

102. Keener, rightly, observes, "The extent to which 'apocalyptic' can characterize Galatians is largely a matter of definition" (*Galatians*, 5).

103. Dunne criticizes Martyn and de Boer for not emphasizing suffering in their understanding of apocalyptic ("Suffering and Covenantal Hope," 1–15).

104. Middleton, *Radical Martyrdom*, 136–46.

105. Baasland, "Persecution," 135.

106. Baasland, "Persecution," 135.

Jesus. Baasland summarizes, "Paul now suffers as a righteous Christian, not as a cursed Jew.... A blessed man is now the man not living ἐν νόμῳ, but in the cursed man Jesus Christ."[107] Baasland's main contribution is to highlight, as he himself states, a neglected theme. But due to the brevity of the article, Baasland began a project that he left for others to complete. Moreover, Baasland's work remains largely unaffected by the New Perspective and its aftermath. In fact, as a Norwegian Lutheran, the article suffers from certain Lutheran dogmatic tendencies. Most prominently is his negative view of the law in contrast with the gospel and thus of Judaism in contrast with Christianity.[108] Baasland's arguments are insufficient in the current scholarly atmosphere on the topic of Paul's relation to Judaism.

Two monographs have, however, sought to build upon Baasland's emphasis on the curse: Davis's *Christ as Devotio* (2002) and Wilson's *The Curse of the Law and the Crisis in Galatia* (2007).[109] Davis attempts to understand the curse of the Mosaic law by way of the Greco-Roman curse tablets called *defixiones*.[110] Christ is the *devotio* sacrifice that rescues persons from imminent disaster.[111] Davis reviews the theme of persecution in his sixth chapter.[112] Building on Baasland's argument, Davis focuses specifically on 3:1–14. He views the order of Paul's questions in 3:4–5 as a retelling of the gospel of Christ. First, suffering must take place, and then the blessing of the Spirit may come.[113] He concludes, "Paul reminds the Galatians that they too were in solidarity with him in his suffering, a solidarity which was the causal link between their acceptance of his gospel of the crucified Christ and their reception of the Spirit."[114]

Wilson's main aim is to counter the view that the law is irrelevant to the Christian in 5:13—6:10. He explains, "Paul's aim is to assure the Galatians of the sufficiency of the Spirit to enable them to fulfil the Law

---

107. Baasland, "Persecution," 147.

108. Baasland, "Persecution," 135, 144, 146–47. Similarly, Baasland, following Lutheran orthodoxy, simply equates reception of the Spirit with baptism ("Persecution," 145).

109. Davis, *Christ as Devotio*; Wilson, *Curse of the Law*.

110. Davis, *Christ as Devotio*, 119–200.

111. Davis, *Christ as Devotio*, 119–220.

112. Davis, *Christ as Devotio*, 201–6.

113. Davis, *Christ as Devotio*, 210–20.

114. Davis, *Christ as Devotio*, 249–50.

and thereby avoid its curse."[115] Wilson addresses persecution in chapter 4 of his work by beginning with a review of Baasland's article.[116] Wilson appeals to epigraphic evidence that devotees to Anatolian religion would often attribute their personal suffering to divine curses, and therefore the Galatians would have been particularly susceptible to fear of the curse.[117] By undergoing circumcision, therefore, the Galatians were attempting to avoid the curse of the law and its manifestation in their suffering. Paul however contends, according to Wilson, that the curse is avoided through the Spirit.[118] In summary, while Baasland et al. adequately demonstrate connections between the themes of persecution and curse, readers should ask if "curse" is the primary motif in which Paul's emphasis on persecution fits.

Power dynamics: John Muddiman (1994). In a brief essay, Muddiman uses the analogy of anatomy to describe the purpose and structure of Galatians, making persecution a unifying feature. Muddiman begins by examining 6:11–17, concluding that "the trouble in Galatia stems from a group which advocates observance of certain, outward features of Jewish practice ('making a good showing in the flesh'), not because they believe that eternal salvation depends upon them, but because they wish to avoid persecution."[119] He then shifts his focus to the autobiography of 1:13–14. Based on 1:13–14 and comparison with 4:29 and 5:11, he deduces that the persecution feared by Paul's opponents came from the same "fanatical Diaspora brand of Pharisaism" once held by Paul himself.[120] This historical reconstruction allows him to offer a unique solution to the identity of the ψευδάδελφοι in 2:4. Muddiman contends that they are undercover spies employed by the Pharisaical authorities in Jerusalem to infiltrate the Jerusalem church and "to find out how far from traditional Torah obedience the new group was prepared to go."[121] He uses this reconstruction of the Jerusalem situation to offer a similar reconstruction of the conflict

---

115. Wilson, *Curse of the Law*, 139.

116. Wilson, *Curse of the Law*, 80–81.

117. Wilson, *Curse of the Law*, 91. He cites Schnabel, "Divine Tyranny," 160–88. These inscriptions, however, do not demonstrate *particular* susceptibility in Anatolia to fear of curses. Such fear is pervasive in pagan and folk religion globally.

118. Wilson, *Curse of the Law*, 94–96.

119. Muddiman, "Anatomy of Galatians," 259.

120. Muddiman, "Anatomy of Galatians," 260.

121. Muddiman, "Anatomy of Galatians," 263.

in Galatia. Paul's opponents correspond to Peter and James. They agree with Paul theologically but disagree pragmatically on how to relate to the Pharisees.[122] Therefore, Paul's theological arguments in the central section of Galatians are aimed past the Jewish Christians toward the Pharisees that those Christians feared. Muddiman writes, "Paul the Pharisee and Paul the Apostle of Christ struggle to the death in this central section; Paul as it were conducts his own autopsy, and takes the Pharisee apart limb from limb before our eyes, replacing him with a whole new man."[123] Muddiman speculates about the motivation of these Pharisaical persecutors. Paul's missionary success has provoked them and has become a "major threat to the whole movement."[124] Paul's efforts had siphoned off "influential 'God-fearers'" from their synagogues, which threatened their power and the stability of their movement within their Greco-Roman communities.[125]

Muddiman offers a creative reading of Galatians, but his reconstruction faces three specific difficulties. First, Muddiman bases his reconstruction almost completely on a mirror-reading of the text of Galatians. He makes no appeal to external historical evidence to confirm his hypothesis. As Barclay has demonstrated, diaspora Judaism was a complex phenomenon with a variety of responses to the difficult task of maintaining Jewish identity within Greco-Roman communities.[126] Thus it is not at all clear that a zealous band of Pharisees would have exercised the influence that Muddiman's reconstruction requires. Second, Muddiman's hypothesis does not take seriously the theological convictions of either the Pharisees or the Jewish Christians. He speculates that the Pharisees were motivated by a desire for power. But Pharisaism was not merely a political movement (as if the various sectors of life and motivations of action could easily be distinguished in the ancient world, or in the modern world for that matter). Many Pharisees would have seen corporate faithfulness to Torah as a prerequisite for the fulfillment of God's promises to the nation (e.g., 2 Bar. 78:5–7; 84:8; 85:14–15). Furthermore, it is highly probable that Paul's opponents at Galatia held to a version of

---

122. Muddiman, "Anatomy of Galatians," 270.

123. Muddiman, "Anatomy of Galatians," 266–67. Muddiman argues that this reconstruction of the Galatia situation should also be applied to the "faith-righteousness" issues found in Romans and Philippians ("Anatomy of Galatians," 269).

124. Muddiman, "Anatomy of Galatians," 268.

125. Muddiman, "Anatomy of Galatians."

126. See especially Barclay, *Jews in the Mediterranean Diaspora*, 320–35.

this theology with the slight modification of affirming Jesus of Nazareth as the Messiah. Finally, Muddiman's explanation does not adequately explain the harsh polemic that Paul employs against those who avoid persecution. If Paul does not disagree with his opponents theologically but merely pragmatically, why does he wish for their emasculation (5:12)? Why does he insist that the blade of circumcision—a mere pragmatic choice—in fact severs them from Christ (5:4)?

A hermeneutical key: Jeff Hubing (2015). Following Hans Dieter Betz's comments, Hubing, in his published dissertation, argues that 6:11–17 functions as "a hermeneutical key" to Paul's intentions in Galatians.[127] By using this hermeneutical key, Hubing thus highlights the importance of persecution throughout the letter. He writes that persecution is "a central concern of the letter, both in terms of its impact on the Galatian situation and in terms of its theological and practical significance to Paul himself."[128] He spends one chapter analyzing explicit references to persecution (1:13–14, 21–24; 4:28—5:1; 5:7–12),[129] and he concludes that the Galatians did not endure "physical violence" but rather "a combination of pressure, persuasion, and manipulation that is designed to interrupt their continued progress in the faith."[130] He then takes an additional chapter to examine passages where persecution is implicit (1:7; 2:1–5; 3:1–5; 4:12–18; 5:4).[131] Hubing claims that persecution "plays a pivotal role" in the letter because all parties in the crisis are involved in it in some way, and thus persecution is "an index that measures the degree of one's conformity to the truth of the gospel."[132] In Gal 6:11–17, Paul creates a "stark contrast between the agitators and himself regarding the cross of Christ and the persecution that inevitably comes to those who make it their boast."[133] Hubing, therefore, reads 6:11–17, not as a summary of previously made points, but as the logical conclusion of Paul's argument

---

127. Hubing, *Crucifixion and New Creation*, 258. For the description "hermeneutical key," see Betz, *Galatians*, 313.
128. Hubing, *Crucifixion and New Creation*, 84.
129. Hubing, *Crucifixion and New Creation*, 118–58.
130. Hubing, *Crucifixion and New Creation*, 157–58.
131. Hubing, *Crucifixion and New Creation*, 159–87.
132. Hubing, *Crucifixion and New Creation*, 186.
133. Hubing, *Crucifixion and New Creation*, 189.

in the body of the letter.¹³⁴ While the term "hermeneutical key" may be an overstatement, Hubing's emphasis on the closing section of Galatians means that he does not adequately synthesize Paul's theology throughout the letter. Consequently, he does not offer an explanation of the interpretive framework that makes sense of the contrast in 6:11–17.

The Isaianic servant: John Anthony Dunne (2016). In three articles and his doctoral thesis, Dunne has done more toward putting together persecution in Paul's theology than any other scholar. Dunne published two articles in 2013 focusing on the exegesis of difficult texts, 3:4 and 4:30.¹³⁵ In a third article in 2015, he critiques the apocalyptic reading of Galatians. Martyn and de Boer's reading of Galatians emphasizes discontinuity with previous history and a strong dichotomy between revelation and religion. Dunne rightly points out that these features owe more to Barth than apocalyptic literature.¹³⁶ Following N. T. Wright, Dunne sees the story of Israel, especially exodus and exile, as underlying Paul's arguments in Gal 3–4.¹³⁷ Nonetheless, discontinuity and dichotomy can be found in Galatians, but it is specifically the discontinuity of the law and the dichotomy of the two ages.¹³⁸ Dunne's unique criticism of the apocalyptic reading, however, is their neglect of the theme of suffering. He correctly identifies the function of apocalyptic literature as confronting suffering and oppression.¹³⁹ He then argues that the exodus narrative was central for apocalyptic texts and concludes that "the apocalyptic and exodus imagery in Galatians converge around suffering, as they often do in apocalyptic literature."¹⁴⁰ He then argues that the Abba cry in Gal 4:6 echoes the cry of Israel in Egypt in Exod 3:7.¹⁴¹ In conclusion, Dunne claims that the theme of persecution "helps demonstrate that Paul's apocalyptic

---

134. Hubing, *Crucifixion and New Creation*, 257.

135. These articles will not be discussed in detail here because their substance appears in his doctoral thesis. See Dunne, "Cast Out," 246–69; "Suffering in Vain," 3–16.

136. Dunne, "Suffering and Covenantal Hope," 3.

137. Dunne, "Suffering and Covenantal Hope," 7–8; Wright, *Climax of the Covenant*, 140.

138. Dunne, "Suffering and Covenantal Hope," 8.

139. Dunne, "Suffering and Covenantal Hope," 9–12.

140. Dunne, "Suffering and Covenantal Hope," 12–13.

141. Dunne, "Suffering and Covenantal Hope," 13–14.

perspective in Galatians and his covenantal theology are two parts of a larger whole."[142]

In his published doctoral thesis, Dunne attempted a comprehensive account of the theme of persecution in Galatians. He seeks to demonstrate that "in Galatians, Paul is informed by the Christ-event and the full implications of participation with Christ in such a way that he sees suffering for the sake of the cross not as incidental, but as one of the alternative marks to circumcision, which demarcates the true people of God, and sets them apart for future blessing."[143] By examining 3:4, 4:6–7, and 4:29, Dunne claims that suffering marks Christian identity (sonship) and destiny (inheritance).[144] Furthermore, on the basis of 6:11–17, Dunne argues that suffering serves as a means of "participation in the cross" and thus indicates "who will therefore be vindicated at the final judgment."[145] In particular, "the language of *bearing* the 'marks of Jesus' should probably be interpreted against the backdrop of the final judgment."[146] Paul bears the marks of a slave of Christ (1:10; 6:17), and he expects the Galatians to become slaves as well (6:2).[147] Dunne claims that Paul's emphasis on suffering and slavery in Galatians echoes Isaiah. In this claim, he builds on the earlier work of Harmon.[148] Dunne's argument can be summarized in three steps: (1) Paul echoes Isa 53 when he describes Jesus's death (Gal 1:3; 2:20; cf. Isa 53:5–6, 10, 12).[149] (2) Paul presents himself as the Isaianic servant from Isa 49 (Gal 1:10, 15–16, 24; 2:2; cf. Isa 49:1–6). He is thus the servant of the Servant, displaying the Servant's suffering and indwelt by his Spirit.[150] (3) Finally, Paul calls on the Galatians to imitate him as suffering servants (Gal 4:12–5:1; Isa 49–54).[151] Following Harmon again, Dunne believes that in the allegory Paul gives an "Isaianic reading" of Genesis.[152] He summarizes, "Paul's reading of Genesis through the lens

---

142. Dunne, "Suffering and Covenantal Hope," 15.
143. Dunne, *Persecution and Participation*, 4.
144. Dunne, *Persecution and Participation*, 43–87.
145. Dunne, *Persecution and Participation*, 88.
146. Dunne, *Persecution and Participation*, 104.
147. Dunne, *Persecution and Participation*, 126.
148. Harmon, *She Must and Shall Go Free*.
149. Dunne, *Persecution and Participation*, 135–36.
150. Dunne, *Persecution and Participation*, 136–79.
151. Dunne, *Persecution and Participation*, 155–82.
152. Dunne, *Persecution and Participation*, 182–91; Harmon, "Allegory, Typology," 144–58.

of Isaiah demonstrates how Isaiah has been informing much of Paul's thinking in Galatians."[153]

Dunne's research represents the most comprehensive attempt to understand the topic of persecution in Galatians, and the quality of his research only serves to buttress the value of his work. This monograph shares some important observations with Dunne's work: (1) We both agree that 4:29 is a key text for understanding the theological purpose of the persecution theme in Galatians.[154] In this, of course, we have both been preceded by Baasland.[155] (2) We both agree that the emphasis on curse found in the works of Baasland et al. is insufficient for explaining all that Paul intends to do with the theme.[156] (3) Finally, we both acknowledge that persecution in Galatians, in part, replaces circumcision as a mark of identity for God's true people and thus also concerns the issue of inheritance as well.[157]

Nonetheless, several differences between Dunne's thesis and the present project merit further research: (1) Dunne shows little concern for understanding the historical questions about persecution in Galatia. He acknowledges this in his conclusion by identifying historical reconstruction as an area for further research.[158] This issue, however, cannot be isolated from exegesis. First, two recent trends—Paul within Judaism and Paul and Empire—demonstrate how significant historical reconstruction is to understanding the theology of the text. These trends offer unique readings of Galatians based on particular understandings of the historical evidence.[159] Second, without historical reconstruction the interpreter cannot easily identify instances when Paul might be using the theme to accomplish polemical purposes. What if Paul is using διώκω in 4:29 polemically to refer to false teaching rather than physical or social hostility? This would tell us something significant about Paul's understanding of the concept of persecution. Dunne attempts to evade the issue, and

---

153. Dunne, *Persecution and Participation*, 191.
154. Dunne, *Persecution and Participation*, 47–48.
155. Baasland, "Persecution," 135.
156. Dunne, *Persecution and Participation*, 29–31.
157. Dunne, *Persecution and Participation*, 43–87.
158. Dunne, *Persecution and Participation*, 195.
159. For Paul within Judaism in Galatians, see Nanos, *Irony of Galatians*. For Paul and Empire in Galatians, see Winter, *Seek the Welfare*; Winter, *Divine Honours*; Hardin, *Galatians and the Imperial Cult*; Lopez, *Apostle to the Conquered*; Prokhorov, "Taking the Jews Out," 172–88; Kahl, *Galatians Reimagined*.

thus he must interpret 4:29 at face value.[160] (2) While Dunne argues for a modified apocalyptic reading in his 2015 article,[161] he does not give particular emphasis to an apocalyptic reading in his thesis. His primary focus remains salvation historical. This monograph, following Middleton, gives greater weight to the apocalyptic reading.[162] (3) Dunne, following Harmon, appeals to broad echoes of Isa 49–54 throughout the book of Galatians as the basis of Paul's theology of persecution. This monograph will seek a simpler and clearer explanation of persecution in Paul's theology: the cosmic conflict between God and the present evil age that is explicit and central to the letter. While some have pointed out methodological weaknesses with Dunne and Harmon's Isaianic approach,[163] I would argue that, while some (but not all) of the broad Isaianic echoes identified by Dunne and Harmon exist, they fit within the larger, explicit category of cosmic conflict. (4) Finally, this monograph demonstrates continuity between Paul's understanding of cosmic conflict and Second Temple Judaism. This is a serious shortcoming in both Harmon and Dunne's approach. They generally move directly from Isaiah to Galatians (and then back from Galatians to Genesis through Isaiah), but they do not give significant evidence that other Jewish authors read Isaiah (or Genesis) in the way they propose. This shortcoming does not disprove the echoes of Isaiah that they propose, but it does represent a failure to make their case as strong as they could have done.[164] This monograph shows that cosmic conflict is not merely a thematic parallel between two or three texts but between a number of early Jewish sources.

---

160. Dunne, *Persecution and Participation*, 50–51.

161. Dunne, "Suffering and Covenantal Hope."

162. Middleton, *Radical Martyrdom*.

163. E.g., Ciampa writes concerning Harmon, "The method focuses on looking for any possible parallel between Isaiah and Galatians and then looking for patterns in the parallels. (Although it is not an intentional part of the method, it seems to me that there is also a tendency to highlight similarities and to ignore or downplay significant differences.) In my view, the problem with the methodology is that alternative sources for influences on Paul's thought are not given significant attention" (Review of *She Must and Shall Go Free*, 200).

164. Williams demonstrates thematic parallels between Isa 53 and several Second Temple texts (LXX Dan, 2 Macc, 4 Macc) on the topic of atonement. One wonders if Harmon and Dunne could have utilized these same parallels to strengthen their case (Williams, *Christ Died for Our Sins*, 35–104).

Conclusion. These studies on persecution in Galatians have revealed three perspectives on Paul's theology—curse, power, the Isaianic servant. This monograph, following the historical work of Middleton, proposes a different category that is able to encompass many other perspectives, namely the theme of cosmic conflict.[165]

BIBLICAL-THEOLOGICAL METHOD

This monograph is a work in Pauline theology, which I understand to be a sub-unit of the broader field of biblical theology. I recognize that biblical theology can be a problematic term, which represents many different things to different scholars.[166] I believe biblical theology to be primarily, although not exclusively, historical and descriptive in orientation. The task of Pauline theology in particular is to describe Paul's own theological worldview through an exegetical examination of primary sources, namely, Paul's letters. The goal then is to reconstruct, as much as possible, Paul's own thinking from the literary evidence he left behind and to understand Paul's thinking within his literary, cultural, historical, and theological contexts.

Exegesis of Paul's letters however will quickly require particular attention to Paul's interpretation of earlier Scripture. Whatever else may be said about Paul, he understood himself as called by the God of Israel's Scriptures and as serving a critical role in Yahweh's purpose for the cosmos. Examining Paul's hermeneutic allows us to observe not only how he understood the earlier texts of Scripture but also how he understood the character and actions of the God of Israel who revealed himself in those texts. Nonetheless, this divinely given vocation did not isolate Paul from his Jewish and Greco-Roman contexts. Paul was an interpreter of Scripture among interpreters of Scripture, and, although we may never know to what extent Paul knew the Second Temple texts that we now possess, we may assume that those texts serve as a representative sample of the type of theologizing which occurred in Paul's day. Examining how other Jews in the period interpreted similar passages of Scripture and employed similar themes helps us to see more vividly how Paul interpreted Scripture, both in ways similar and different.

---

165. Middleton, *Radical Martyrdom*.

166. For an attempt to catalogue various approaches, see Klink and Lockett, *Understanding Biblical Theology*.

In examining Paul's interpretation of Scripture and his theological context, I employ Harmon's concept of "thematic parallel." Harmon explains, "Thus with thematic parallels we are dealing with ideas/concepts shared between texts that transcend precise verbal relationships."[167] Thematic parallels are weaker connections between texts than citations, allusions, or echoes.[168] Thematic parallels do not necessarily originate directly from a specific text. Rather they are "part of the larger shared scriptural background that shaped the very conceptual framework of Paul."[169] I contend that cosmic conflict is a thematic parallel between Paul and other Jewish texts—both the OT and Second Temple texts. But even more than that, due to the divine authorship of Scripture, a thematic parallel such as cosmic conflict, which can be found across the canon, instructs believers both in the proper interpretation of earlier Scripture as well as the right understanding of the world that we live in.

EXAMINING GALATIANS AND EARLIER SCRIPTURE

The following chapters build upon one another in order to demonstrate that persecution in Galatians manifests the cosmic conflict between God and the present evil age. Chapters 2–4 focus on a theme of cosmic conflict in Galatians and other Jewish texts. Chapter 2 demonstrates that an apocalyptic cosmic conflict is a significant theme in Galatians and defines the nature of that conflict in the letter. In Galatians, Paul utilizes the theme of cosmic conflict to place the crisis in Galatia within a broader context. Middleton's definition of cosmic conflict unnecessarily limits the theme to a war between God and a personal being named Satan.[170] This exegetical investigation, however, establishes that Paul sees himself and the Galatian Christians as part of a cosmic conflict between God who has inaugurated the new creation within the present time and an impersonal

---

167. Harmon, *She Must and Shall Go Free*, 30. For criteria for recognizing thematic parallels, see Harmon, *She Must and Shall Go Free*, 31–36.

168. Harmon, *She Must and Shall Go Free*, 29.

169. Harmon, *She Must and Shall Go Free*, 30. Harmon is applying to Paul the language of parallel used by literary scholars Altick and Fenstermaker. They write, "While certain features of poem *y* are indeed found in *x*, they occur fairly often in preceding or concurrent literature, and the fact that they are found in *y* may equally well—in the absence of more specific indications—be due to antecedents floating at large in the nebulous realm of literary tradition or intellectual milieu" (*Art of Literary Research*, 111).

170. Middleton, *Radical Martyrdom*, 6.

yet personified entity called "this present evil age" (1:4). In Galatians, Paul identifies three primary ways that this cosmic conflict manifests itself in the Galatian crisis: (1) within the believer and the community, (2) between Jew and gentile, and (3) between persecutor and persecuted.

Chapters 3–4 examine Paul's theological context by identifying cosmic conflict as a thematic parallel between Galatians and a sample of earlier Jewish texts. These chapters also compare Paul's depiction of cosmic conflict with the theme in these other documents. Chapter 3 examines a theme of cosmic conflict in the OT. The chapter focuses on OT books that influenced Paul as evidenced by quotations or allusions in Galatians: Genesis, Psalms, Isaiah, and Habakkuk. The examination identifies three loci of the theme: (1) the polarity of the righteous/wicked, (2) the problem of sin and suffering, and (3) the solution of God's invasive action. Chapter 4 examines cosmic conflict in early Jewish texts that Paul does not cite. Three types of texts are reviewed: (1) Apocalyptic Genre (Daniel; 1 Enoch; 4 Ezra; 2 Baruch), (2) Other Apocryphal and Pseudepigraphal Texts (Jubilees; 1 Maccabees; 2 Maccabees; 4 Maccabees), and (3) Dead Sea Scrolls (1QS; CD; 1QM). This survey reveals a general unity around a theme of cosmic conflict as well as broad diversity concerning the details of the conflict. By comparison, Paul transforms the theme in significant ways.

Chapter 5 shifts to the topic of persecution in Galatia and answers the historical questions about the persecution referred to in the letter. The letter refers to four possible instances of persecution or likely persecution: (1) Paul's persecution of the church before the revelation of Christ (1:13, 23), (2) the persecution that Paul endured after the revelation of Christ (3:1; 4:13, 19; 5:11; 6:17), (3) the potential persecution that Paul's opponents avoid (6:12), and (4) the persecution of the Galatian Christians (3:4; 4:17–18, 29). A careful historical reconstruction is necessary to understand how the theme of persecution contributes to Paul's polemical purposes in the letter.

Chapter 6 brings together the earlier studies on the theme of cosmic conflict (chs. 2–4) and persecution in Galatia (ch. 5) in order to discover Paul's theological understanding of persecution in Galatians. In Galatians, persecution manifests the cosmic conflict between God and the present evil age. Galatians 4:29 directly connects the phenomenon of persecution with the broader cosmic conflict. Paul does so by identifying Gen 21:9 as an earlier type of the persecution experienced in Galatia. Most commentators, following Richard N. Longenecker, posit that Paul uses rabbinic interpretations or methods when alluding to Gen 21:9.[171] The typology that Paul identifies in Gen 21:9, however, fits within a unified reading of Genesis. Genesis itself sees fraternal strife as a manifestation of cosmic conflict, and, therefore, Paul rightly understands Ishmael's laughter as threatening to the true heir of Abraham, Isaac. The Galatian believers, therefore, are not in a conflict *similar* to Isaac. They are in the *same* conflict as Isaac. In order to receive their inheritance and stand in their freedom, they also must obey Sarah's protective command (4:30; Gen 21:10). After examining 4:29, the chapter reexamines other significant passages within this cosmic conflict reading: 1:13, 23; 3:4; 5:11; 6:12, 17.

Chapter 7 summarizes the argument of this monograph and suggests three results of Paul's understanding of persecution as cosmic conflict. In conclusion, the significance of the thesis for global Christianity today will be highlighted.

---

[171]. Longenecker, *Galatians*, 216–17.

2

Cosmic Conflict in Galatians

PAUL WROTE GALATIANS TO correct the eschatology of the Galatian Christians. Certainly, he intended also to correct their soteriology, as the Reformation tradition has emphasized, as well their ecclesiology, as the New Perspective has brought into focus. However, the soteriology and ecclesiology of Galatians is built upon the foundation of Paul's eschatology. At first glance, though, Galatians seems to have almost nothing to do with eschatology. It does not mention the imminent return of Christ or the future resurrection and only alludes to a future expectation in passing (5:5, 21; 6:8, 16). For this reason, J. Christiaan Beker claims that Galatians threatens the coherence of Paul's apocalyptic thought, writing, "Because the Christocentric focus of Galatians pushes Paul's theocentric apocalyptic theme to the periphery, Galatians cannot serve as the central normative guide for all Paul's letters and theology."[1] Beker concludes that Galatians focuses on the "eschatological present," but he is nonetheless troubled by what he sees as the failure of Galatians to address future apocalyptic events.[2]

In response, J. Louis Martyn has sought to demonstrate the importance of apocalyptic eschatology to Galatians. Martyn writes that the "crucial issue of the entire letter" is the question "What time is it?"[3] He argues that Paul believes it is the time of a "war of liberation commenced

---

1. Beker, *Paul the Apostle*, 58.
2. Beker, *Paul the Apostle*.
3. Martyn, "Apocalyptic Antinomies," 418.

by the Spirit."[4] Paul reminds the Galatian Christians "where the front line of that cosmic warfare actually lies" and summons them "back to their place on that battle front."[5] Martyn successfully reframed the debate over Galatians. For many scholars, the question is no longer, "Is Galatians apocalyptic in nature?" but rather "What sort of apocalyptic is Galatians?"[6]

Key to apocalyptic readings of Galatians is the theme of cosmic conflict.[7] Since this theme is often identified without careful exegetical definition, this chapter will demonstrate and define the significance of this key element of Paul's apocalyptic eschatology in Galatians based upon a surface reading of the letter. To do this, two issues must be addressed: First, it must be demonstrated in what sense Galatians is about the cosmos. Second, it must be shown how the specific conflict in Galatia, which the letter confronts, relates to the larger conflict in the cosmos.

THE COSMOS AND THE CROSS

Paul designs the beginning and the end of Galatians to complement one another in order to demonstrate that the gospel that he is defending in the letter concerns the cosmos.[8] By doing this, he sets the contents of Galatians within a cosmic frame. In 1:4, he speaks of Christ rescuing believers from "the present evil age" while in 6:15 he mentions the "new creation." Both entities are connected to the work of Christ on the cross: Christ "gave himself for our sins to rescue us from the present evil age" (1:4). So also, the new creation supplants the value of circumcision because of the work of Christ on the cross (6:15). The crucifixion of Christ

---

4. Martyn, "Apocalyptic Antinomies," 418.

5. Martyn, "Apocalyptic Antinomies," 421.

6. See, for example, Wright: "I believe Paul's message is thoroughly 'apocalyptic,' in the sense that he believed that the events concerning Jesus constituted the long-promised and long-awaited moment when the divine saving purpose for Israel and the world was at last revealed. . . . So, if I am faced with the choice between an 'apocalyptic' and a 'non-apocalyptic' Paul, I unhesitatingly and enthusiastically choose the former" (*Paul and His Recent Interpreters*, 184). It should be noted that the very question "What time is it?" enables a degree of unity between apocalyptic and salvation historical readings of Galatians. The conflict that is highlighted by apocalyptic readings has clear basis in the temporal transitions taking place in salvation history.

7. For an explanation of the term "cosmic conflict" borrowed from Middleton, see chapter 1 (*Radical Martyrdom*).

8. Schreiner identifies the correspondence as an inclusio (*Galatians*, 77).

was in fact a dual crucifixion of the present "world" to Paul and Paul to "the world" (6:14). The theme of Galatians is "cosmic" in the sense that it is concerned with God's invasive action, which is transitioning the cosmos from this age/world into the new creation.[9] To understand this cosmic nature of the letter, three words deserve further attention: αἰών, κόσμος, and κτίσις. Special consideration of these words is necessary to determine both what Paul means by them and how he understands them in relation to one another.

Αἰών

The noun αἰών occurs three times in 1:4–5 while the adjectival form αἰώνιος occurs in 6:8. In 1:5, it occurs twice in the expression εἰς τοὺς αἰῶνας τῶν αἰώνων, which simply means "forevermore" and often appears in doxologies.[10] In 6:8, the adjective modifies ζωή attributing the quality of eternality to life.[11] The NT abounds with uses of the nominal and adjectival forms of αἰών that communicate the concept of "forever" or the attribute of eternality.

However, the occurrence of αἰών in 1:4 exemplifies a different usage of the word, translated by either the temporal term "age" or the spatial term "world."[12] Paul uses αἰών in this way often (Rom 12:2; 1 Cor 1:20; 2:6–8; 3:18; 10:11; 2 Cor 4:4; Eph 1:21; 2:2, 7; 3:9; Col 1:26; 1 Tim 1:17; 6:17; 2 Tim 1:9; 4:10; Titus 1:2; 2:12). In some instances, the temporal aspect of the term is clearly in view. Believers are those on whom τὰ τέλη τῶν αἰώνων have come (1 Cor 10:11). Divine actions can be said to have occurred πρὸ χρόνων αἰωνίων (2 Tim 1:9; Titus 1:2). Likewise, God hid the mystery of gentile salvation ἀπὸ τῶν αἰώνων (Eph 3:9; Col 1:26). Believers will praise Christ ἐν τοῖς αἰῶσιν τοῖς ἐπερχομένοις (Eph 2:7). In Eph 1:21, Paul explicitly indicates his belief in two ages: this age and the one to come. Three times in the Pastoral Epistles Paul modifies αἰών with

---

9. Again, Wright: "I fully agree with Martyn and the others that this event is *cosmic* in the sense that the unseen suprahuman powers that have tyrannized the world have been overcome" (*Paul and His Recent Interpreters*, 184).

10. Cf. Phil 4:20; 1 Tim 1:17; 2 Tim 4:18. See BDAG, s.v. "αἰών"; Burton, *Galatians*, 429.

11. Burton, *Galatians*, 426–27, 432. Contra Wright who translates the phrase "the life of the age [to come]" (*Paul and the Faithfulness of God*, 1060).

12. Note that Louw and Nida categorize the usage of αἰών into four categories: geographical features (i.e., the universe), supernatural powers, behaviors and related states, and time. See L&N, 1.2; 12.44; 41.38; 67.143; Burton, *Galatians*, 430.

the temporal adverb νῦν (1 Tim 6:17; 2 Tim 4:10; Titus 2:12). Ὁ νῦν αἰών in the Pastoral Epistles is equivalent to ὁ αἰών οὗτος in Eph 1:21. It is the current state of the world in which all persons, including believers, live (1 Tim 6:17; Titus 2:12).

In addition to the temporal sense, "this present age" is also a system of values that someone might love and by doing so desert Christ (2 Tim 4:10). In Rom 12:2, αἰών indicates a system of thinking to which believers must not be conformed.[13] Similarly, in 1 Cor 1:20, Paul asks, ποῦ συζητητὴς τοῦ αἰῶνος τούτου; The question contrasts a human way of thinking with the divine logic of the cross (cf. 1 Cor 2:6–8; 3:18). In 2 Cor 4:4, ὁ θεὸς τοῦ αἰῶνος τούτου exercises his power by blinding "the minds of the unbelievers."

Paul's conception of two ages—the present one dominated by sin and a coming one of righteousness—aligns with Jewish thinking generally at his time.[14] But did Paul conceive of these two αἰῶνες as primarily temporal or spatial? Citing Jewish apocalyptic literature, Martinus C. de Boer asserts that "the two ages are not simply, or even primarily, temporal categories, referring to two successive, discontinuous periods of world history ('ages'); they are also spatial categories, referring to two spheres or orbs of power, both of which claim sovereignty over the world."[15] While de Boer risks minimizing the temporal aspect of the word too much, he does accurately describe the two ages as "spheres or orbs of power."[16]

One need not read apocalyptic literature broadly, however, to reach this same conclusion about Paul's use of the word. First, in Gal 1:4, Paul clearly has the temporal aspect in mind when modifying αἰών with the participle τοῦ ἐνεστῶτος.[17] The age is temporally present. Second, Paul attributes a moral quality to this present age. It is πονηρός, possessing a character of human sinfulness.[18] Third, and perhaps most significantly, Paul describes—even personifies—the age as possessing a certain power

13. See Keener, *Mind of the Spirit*, 143–72.

14. For a nuanced examination of the two-ages in apocalyptic literature, see Davies, *Paul among the Apocalypses?*, 72–112.

15. De Boer, *Galatians*, 33.

16. De Boer, *Galatians*.

17. See Rom 8:38; 1 Cor 3:22. So deSilva: "Especially in the perfect tense, ἐνίστημι refers to conditions contemporaneous with the time of speaking, etc." (*Galatians: Handbook*, 5). See also Burton, *Galatians*, 432–33; Schlier, *Brief an die Galater*, 9.

18. By stating πονηρός rather than simply assuming the age's evil character, Paul gives the moral character of the age special emphasis (see Rom 12:2; 1 Cor 1:20). See Calvin, *Galatians and Ephesians*, 27; Burton, *Galatians*, 13; Longenecker, *Galatians*, 9.

to enslave persons.[19] The Galatian believers needed to be delivered from this present evil age by the work of Christ on the cross.[20] To Paul, this age is temporally present, morally evil, and powerfully oppressing.

Κόσμος

The word κόσμος appears three times in Galatians. In 4:3, it appears in the difficult expression τὰ στοιχεῖα τοῦ κόσμου. The word occurs twice in 6:14 when Paul describes the cross of Christ as a mutual crucifixion of the κόσμος to him and him to it. Paul uses the noun κόσμος forty-seven times in his corpus. Twenty-one of those instances appear in 1 Corinthians alone. Several times in 1 Corinthians Paul uses the word as a geographical term (1 Cor 3:22; 4:9, 13; 5:10; 8:4; 14:10). But at other times it signifies a system that is opposed to God and his wisdom (1 Cor 1:20–28; 3:19). As a system of human evil, Paul uses κόσμος and αἰών synonymously.[21] Through his rhetorical questions, Paul asserts that the debater of this "age" operates from the wisdom of the "world," which God has made folly (1 Cor 1:20–21). In 1 Cor 2:6, he switches from "the wisdom of the world" to "the wisdom of this age." Likewise, in 1 Cor 3:18–19, the one who is wise ἐν τῷ αἰῶνι τούτῳ possesses ἡ σοφία τοῦ κόσμου τούτου. For Paul, the world stands in absolute opposition to God and is thus under divine judgment. He contrasts τὸ πνεῦμα τοῦ κόσμου with the Spirit of God (1 Cor 2:12) and τὰ τοῦ κόσμου with τὰ τοῦ κυρίου (1 Cor 7:33–34). In its opposition to God, the κόσμος is "condemned" (1 Cor 11:32), "passing away" (1 Cor 7:31), and will be judged by the saints (1 Cor 6:2).

As with its near synonym αἰών, the question arises as to whether the term should be taken temporally or spatially. Rudolf Bultmann claimed that κόσμος "is much more a time-concept than a space-concept; or, more exactly, it is an *eschatological concept*."[22] Similar to de Boer's comment

---

19. To take this personification as referring overtly to demonic forces goes beyond what is explicitly stated in the text. Contra Luther, "Lectures on Galatians," 26:39–43; Betz, *Galatians*, 42.

20. Only here does Paul use the verb ἐξέληται. In Acts, Luke uses it for rescue from peril (cf. Acts 7:10, 34; 23:27; 26:17). The LXX also uses the verb for rescue from peril (e.g., Gen 32:12; 1 Sam 17:37; Ps 58:2). See Longenecker, *Galatians*, 7; Dunn, *Galatians*, 35; Martyn, *Galatians*, 90.

21. Schlier, *Brief an die Galater*, 9; Fung, *Galatians*, 41; Longenecker, *Galatians*, 9; Dunn, *Galatians*, 340; deSilva, *Galatians: Handbook*, 143.

22. Bultmann, *Theology of the New Testament*, 256.

above on αἰών, Bultmann makes the mistake of setting time and space against each other. When Paul uses κόσμος and αἰών to describe the system opposed to God, the words possess both temporal and spatial elements since the system of evil is present in the here and now. Certainly, Paul's emphasis is on the moral element of the terms, but not exclusively so. The present here and now is dominated by sin.

As in 1 Corinthians, in Galatians also κόσμος and αἰών are synonymous and describe a system of moral evil that is in place in the present time and within the present creation. In Gal 4:3, κόσμος appears in the genitive modifying τὰ στοιχεῖα. In terms of syntax, τοῦ κόσμου is either a simple attributive genitive, "the worldly elements," or a possessive genitive, "the world's elements." Either possibility continues to leave the weight of the meaning of the phrase to one's understanding of τὰ στοιχεῖα. Typically, when described by κόσμος, στοιχεῖα refers to the physical elements that compose the world—earth, water, air, and fire.[23] Nonetheless, it is clear from context that Paul has more in mind than these physical elements as such.[24] He asserts that the Galatian believers were "enslaved under the elements of the world," but the sending of the Son into the world redeemed them from their slavery (4:4–5). The synonymous usage of κόσμος and αἰών along with the shared language of slavery and rescue point to the fact that Paul describes in 4:3–5 the same reality he had described only briefly in 1:4. The world in 4:3 is the present evil age of 1:4. What, then, are the στοιχεῖα of this world/age? The word's second occurrence in 4:9 sheds light on its initial appearance in 4:3. In 4:8, Paul describes their slavery as being under those things or beings "who by nature are not gods." In 4:9, he switches back to describing their slavery as being under the στοιχεῖα, which he describes now as "weak and poor." Thus, στοιχεῖα indicates an impotent, enslaving force that does

---

23. E.g., Wis 7:17; 19:18; 2 Pet 3:10, 12; Philo, *Aet.* 107. See Blinzer, "Τὰ Στοιχεῖα," 2:429–43; Schweizer, "Slaves of the Elements," 455–68; Rusam, "Στοιχεῖα," 119–25. The use of στοιχεῖα τοῦ κόσμου as a technical term in the period undercuts two alternative interpretations: (1) "elementary principles," i.e., basic principles of a subject that should be learned. (2) "elemental spirits," i.e., gods or demons. For the "elementary principles" view, see Longenecker, *Galatians*, 165–66; Bundrick, "Ta Stoicheia," 353–64; Witherington, *Grace in Galatia*, 285–86. For the "elemental spirits" view, see Betz, *Galatians*, 213–15; Cousar, *Galatians*, 92–93; George, *Galatians*, 295–96; Arnold, "Returning to the Domain," 55–76.

24. Martyn argues that readers would have grown to understand this through subsequent readings, in which they would have come to understand a contrast between the elements of the present world and the value system of the new creation. See Martyn, "Elements," 31–32.

not share in the divine nature. Paul, likely, intends for the Galatians to recall the idolatrous pagan worship that they participated in prior to faith in Christ. This worship venerated the physical elements of the universe and ordered calendrical observances on the basis of these elements.[25] But the real surprise comes when he describes how they are attempting to turn back to this slavery: by observing days, months, seasons, and years (4:10). Since the letter nowhere else indicates a temptation to return to paganism, these calendrical observances most likely refer to elements of the Jewish calendar mandated by the Mosaic law.[26] As de Boer argues, Paul *functionally* equates the calendrical observance of the Mosaic law with the calendrical observance of pagan worship based on the physical elements.[27] Both give the wrong answer to the question, "What time is it?" or "In what cosmos do we actually live?" since both base their time-keeping on the present world, ignoring that the time of faith has come (3:23–25).[28] Furthermore, both Torah and pagan calendrical observances are "weak and worthless," being unable to solve the problem of sin and thus contributing to humanity's enslavement within the present evil age.[29]

Galatians 6:14–15 continues the theme of the liberating work of the cross from the power of this world/age.[30] Paul boasts in the work of Christ on the cross because it enacted a mutual death between himself and the world. The dual crucifixion of 6:14 builds upon two earlier descriptions of the believer's crucifixion.[31] In 2:19–21, Paul describes himself as being crucified with Christ, and through this self-crucifixion, Paul has died to the law and come to live to God. Paul's death to the law has cancelled the value of the law's requirement of circumcision. In 5:24, Paul says that "those who belong of Christ Jesus have crucified the flesh with

25. Wis 7:17–19; 13:1–2; 19:18–20; Philo, *Contempl.* 1.3. See Martyn, "Elements," 22–24; Mitchell, *Anatolia*, 2:10; de Boer, "Τὰ Στοιχεῖα," 218–21; Das, *Galatians*, 444.

26. Contra Martin, "Pagan and Judeo-Christian Time-Keeping," 105–19; Witulski, *Adressaten des Galaterbriefes*, 158–68; 183–214; Hardin, *Galatians and the Imperial Cult*, 116–47. Paul probably uses this general description of time periods to link pagan religious observances to Jewish religious observances, but the present temptation for the Galatian churches is observance of the Jewish law. So Betz, *Galatians*, 217–18; de Boer, *Galatians*, 276.

27. De Boer, "Τὰ Στοιχεῖα," 222–24.

28. Martyn, "Apocalyptic Antinomies," 418; Martyn, *Galatians*, 23; de Boer, "Τὰ Στοιχεῖα," 224.

29. Woyke, "Elementen," 221–34.

30. Betz calls this "a summary of [Paul's] soteriology" (*Galatians*, 318). Similarly Matera, *Galatians*, 231.

31. Betz, *Galatians*, 319; Weima, "Gal 6.11–18," 103–5; Moo, *Galatians*, 396.

its passions and desires." The same crucifixion that liberated the believer from the law's requirements also did what the law could never do: It freed the believer from the power of the desires of the flesh.[32] The flesh, law, and sin all belong to the present age or world as a system in which human evil is pervasive and divine judgment has been decreed. But when Paul died to the world and the world died to Paul, the world lost its power over Paul, and thus standards that belonged to its system lost their worth. Only the reality of a new creation is valuable in light of the crucifixion.

Κτίσις

The word κτίσις is rare in the Pauline corpus by contrast with αἰών and κόσμος, occurring only 11 times. Once it denotes the event of creation (Rom 1:20) while more often it indicates the result of that event—that which was created (Rom 1:25; 8:19–22, 39; Col 1:15, 23). Only Paul among NT authors speaks of a καινὴ κτίσις, and he does so only twice (2 Cor 5:17; Gal 6:15).[33] Since Paul gives little explanation of what he means by καινὴ κτίσις in Galatians, two sources serve an important role in uncovering Paul's understanding of the "new creation": Isaiah and 2 Corinthians.[34]

The concept of a "new creation" is an obvious echo of Isaiah's "new heaven and new earth" (Isa 43:18–19; 65:17–18; 66:22).[35] Isaiah 40–66 repeatedly contrasts the former things (ראשנות) with the new things (חדשות; e.g., Isa 43:18–19; 48:1–8; 65:17).[36] In Isa 65:7, Israel's former deeds of idolatry merit for them divine judgment, but in Isa 65:17, God promises that a future day is coming when these former deeds will not be

---

32. Mußner, *Galaterbrief*, 414.

33. References to a new heaven and a new earth occur in 2 Pet 3:13 and Rev 21:1. For more on the word κτίσις, see Lampe, "*Ktisis*," 449–62; Wischmeyer, "ΦΥΣΙΣ und ΚΤΙΣΙΣ," 352–75; Adams, *Constructing the World*.

34. Contra Moo, "Creation and New Creation," 52.

35. The two parts of creation are often used in the OT to stand for the whole of creation (e.g., Gen 1:1; Deut 4:26; 1 Chron 16:31; Ps 146:16). Note that the phrase "new creation" occurs rarely in the Pseudepigrapha: 1 En. 72:1; Jub. 1:29; 4:26; 2 Bar. 44:12. Moyer V. Hubbard argues that the description of conversion in Jos. Asen. utilizes new creation imagery, even though the phrase itself is absent (*New Creation*, 54–76). Craig S. Keener notes that some rabbinic Jewish teachers applied the "new creation" language to personal transformation (*1–2 Corinthians*, 185).

36. Jackson, *New Creation*, 22.

remembered.[37] The ultimate deliverance of Israel from its sin problem will be the complete renewal of creation.[38] Thus, in Isaiah, the new creation is "both anthropological and cosmological in scope" as Isaiah "speaks of a transformed people (40–55) in a transformed universe (65–66)."[39]

Paul follows Isaiah in describing the new creation as both anthropological and cosmological in scope, but Paul makes a modification. For Paul, the new creation has already come in the past event of Christ's death and resurrection.[40] Christ's redemptive work makes Christ the sphere where the eschaton has broken into the present world.[41] Therefore, when he speaks of the "new creation" in 2 Cor 5:17, he speaks of it as a personal reality for those who are "in Christ." The Greek is somewhat ambiguous on the relationship of "a new creation" to "anyone who is in Christ." Is Paul identifying the person who is in Christ as a new creation or is he simply saying that the new creation has become a reality for those in Christ?[42] Either interpretation—identification as the new creation or participation in the new creation—signifies a deeply personal transformation that changes the way a person thinks about humanity generally and Christ in particular.[43] That said, 2 Cor 4:6 speaks of God's new creative act as occurring within a person's heart, giving weight to the interpretation that believers themselves are an early installment of the new creation.[44] Secondly, Paul contrasts the "new creation" with "the old" which has passed away. The old is conceptually linked with σάρξ in the previous

---

37. Jackson, *New Creation*, 21–31.

38. Matthew S. Harmon describes the new creation in Isaiah as "the goal towards which Yahweh's various actions described in Isaiah have been pressing" (*She Must and Shall Go Free*, 232).

39. Hubbard, *New Creation*, 17.

40. Jackson calls this "Paul's Modification of 'Jewish Apocalyptic Eschatology'" (*New Creation*, 100–103).

41. Barnett, *Second Epistle to the Corinthians*, 298; Seifrid, *Second Letter to the Corinthians*, 252.

42. Most English translations have "he is a new creation" (e.g., KJV, NASB, ESV, CSB). NIV has "the new creation has come" (similarly NRSV). For the identification view, see Best, *Second Corinthians*, 54–55; Matera, *2 Corinthians*, 137; Harris, *Second Epistle to the Corinthians*, 432–33. For the participation view, see Furnish, *II Corinthians*, 333; Adams, *Constructing the World*, 227–28; Moo, "Creation and New Creation," 51–55; Seifrid, *Second Letter to the Corinthians*, 252–53.

43. The emphasis on the mind reflects the allusion that Paul is making to Isa 43:8 and 65:17. See Beale, *New Testament Biblical Theology*, 302.

44. The anthropological emphasis of the new creation in 2 Cor 5:17 should in no way diminish the cosmological emphasis that Paul draws from Isaiah. See Moo, "Creation and New Creation." Contra Matera, *2 Corinthians*, 137; Hubbard, *New Creation*, 183.

verse. Once believers thought κατὰ σάρκα, but now they are a "new creation."[45] Thirdly, the new creation has come into the lives of believers by the work of Christ on the cross: He died "that those who live might no longer live for themselves but for him" (2 Cor 5:15). God "through Christ reconciled us to himself" (2 Cor 5:18). "In Christ God was reconciling the world to himself" (2 Cor 5:19).[46] These three observations fit with the way that Paul uses "new creation" in Galatians.[47] When writing Galatians 6:15, Paul echoes his earlier assertion in 5:6. Both verses deny the value of the fleshly sign of circumcision, removing ethnic boundaries.[48] Instead the Galatians should concern themselves with something else, described as "faith working through love" in 5:6 and a "new creation" in 6:15.[49] The reader is thus invited to see these two phrases as mutually explanatory. Believers experience the "new creation" through faith in Christ that works itself out in love, which is expounded even more fully as the fruit of the Spirit (5:22–23).[50] Paul teaches believers to expectantly hope for the coming of a new universe freed from sin and judgment in the future (5:5, 21; 6:8, 16).[51] But he also claims that this new creation has already begun in the believer.[52]

---

45. Furnish translates κατὰ σάρκα as "according to worldly standards," explaining "Those who are *in Christ* have not only abandoned *worldly standards* of judgment (v. 16); they have also become part of a wholly *new creation*" (*II Corinthians*, 332; italics original). See also Martyn, "Epistemology," 106; Matera, *2 Corinthians*, 135.

46. Also, implicit from the broader context of both 2 Cor 5:17 and Gal 6:15 is that the Spirit brings about this new creation. See Yates, *Spirit and Creation*, 114–21.

47. For a more comprehensive comparison between 2 Cor 5:17 and Gal 6:15, see Moo, "Creation and New Creation."

48. De Boer, *Galatians*, 402; Das, *Galatians*, 644.

49. Schlier, *Brief an die Galater*, 209; Fung, *Galatians*, 308; Silva, "Eschatological Structures," 158; de Boer, *Galatians*, 402–3; Rosner, *Paul and the Law*, 128–31.

50. Simon Butticaz writes, "En clair: l'éthique n'est pas, pour l'apôtre, un appendice secondaire de la foi. C'est au contraire le lieu où est appelée à se dévoiler et à se vérifier l'identité neuve du croyant—la «nouvelle création»" ("Vers une Anthropologie Universelle?" 522). See also Cousar, *Galatians*, 154–56; Harmon, *She Must and Shall Go Free*, 230–31; Beale, *New Testament Biblical Theology*, 583–88.

51. Silva, "Eschatological Structures."

52. Paul does not see merely an analogy between the believer and the new creation. To Paul, "Christians are the actual beginning of the end-time new creation" (Beale, *New Testament Biblical Theology*, 303).

The Fullness of Time

To summarize, Paul uses αἰών and κόσμος interchangeably. Thus, in Galatians, "this present evil age" in 1:4 is the same entity as "the world" referred to in 4:3 and 6:14. The "new creation" in 6:15 is the opposite of that entity and corresponds to the new reality that has come about by the work of the Son and the Holy Spirit.[53] What "counts" for the Galatian Christians is their relationship to these two systems of reality (6:15). Paul stresses the present experience of the believer as a new creation through faith in Christ and reception of the Spirit. Nevertheless, he hints at the future consummation of the new reality in three verses: Believers "eagerly wait for the hope of righteousness" (5:5). They will "inherit the kingdom of God" (5:21), and they will "reap eternal life" (6:8). Thus, Galatians serves as a prime example of the already/not yet eschatology of the NT. The situation in Galatia required a theological response which focused primarily on the transition between this age and the new creation that is being experienced in the present time within individual believers and among churches.

But it is not sufficient to discuss these two ages as passive markers of time. Paul personifies the present evil age as a powerful and oppressive moral force. From this personified age, persons need to be freed from slavery (1:4; 4:3, 8–11). So also, Paul portrays the world as an individual that can be crucified (6:14). He uses such personification because this age/world stands essentially as shorthand for a complex of entities that define the human condition: flesh, sin, law, and curse.[54] This age is the age of human sinners who have been condemned by the law and are under the curse of God, and to this system of human sinfulness and divine condemnation humans are enslaved.[55] Apart from the Jerusalem above in 4:26, the new creation is not similarly personified. This is because a Trinity of actors exist already for Paul's discourse: God the Father, Christ,

---

53. Wischmeyer writes, "Es gibt für Paulus also keinen neuen κόσμος mit einer Teilhabe des Menschen, sondern eine neue κτίσις und eine neue vollendete Existenz der Menschen bei Gott. D.h., der κόσμος braucht und erfährt καταλλαγή, die κτίσις erfährt Erneuerung und Vollendung. Dabei wird deutlich, daß die κτίσις als καινή κτίσις ins Eschaton hinüberreicht. Denn die κτίσις war, ist und bleibt die dem Menschen zugewandte und grundsätzlich erkennbare Seite Gottes selbst und kann als solche nicht vergehen. Der κόσμος dagegen als eigenmächtiges Schöpfungsprodukt wird nicht Bestand haben, sondern dem Gericht verfallen" ("ΦΥΣΙΣ und ΚΤΙΣΙΣ," 366–67). See also Adams, *Constructing the World*, 221–32.

54. Mußner, *Galaterbrief*, 51.

55. McKnight, *Galatians*, 50.

and the Spirit. God has liberated persons from the oppression of the present evil system and brought about a new creation (1:4; 4:3–7; 6:14–15). Nowhere does the relation of God to Paul's cosmology come into sharper focus than in 4:4–7. God has acted in time and space. If the "crucial issue of the letter" is the question "What time is it?"[56] then Paul provides an unmistakable answer: It is τὸ πλήρωμα τοῦ χρόνου (4:4).[57] This appointed time is identifiable by the invasive acts of God who spatially "sent forth" (ἐξαπέστειλεν) first "his Son" and second "the Spirit of his Son" (4:4–5).

At the center of God's invasive actions—and thus at the center of Paul's eschatology—is the redemptive death of the Son on the cross. Paul's gospel, to put it colloquially, was that when Jesus died on the cross everything—literally everything—changed.[58] The oppressive power of the present evil system died, and a new creation, freed from sin and guilt before the law, was born.[59] The work of the cross thus constitutes the content of Paul's gospel. To possess life by faith in the gospel is to be "crucified with Christ" (2:20–21). To proclaim the gospel is to publicly portray Christ as crucified (3:1). To preach circumcision is to remove the offense of the cross (5:11). He boasts in the cross alone (6:14). Douglas J. Moo writes, "The cross, and especially the epochal significance of the cross, is the fulcrum of Paul's strategy for persuading the Galatians to reject the overtures of the false teachers."[60] This epochal significance of the cross is *the issue* in Galatia. That is to say, in Galatians, Paul was contending for the truth of the world-changing gospel.

THE CONFLICT

To name conflict as a central aspect of the letter of Galatians is no unique assertion. The conflict appears on the surface of the text when Paul skips the typical thanksgiving for his readers and begins unleashing anathemas

---

56. Martyn, "Apocalyptic Antinomies," 418.

57. Barclay, *Paul and the Gift*, 413.

58. Schlier, *Brief an die Galater*, 10; Tannehill, *Dying and Rising with Christ*, 64; Betz, *Galatians*, 42; Bruce, *Galatians*, 76; Weima, "Gal 6.11–18," 94; Martyn, *Galatians*, 564; Schreiner, *Galatians*, 77. Contra Kwon, *Eschatology in Galatians*, 156–61.

59. The present age itself remains, but its power has been destroyed. Therefore, the emphasis of Galatians is on liberation (cf. 1:4; 5:1). See Cousar, *Galatians*, 17–18; Fung, *Galatians*, 41; Longenecker, *Galatians*, 8; Weima, "Gal 6.11–18," 101–6; Witherington, *Grace in Galatia*, 76; Hays, "Letter to the Galatians," 344.

60. Moo, *Galatians*, 66. Cf. Martyn, *Galatians*, 90.

against those who would dare distort the gospel (1:6–9).[61] The assertion here, however, is that Paul places this deeply personal conflict between himself, the Galatian churches, and his opponents within the much wider context of a conflict between God and this age.

The truth of the world-changing gospel is at stake in the situation in Galatia.[62] Paul accuses his opponents of "desiring to distort the gospel of Christ" (1:7). The Galatian churches therefore are abandoning Christ and "turning to a different gospel, not that there is another gospel" (1:6–7).[63] In chapter 2, Paul reveals himself as a veteran to this fight. In Jerusalem, he refused to submit to the deceptive "false brothers" because the "truth of the gospel" was at stake (2:4–5). In Antioch, Paul even rebuked Cephas because he and others under his influence were "not walking in step with the truth of the gospel" (2:14). Paul now finds himself in the same position with his Galatian converts. He is at risk of becoming their enemy by proclaiming to them the truth (4:16). For their part, formerly they had been "running well" but now they are being hindered from "obeying the truth."[64]

Opposing Polarities

The gospel is the truth, and there is no other gospel (1:7). Therefore, any deviation from or addition to the world-changing gift of the cross places one under the curse of God (1:8–9). Throughout the letter, Paul paints the situation in monochrome. One must choose between the human or the divine, works of the law or faith of Christ, law or promise, slavery or freedom, the flesh or the Spirit. Martyn labels these pairs of opposites "apocalyptic antinomies."[65] Paul utilizes antinomies or polarities to help the Galatian churches perceive reality correctly in light of Christ and the Spirit and thus win the battles they face.[66] This section examines the

61. Contra van Voorst, "Why Is There No Thanksgiving Period?" 153–72.
62. Silva, "Truth of the Gospel," 51–61.
63. Das, *Galatians*, 103. Contra Vanhoye, "La Définition," 392–98.
64. Πείθω means "to obey because one has been persuaded," which explains differences in translation between "obey" (ESV, KJV, NASB, NIV) and "persuaded" (CSB). See BDAG, s.v. "πείθω"; Wallace, *Greek Grammar*, 416.
65. Martyn, "Apocalyptic Antinomies," 413.
66. Martyn, "Apocalyptic Antinomies," 421. Barclay utilizes "polarities" as a synonym for antinomies. He writes that Paul uses polarities in Galatians to remap "reality with a cartography capable of blurring traditional categories by means of newly minted distinctions" (*Paul and the Gift*, 337–39). The term "polarities" is preferred here for

primary polarities in the letter in order to see, first, how they relate to one another and, second, how Paul uses them to characterize the cosmic conflict he describes.

Human or divine. The cosmic conflict is between that which is human—operating from the values of the present cosmic system—and that which is divine. Paul transitions to the body of the letter by inviting the Galatians to judge him as either seeking to please humans or God (1:10).[67] Paul then claims that the two are irreconcilable opposites: "If I were still attempting to please humans, I would not be a servant of Christ" (1:10).[68] But he is not seeking human approval because he is not proclaiming "a human gospel" (1:11).[69] Paul received his gospel as a direct revelation of God (1:12).[70] His previous way of life had been lived with reference to humans his own age among his own ethnic group and had been motivated by zeal for human ancestral traditions (1:14).[71] God, having chosen Paul before he was even in a human womb, "revealed his Son" to Paul (1:15–16a).[72] So, Paul did not need any human validation of his gospel from the Jerusalem apostles or anyone else for that matter (1:16b–17). In fact, he remained relatively unknown (1:22), and all that was known about Paul by the Judean churches reflected the divine origin

---

clarity.

67. While the second rhetorical question in 1:10 is clear, the first can be interpreted in various ways. See Williams, *Galatians*, 41; Das, *Galatians*, 111–13.

68. McKnight, *Galatians*, 63; Martyn, *Galatians*, 139–41; Hunn, "Pleasing God?," 48; de Boer, *Galatians*, 65; Barclay, *Paul and the Gift*, 353–56.

69. Gal 1:11 is a "thesis statement" that answers the questions asked in 1:10. See Longenecker, *Galatians*, 20; Schreiner, *Galatians*, 92. The phrase κατὰ ἄνθρωπον may indicate either human in quality (Schlier, *Brief an die Galater*, 17; Burton, *Galatians*, 37–38; Moo, *Galatians*, 93; Das, *Galatians*, 116) or human in origin (Matera, *Galatians*, 52–53; Dunn, *Galatians*, 52; de Boer, *Galatians*, 76).

70. Peter Oakes writes, "Paul repeatedly emphasizes both lack of human origin and lack of human agency in his commissioning and message" (*Galatians*, 52; cf. Mußner, *Galaterbrief*, 65).

71. "Ancestral traditions" focuses on the oral Pharisaic traditions to which Paul devoted himself (cf. Mark 7:5; Acts 22:3; Josephus, *Ant.* 13.297, 408). So Dunn, *Galatians*, 60; Schreiner, *Galatians*, 99–100. Contra Martyn, *Galatians*, 155; Barclay, *Paul and the Gift*, 358. On the relation of the autobiography to this and other polarities, see Gaventa, "Galatians 1 and 2," 315; Koptak, "Rhetorical Identification," 109; Hunn, "Pleasing God?," 36–37.

72. The allusions to Isa 49:1 and Jer 1:5 emphasize the divine nature of Paul's prophetic calling. See Schreiner, *Galatians*, 101; Oakes, *Galatians*, 55–56.

of his gospel, which resulted in the divine end: the glorification of God (1:23–24).

When Paul finally did make a significant trip to Jerusalem after fourteen years, he was opposed by false brothers who concerned themselves with a physical identity marker that belongs to the value system of the present age (2:3–4; cf. 5:6; 6:15). One of the purposes of this trip was to present his gospel to the other apostles (2:2). Paul recognizes that this could be interpreted as seeking human validation of his gospel from those who "seemed influential" (2:2 ESV).[73] Paul repudiates this interpretation of the visit. He did not care about their human positions because "God shows no partiality," and they contributed nothing to him (2:6). Rather the group of apostles simply perceived the divine grace and recognized one another's unique divine callings (2:7–10).[74]

By contrast, Cephas came under human influence at Antioch. He was eating with the gentiles until "certain people came from James" at which point he withdrew because he feared other human beings that Paul identifies as "the circumcision party" (2:12).[75] Besides being motivated by fear of other human beings, Cephas's withdrawal violated the gospel's truth in one additional way: His actions wrongly placed value in human ethnic distinctions that are reevaluated by the gospel of Christ (2:14). In summary, the biographical recollections found in chapters 1–2 serve to demonstrate that Paul himself has been freed from valuing or fearing that which is human and that he now preaches and lives the divine revelation of God's Son.

Works of the law or faith of Christ. In 2:16, Paul supplements the human/divine polarity with the works of the law/faith of Christ polarity. The

---

73. Lightfoot, *Galatians*, 103; Burton, *Galatians*, 71; Longenecker, *Galatians*, 48; Schreiner, *Galatians*, 121; Moo, *Galatians*, 124.

74. Paul and the Jerusalem apostles mutually recognized their unique divine gifts. The identification of Paul as the apostle to the gentiles was not a decision handed down by the Jerusalem apostles. See Mußner, *Galaterbrief*, 116–18; Betz, *Galatians*, 96; Dunn, *Galatians*, 112; Martyn, *Galatians*, 192; Schreiner, *Galatians*, 128; Das, *Galatians*, 189.

75. DeSilva explains, "Paul is accusing Peter of outright cowardice (as Paul does the rival teachers in 6:12 and denies in his own case in 5:11 and 6:17) or people-pleasing (as Paul does the rival teachers in 6:13 and denies in his own case in 1:10)" (*Galatians*, 37). Peter likely feared possible persecution from other Jews. So Jewett, "Agitators and the Galatian Congregation," 340–41; Dunn, "Incident at Antioch," 7–11; Schreiner, *Galatians*, 144; Moo, *Galatians*, 147–49; Das, *Galatians*, 208, 230–32. The precise source of this possible persecution will be discussed in ch. 5.

verse has been a thorny one for interpreters with debates raging about the meaning of δικαιόω, ἔργα νόμου, and πίστις Χριστοῦ. The point here, however, must focus on how the works of the law/faith of Christ polarity supplements the human/divine polarity, and therefore, this discussion will focus on ἔργα νόμου, and πίστις Χριστοῦ.[76]

In 2:15, Paul points out to Cephas the advantage of their human birth: "We are Jews by nature and not Gentile sinners." Yet, such a human advantage was insufficient to obtain justification. Like the gentiles, they also were justified by faith rather than by ἔργα νόμου (2:16). The phrase is an objective genitive: the works done in obedience to Torah.[77] But as Moo points out, "The real debate is over the significance of the phrase or, more particularly, *why* this doing of the law cannot justify."[78] James D. G. Dunn has argued that the emphasis is on those commands that function to mark the boundary between Jew and gentile.[79] Certainly the bound-

---

76. The meaning of δικαιόω is not insignificant, but it is less central to this argument. The word appears eight times in the letter (2:16, 17; 3:8, 11, 24; 5:4). Four primary interpretations have been offered historically: (1) Roman Catholics have traditionally held that justification, while certainly referring to forgiveness of past sins, refers to the actual ethical status of the righteous person. (2) By contrast, the Reformers held to a forensic understanding of justification. To be justified is to be declared righteous by God and thus given a status that one has not merited (see Das, *Galatians*, 244; Longenecker, *Galatians*, 84). (3) Martyn argues for the translation "rectification," which means "making right what has gone wrong." Martyn's understanding joins with the subjective genitive interpretation of πίστις Χριστοῦ. Rectification occurred already in the faithful act of Christ's death. It is not a response to either human faith or works. It is God's initiatory act that brings about the restoration of his people (*Galatians*, 250, 263–75; Martyn, "God's Way," 141–56). (4) More recently, N. T. Wright has argued that justification means "to be reckoned by God a true member of his family" (*Justification*, 116). For the purposes of this chapter, it is sufficient to note two lines of evidence. First, Paul's use of δικαιόω reflects the Hebrew verb צדק. In the Hiphil form, צדק refers to the forensic declaration that a person is righteous or just. Second, forensic justification best explains the citation of Gen 15:6 in Gal 3:6 in which righteousness is "counted" to Abraham. See especially Schreiner, *New Testament Theology*, 351–67; Schreiner, *Galatians*, 155; Moo, *Galatians*, 161; Westerholm, *Justification Reconsidered*. Forensic justification is "a proleptic manifestation of God's righteous verdict" on the last day (Silva, "Eschatological Structures," 149).

77. Dunn, *Galatians*, 135; Dunn, *Beginning from Jerusalem*, 475; Moo, *Galatians*, 175.

78. Moo, *Galatians*, 158. Don B. Garlington argues that the preposition ἐκ possesses a partisan sense. On this basis, he claims that Paul's opponents were not concerned with works-righteousness but whether one belonged to the eschatological people of God as marked out by the works of the law ("Paul's 'Partisan Ἐκ,'" 567–89). In Paul, however, ἐκ commonly signifies instrumentality. See Lambrecht, "Critical Reflections," 135–41.

79. Dunn, *Galatians*, 135–39. Contra Bachmann, "4QMMT und Galaterbrief," 91–113.

ary between Jew and gentile became the flashpoint in Antioch (2:11–21) and lies behind the obsession with circumcision by Paul's opponents in Galatia. Nonetheless, Paul's use of the phrase ἔργα νόμου in response to these boundary issues is not limited to the boundary markers of Torah. Instead, Paul responds to boundary marker controversies by demonstrating the failure of the Jewish people, like the gentiles, to keep the entire law (3:10). Why have the Jews failed to keep the entire law? The fault is not with the law. Rather the problem is human frailty as is hinted at in 2:16 where Paul alludes to Ps 143:2, "Do not bring your servant into judgment, for no one living (ζῶν) is righteous before you." Paul changes ζῶν in the LXX to σάρξ in order to emphasize human frailty and create a link with the emphasis on the flesh at the end of the letter.[80] Paul makes an anthropological argument: The failure of Torah obedience to justify is a *human* failure.[81]

Since one cannot be declared righteous by Torah obedience because of human frailty, one can only be declared righteous through πίστις Χριστοῦ. But does πίστις Χριστοῦ signify the faithfulness accomplished by Christ (subjective genitive) or faith in the person and work of Christ (objective genitive)?[82] While certainly not denying that persons are justified on the basis of Christ's obedience, context points toward the objective genitive interpretation here. The Galatians received the Spirit ἐξ ἀκοῆς πίστεως (3:2), and Abraham ἐπίστευσεν τῷ θεῷ (3:6).[83] The emphasis in the context is on the response of faith to the divine revelation, and it is in this way that the phrase builds upon the earlier human/divine polarity. Justification cannot come by Torah obedience because of human frailty. It comes by a faith response to the divine revelation of the gospel of Christ. In fact, were the Galatians to seek justification by works of the law, they would be forgetting the revelation of the cross and the way they received the Spirit (3:1–2). Abraham serves as the precedent.[84] Having

---

80. Thielman, *From Plight to Solution*, 63–65; de Boer, *Galatians*, 152; Moo, *Galatians*, 159. Contra Dunn, who argues that σάρξ here speaks not only of human frailty but of human ethnic origin, despite lack of evidence for the claim (*New Perspective on Paul*, 116).

81. See Kim, *Paul and the New Perspective*, 61–66; Westerholm, *Perspectives Old and New*, 366–84; Moo, *Galatians*, 160.

82. For the subjective genitive view, see Hays, *Faith of Jesus Christ*. So also Martyn, *Galatians*, 263–73; Martyn, "God's Way"; de Boer, *Galatians*, 148–50.

83. For a more in depth discussion of the debate, see Bird and Sprinkle, *Faith of Jesus Christ*.

84. Betz, *Galatians*, 141; Longenecker, *Galatians*, 112; Dunn, *Galatians*, 160–61;

received the divine revelation, he responded in faith and was declared righteous (3:6), and now all who respond to the divine revelation in the same manner belong to his line (3:7–9).[85] On the other hand, those who revert to reliance on Torah works reject the revelation of the cross and remain under the divine curse against human sin (3:10–13). The blessing of Abraham, which is experienced through the promised Spirit, comes to the gentiles only "in Christ Jesus" and "through faith" (3:14).

Law or promise. In 3:15–29, Paul shifts focus again to a third polarity, law or promise. This polarity builds upon the previous two, but as becomes clear in 3:21–22, the pair must be more nuanced than either of the previously discussed ones. Paul begins by defending the primacy of the covenant promises made to Abraham. He does this first on the basis of chronology: "the law that came 430 years later does not annul a covenant previously established by God" (3:17). God gave the law τῶν παραβάσεων, a difficult phrase that likely means that God gave the law to "increase the trespass" (Rom 5:20).[86] It served this function "until the Seed would come to whom the promise was made" (3:19). So, the law is secondary to the promise, not merely because of chronology, but also since the law served its purpose only until the coming of the Seed. Paul notes that this was also evident in the way the law was established, that is "through angels by an intermediary" (3:19).[87]

Unlike the other polarities, the law and promise are not absolutely opposed to one another. Paul expects the question: "Therefore, is the law opposed to the promises of God? Certainly not!" (3:21). The difference between law and promise is much more complicated than simply labeling one bad and the other good.[88] Both have their place in God's plan,

---

McKnight, *Galatians*, 151.

85. In Paul's argument, Abraham and the Christian place their faith in a common object, God's promise. So Betz, *Galatians*, 153; Longenecker, *Galatians*, 113. Contra Schlier, *Brief an die Galater*, 141; Matera, *Galatians*, 116; de Boer, *Galatians*, 191.

86. See especially Das, *Galatians*, 358–61.

87. Albert Vanhoye argues that the mediation of the law serves "pour rabaisser ainsi la Loi à un niveau qui n'est pas réellement divin" ("Médiateur des anges," 411).

88. Mußner comments, "Deshalb begnügt Paulus sich auch nicht mit einer raschen Zurückweisung, sondern begründet (vgl. rap) in V 21b ausdrücklich, warum das Gesetz nicht ein Konkurrent der Verheißungen sein kann: weil das Gesetz in Wirklichkeit nicht das Heil zu bringen vermag" (*Galaterbrief*, 251). See also Fung, *Galatians*, 162. Contra de Boer, *Galatians*, 232. Nevertheless, Paul's functional elevation of promise over Torah would have been "entirely *unnatural* for anyone reared in the Jewish

but both must be kept in their place to serve their own respective roles. Functionally, law and promise serve opposite purposes. The law condemns while the promise looked ahead to justification through Christ. For this reason, Paul argues, the law should not be used for a function for which it was not designed. The law could never bring about life and righteousness (3:21). Instead, the law served as a παιδαγωγός until the coming of Christ (3:24). Within the present evil age—the time "before faith came" (3:23)—the law had a positive imprisonment function. God, who stands behind the personified Scripture, "imprisoned everything under sin" (3:22; cf. Rom 11:32).[89] But for those who have become "heirs according to promise" the time has come to leave behind such captivity and enjoy the freedom of sons (3:25-29). To put it differently, while both law and promise came within this present evil age, the function of the law was limited to the present evil age while the promise always pointed beyond the present to the future coming of the Seed.[90]

Slavery or freedom. The fourth primary polarity, slavery/freedom, appears as early as 1:4 where Paul speaks of rescue from this present evil age, but the polarity takes center stage beginning in 3:22 and becomes even more important in chapter 4.[91] Paul further explicates the παιδαγωγός illustration in 4:1-2, emphasizing that the pseudo-slavery of an heir is only a temporary state within his father's plan. Unlike the illustrative heir, the slavery of the Galatians was all too real. They "were enslaved to the cosmic elements" (4:3). Paul portrays slavery as the natural activity of this present evil age while freedom is obtained only by divine intervention

---

tradition" (Barclay, *Paul and the Gift*, 401; italics original).

89. So Warfield, *Inspiration and Authority*, 299-348; Schlier, *Brief an die Galater*, 121; Martyn, *Galatians*, 372-73; Schreiner, *Galatians*, 244-45. Similarly Das, *Galatians*, 368. Contra those who hold that "Scripture" refers to a particular text in Paul's mind (Longenecker, *Galatians*, 144) or those who hold that "Scripture" refers to the law or Scriptures generally (Dunn, *Galatians*, 194; Moo, *Galatians*, 239).

90. On the temporal function of the law, see Bruce, *Galatians*, 183; Longenecker, *Galatians*, 148-50; Matera, *Galatians*, 137; McKnight, *Galatians*, 182; Schreiner, *Galatians*, 248; Wright, *Paul and the Faithfulness of God*, 866; Barclay, *Paul and the Gift*, 402-4.

91. Longenecker identifies freedom as "the essence of the Christian proclamation" (*Galatians*, 225; cf. Longenecker, *Paul, Apostle of Liberty*). Betz calls freedom the "central theological concept which sums up the Christian's situation before God" (*Galatians*, 255). See also Luther, "Freedom of a Christian," 31:327-77; Mußner, *Theologie der Freiheit*; Epp, "Paul's Diverse Imageries," 100-116; Silva, "Eschatological Structures," 155-57; Schreiner, *Paul, Apostle of God's Glory*, 219-50.

through Christ. God the Father liberated and adopted the Galatians into his family by sending the Son and then later the Spirit (4:4–7). Before the divine intervention, they were alienated from God and worshiped idols (4:8), but now everything has changed as God knows them and they know God (4:9). The problem in Galatia then is startling: They are tempted to return to their enslaved status under the oppression of the cosmic elements (4:9). How? By seeking to observe the law that belongs to the present evil age (4:10).[92]

After making a personal appeal (4:12–20), Paul points the Galatians to the law itself. In the narrative of Abraham, Sarah, and Hagar, Paul finds all his themes coalescing. One woman is a slave, and one is free (4:22). The slave gives birth to a son through the flesh, that is by human action and the natural processes of the present age, but the free woman gives birth to a son through the divine promise that was believed (4:23). Paul then identifies an allegory: each woman represents a different covenant (4:24).[93] The Sinai law bears children for slavery because it gives no way to escape the problem of human frailty (4:24). So also, Jerusalem within the present age produces slaves because Torah cannot give the freedom of righteousness and life (4:25). But the heavenly Jerusalem, the one not of this age or this creation, is free and has given birth to free children through God's promised action (4:26–27).[94] Like in Genesis, it is those who are free now, not the enslaved, who will receive the inheritance (4:30–31).[95] Therefore, Paul pleads with the Galatian Christians to "stand" in their freedom, which is a gift from Christ, and not to "submit again to a yoke of slavery" (5:1).[96] By accepting circumcision, they would be returning to slavery under the law and rejecting the advantages of freedom

---

92. On the functional equation of the calendrical observances of the Mosaic law and pagan worship, see de Boer, "Τὰ Στοιχεῖα," 222–24.

93. The nature of the allegory will be discussed in chap. 6. See Caneday, "Covenant Lineage," 50–77; Harmon, "Allegory, Typology," 144–58.

94. Cf. Tob 13:16–17; Heb 11:10, 16; 12:22; 13:14; Rev 3:12; 21:2, 10–21; 2 Bar 4:2–6; 4 Ezra 7:26. On the growth of the concept of a heavenly Jerusalem, see Longenecker, *Galatians*, 213–15; Witherington, *Grace in Galatia*, 334–35; Dow, *Images of Zion*; de Vos, "Jerusalem," 326–37.

95. Although wrongly denying the imperative function of Sarah's words to cast out the false teachers, on the importance of inheritance in 4:30, see Eastman, "'Cast Out the Slave Woman,'" 309–36.

96. Gal 5:1 is "syntactically independent" (Fung, *Galatians*, 216). While the verse is obviously transitional in nature, it is also a climactic summation of the book's argument. See Betz, *Galatians*, 256; Longenecker, *Galatians*, 223; Matera, *Galatians*, 198; McKnight, *Galatians*, 243; deSilva, *Galatians: Handbook*, 101–2.

that Christ has won for them (5:2-6). Within the present age, humanity cannot escape the condemnation declared by the law. Only through the divine fulfillment of divinely revealed promises can persons receive the freedom of blessed sons.

Flesh or Spirit. In 5:13, Paul shifts to the final major polarity: the flesh and the Spirit. Despite the shift in vocabulary, 5:13—6:10 continues to supplement the cosmic conflict theme that has taken up the whole letter.[97] The law could never cure human frailty, and thus it only served to place humanity under the curse. Despite human shortcomings, the law itself accurately communicated God's desire for his people as summarized in the command to love neighbor (5:14). Freedom from the law then should not be taken as freedom to indulge the flesh but freedom to please God by loving others (5:13-15).[98] Believers "walk by the Spirit" (5:16), but set against the Spirit are "the desires of the flesh" (5:17).[99] The desires of the flesh and the desires of the Spirit stand in hostile opposition to one another (5:17).[100] When the desires of the flesh are enacted, they become "the works of the flesh," which are those activities condemned by the law and indicative of those who will not inherit the kingdom of God (5:19-21).[101] While the law did not enable persons to overcome the flesh's

---

97. Rightly de Boer: "Believers in Christ now live at 'the juncture of the ages,' the point at which the Spirit of Christ (4:6) comes into conflict with the world of the Flesh" (de Boer, *Galatians*, 328; quotation from Martyn, "Epistemology"). Contra Moo, *Galatians*, 339.

98. Paul's emphasis here does not necessarily indicate a shift toward confronting an antinomian strand in the churches of Galatia. Contra Betz, *Galatians*, 8-9. It is essential to his argument against the opponents to explain that the intention of the law can only be obeyed through the power of the Spirit.

99. De Boer rightly argues that σάρξ is personified by Paul, but he allows the eschatological and cosmological elements of the personification to override the anthropological (*Galatians*, 335-39). On the personification of σάρξ, see also Barclay, *Paul and the Gift*, 427.

100. Gordon D. Fee comments that "the ultimate contrasts in Paul are eschatological: life 'according to the flesh,' lived according to the present age that has been condemned through the cross and is passing away, or life 'according to the Spirit,' lived in keeping with the values and norms of the coming age inaugurated by Christ through his death and resurrection and empowered by the eschatological Spirit" (*God's Empowering Presence*, 431). Although some ignore the anthropological element too much, see also Bruce, *Galatians*, 244; Russell, "Does the Christian Have 'Flesh,'" 179-87; Russell, *Flesh/Spirit Conflict*; Martyn, *Galatians*, 530-31; Das, *Galatians*, 558. On the difficult final clause in 5:17, see Schreiner, *Galatians*, 343-45.

101. Betz, *Galatians*, 283; Fee, *God's Empowering Presence*, 432.

desires, the Spirit does give such power as he produces within persons his fruit and thus transcends the need for the law (5:22–23).[102] Such is not a pessimistic view of life in the Spirit. The desires of the flesh belong to the present evil age and have died on the cross of Christ, and thus believers are free to walk with the Spirit (5:24–25).

Summary. Before the coming of God's invasive action in Christ, reality was determined by those things that belong to the present evil cosmos: Human frailty and the corresponding imperfect works of the law, the flesh and the status of slavery. Even the law finds itself in this realm because it served a temporary and restricted purpose to increase transgressions and imprison everything under sin. On the other side of the fullness of time are those things that belong to the new creation: The divinely revealed gospel and the corresponding faith in that gospel. The Abrahamic promise pointed forward to these things, and the blessed freedom promised to Abraham is now finally experienced even by the gentiles through the Spirit.

Manifestations of the Conflict

This cosmic conflict described in Galatians manifests itself in multiple ways in the lives of believers. In his description of Paul's apocalyptic gospel, Beker describes the conflict as being experienced on two fronts, the macrocosmic—against Satanic forces—and the microcosmic—within the individual.[103] The first problem with this taxonomy when describing Galatians is that the letter says nothing about Satanic forces with the possible exceptions of the "angel from heaven" mentioned in 1:8 and the στοιχεῖα in 4:3 and 8. Second, the microcosmic category limits cosmic conflict too narrowly to the individual. Galatians on the other hand has much to say about social relations. For these reasons, it is better to summarize the conflict as manifesting itself in three areas in the letter of Galatians: (1) Within the believer and the household of faith. (2) Between Jew and gentile. (3) Between persecutor and persecuted.

---

102. Beale, "Old Testament Background," 1–38.
103. Beker, *Paul's Apocalyptic Gospel*, 39; Beker, *Triumph of God*, 28.

Within the believer and the household of faith. Paul emphasizes this manifestation of the conflict in 5:13—6:10. In this section, he describes both the spiritual battle within the individual and the resulting dangers to the community.[104] When Paul speaks of the desires of the flesh and the desires of the Spirit, he calls attention to an inner struggle experienced by every individual believer, and thus there is a need for each individual to examine him or herself (6:4-5). Even so, the individual who walks by the Spirit never walks in isolation, and by indulging the desires of the flesh, the community of faith is put at risk. Believers may consume one another or provoke and envy one another (5:15, 26). They may sin against one another by indulging the desires of the flesh (5:19-21), and therefore, there is a great need for the spiritual in the community to restore those who have fallen (6:1-2).

Between Jew and Gentile. Another manifestation in the conflict is in the relation of Jew and gentile, which is especially prominent in 2:1—3:29.[105] When Paul opposes Peter to his face, it is not on ethical grounds alone. The primary problem is eschatological. Those Jews who withdrew from table fellowship with the gentiles were not "walking in step with the truth of the gospel" (2:14). They wrongly valued human categories that had been divested of relevance by the cross of Christ. Within the new creation, circumcision and uncircumcision are irrelevant (5:6; 6:15), and "there is no Jew or Greek, slave or free, male and female" (3:28a). All have been made "one in Christ Jesus" (3:28b).

Between persecutor and persecuted. A third manifestation of the cosmic conflict is that between persecutor and persecuted. The issue is most prominent in 4:29 where Paul asserts the typological principle that those born according to the flesh persecute those born according to the Spirit.

---

104. John M. G. Barclay's work remains a leading study on this manifestation of the conflict (*Obeying the Truth*). But he now admits that he did not highlight adequately the emphasis on communal life (*Paul and the Gift*, 425). By contrast, J. Louis Martyn, in an otherwise excellent article, risks overemphasizing the community at the expense of the individual ("Daily Life of the Church," 251-66). See also Russell, "Does the Christian Have 'Flesh'"; Russell, *Flesh/Spirit Conflict*.

105. Note, for example, the emphasis on the eschatological transformation of this relationship in these two articles: Donaldson, "'Curse of the Law,'" 94-112; McKnight, "I Am Church," 217-32. For a summary of Paul's theology of racial reconciliation, see Williams, *One New Man*.

This monograph will explore this manifestation of the cosmic conflict in greater detail in the pages ahead.

CONCLUSION

Galatians is about the eschatological transition between two ages: this present cosmos dominated by human sin and the new creation that was inaugurated when God sent the Son and then the Spirit in the fullness of time. As these two cosmic systems overlap,[106] conflict rages because each system stands antithetically opposed to the other. In Galatians, this conflict manifests itself in three primary ways: within the believer and the community, between Jew and gentile, and between persecutor and persecuted.

This overview of the theme of cosmic conflict has demonstrated that Middleton, in his work on early Christian martyrology, wrongly limits cosmic conflict to a war between God and the personal Satan.[107] In Galatians, Paul affirms that the events in Galatia fit within a larger narrative of cosmic conflict, but that conflict is between God and the impersonal yet personified entity labeled, "this present evil age" (1:4). Nevertheless, this study has confirmed other central aspects of the cosmic conflict theme identified by Middleton. Middleton identifies the "deconstruction of spatial and temporal boundaries" as one such aspect.[108] Early Christians lived in a "cosmos without barriers," in which heaven and earth, present and future merged together.[109] Their cosmology was marked by an "eschatological dualism," which served to starkly define the divisions in the cosmic contest.[110] The death of Jesus was a cosmic victory that Christians participated in through their own suffering.[111]

Galatians also reconfigures the cosmic boundaries, identifies stark polarities, and points to the cross as God's invasive cosmic victory. By

---

106. Silva, "Eschatological Structures," 155.
107. Middleton, *Radical Martyrdom*, 6.
108. Middleton, *Radical Martyrdom*, 15.
109. Middleton, *Radical Martyrdom*, 96.
110. Middleton, *Radical Martyrdom*, 141–43. Richard Bauckham says in reference to Johannine studies that dualism "is a slippery term" (*Gospel of Glory*, 109). Note that John G. Gammie has identified ten types of dualism ("Spatial and Ethical Dualism," 356–85). To avoid misunderstanding, I have generally avoided the word "dualism" and described various types of polarities instead.
111. Middleton, *Radical Martyrdom*, 88.

inaugurating the new creation within the present time, God has liberated those who believe in Christ from bondage to this present evil age. The Galatian Christians must resist the ongoing hostility of this age by standing firm in their new creation freedom and not submitting again to their former slavery under the present evil cosmic system (5:1). This resistance occurs through the adoption of the values of the new creation, indicated through the polarities that Paul highlights in the letter. Paul calls on them to choose that which is divine over that which is human, the Spirit over the flesh, the promise over the law, freedom over slavery, and faith in Christ over works of the law.

The next two chapters will answer the contextual questions about Paul's conception of cosmic conflict: Does cosmic conflict in Galatians parallel a theme found in other Jewish texts—both Israel's Scriptures and texts from the Second Temple period? To what degree do these texts speak as a unity about the theme? How do they differ? How does Paul operate within this intellectual context?

3

Cosmic Conflict in Earlier Scripture

IN THE MID-TWENTIETH-CENTURY, KEY scholars like Martin Buber and Gerhard von Rad saw a sharp discontinuity between prophetic and apocalyptic eschatology.[1] In their historical-critical reconstructions, apocalyptic emerges from the influences of Israelite wisdom literature, Persian dualism, and Hellenism. Paul D. Hanson, however, argues that "the rise of apocalyptic eschatology is neither sudden nor anomalous, but follows the pattern of an unbroken development from pre-exilic and exilic prophecy."[2] To Hanson, prophetic eschatology saw the historical realm as the context of divine activity and therefore integrated the prophetic vision with historical realities such as the political and ethical situation of the nation.[3] After the exile, however, Israel's visionaries began to transition to an apocalyptic eschatology that "respiritualized" their religion "by leaving their vision more on the cosmic level of activities."[4] This was due to their "disillusionment with historical realities" and their political disenfranchisement.[5] While Hanson's sociological

---

1. Buber, *Kampf um Israel*, 59–60; von Rad, *Old Testament Theology*, 301–15; von Rad, *Wisdom in Israel*, 277–83; Ringgren, "Jüdische Apokalyptik"; Murdock, "History and Revelation in Jewish Apocalypticism," 167–87. These were largely influenced by the earlier views of Wellhausen, *Prolegomena*, 507–8.

2. Hanson, *Dawn of Apocalyptic*, 7–8. Hanson was preceded in this assessment by his teacher Frank Moore Cross ("New Directions in the Study of Apocalyptic," 157–65). See Oswalt, "Recent Studies," 294; Allen, "Prophetic Antecedents," 15.

3. Hanson, *Dawn of Apocalyptic*, 12, 17.

4. Hanson, *Dawn of Apocalyptic*, 26. Cross had argued that apocalyptic reintroduced myth into Hebrew thought ("New Directions").

5. Hanson, *Dawn of Apocalyptic*, 12, 26. Although he offers a different reconstruction,

reconstruction of apocalyptic and his claim that apocalyptic literature appropriated Canaanite myth have been refuted,[6] the core of his thesis remains convincing, namely that "the visionary element which lies at the heart of apocalyptic extends throughout Israel's religious history; that is, the element of the prophet's vision of the saving cosmic activities of the Divine Warrior and his council."[7]

The depiction of Yahweh as the Divine Warrior is indeed a thematic parallel between OT texts of various epochs and genres (e.g., Exod 15; Judg 5; Ps 68; Hab 3; Zech 14).[8] The conflict in which Yahweh engages is cosmic because the cosmos is "the arena of God's self-revelation."[9] In that arena, the image of the Divine Warrior conveys less about Yahweh's struggle with his enemies than it does about his predetermined victory over them. Diversity exists, however, concerning the nature of Yahweh's victory. Whom or what does Yahweh conquer—pagan nations, sin or evil generally, demonic forces? And what will be the result of Yahweh's victory, that is to say, how is salvation for God's people imagined? John N. Oswalt, after critiquing Hanson, offers a modified version of Hanson's thesis: While the prophetic tradition initially explained Yahweh's salvation "in terms of human historical experience," Yahweh's simultaneous immanence and transcendence made it "increasingly clear that [human historical] experience was finally inadequate to reveal the whole scope of God's salvific intent."[10] Oswalt, therefore, sees the organic growth of Israelite eschatology—as evidence in the transition from prophetic to apocalyptic—not as an escape from history but as a projection of a unified theology upon a larger stage.[11]

While degrees of organic growth will become evident, this investigation does not attempt a precise reconstruction of the development of Israelite eschatology. In Paul Middleton's work on cosmic conflict, he

---

Hanson was influenced by the sociological approach of Otto Plöger (*Theocracy and Eschatology*). See Allen, "Prophetic Antecedents," 17.

6. For a critique of Hanson's sociological reconstruction, see Oswalt, "Recent Studies," 297–300; Cook, *Prophecy and Apocalypticism*. For a critique of the division between history and myth, see Oswalt, "Recent Studies," 294–97; Collins, *Seers, Sibyls, and Sages*, 83–97.

7. Hanson, *Dawn of Apocalyptic*, 16.

8. Miller, *Divine Warrior*; Oswalt, "Recent Studies," 297. On the literary concept of "thematic parallel," see Harmon, *She Must and Shall Go Free*, 29–30; Altick and Fenstermaker, *Art of Literary Research*, 111.

9. Oswalt, "Recent Studies," 293.

10. Oswalt, "Recent Studies," 293.

11. Oswalt, "Recent Studies," 293–94.

attempts such a reconstruction, tracing an arc of development from Israel's holy war theology through the Maccabean conflict to the apocalyptic genre.[12] His reconstruction, however, oversimplifies the evidence and, like much scholarship, fails to appreciate earlier Israelite eschatology.[13] This chapter and the next one, therefore, have more modest goals: (1) to identify cosmic conflict as a thematic parallel between a sample of earlier Jewish documents, (2) to examine elements of continuity, discontinuity, and development on the theme without necessarily arguing for causation, and (3) to set Paul within his intellectual context and thus see his unique contributions to the theme. Since space prohibits a comprehensive examination of all earlier Scripture, this chapter will focus on four books that quotations and allusions in Galatians indicate were important to Paul: Genesis, Psalms, Isaiah, and Habakkuk.[14] While the next chapter will investigate a sample of noncanonical early Jewish writings that Paul does not quote, this chapter examines a sample of books that Paul believed spoke authoritatively into the crisis in Galatia. He introduces them with the phrase "it is written" (3:10, 13; 4:22, 27) or personifies Scripture as speaking to the Galatians (3:8, 22; 4:21, 30). As Richard B. Hays explains, "Paul understands his apostolic vocation to be inseparable from his *apocalyptic interpretation of certain biblical texts* that prefigure the events of the end time."[15] Paul believes the eschaton to be characterized by a cosmic conflict between God and the present evil age *because* he believes that earlier Scripture testified to God's invasive actions that have finally been revealed in the fullness of time.

GENESIS

Paul quotes or alludes to Genesis in Galatians more than any other OT book. Paul incorporates quotations of Genesis in Gal 3:6 (Gen 15:6), 3:8

---

12. Middleton, *Radical Martyrdom*, 128–34.

13. Jonathan Huddleston notes, "The barely-examined assumption that the Pentateuch is uneschatological dominates Pentateuchal studies" (*Eschatology in Genesis*, 2). In this assumption, much of OT scholarship has followed Plöger's dichotomy between theocracy and eschatology (*Theocracy and Eschatology*).

14. Leviticus, Deuteronomy, and Amos also merit examination on the basis of Paul's usage (Gal 2:6//Deut 10:17; Gal 3:10//Deut 27:26; 28:58; 30:10; Gal 3:12//Lev 18:5; Gal 3:13//Deut 27:26; 21:23; Gal 4:16//Amos 5:10; Gal 5:14//Lev 19:18). But including these additional books would result in a more superficial examination of each. In order to balance breadth and depth of examination, the examples have been limited to four books.

15. Hays, *Conversion of the Imagination*, 4.

(Gen 12:3; cf. Gen 18:18; 22:18; 26:4; 28:14), 3:16 (Gen 12:17; 13:15; 17:7; 24:7), and 4:30 (Gen 21:10). Added to these quotations is the allegory that Paul identifies in 4:21—5:1. A. Andrew Das claims, "Most of the scriptural texts that Paul actually quotes to the Galatians appear to have originated in the instruction of these rival teachers."[16] If this is indeed true, then Genesis stands at the epicenter of the controversy that shook the Galatian churches.

Even though Paul almost exclusively cites the Abraham cycle in his letters, Genesis demonstrates a high degree of literary unity.[17] The author of Genesis structures his account of the early history of the world and Israel by using the heading תולדות (2:4; 5:1; 6:9; 10:1; 11:10; 11:27; 25:12; 19; 36:1, 9; 37:2). By combining analysis of תולדות as a textual marker with the thematic transitions from global history to Israelite history and between the patriarchs within Israel's history, a simple structure reveals itself:

I. Primeval History (1:1—11:26)

II. Israelite History (11:27—50:26)

    A. Abraham Cycle (11:27—22:24)

        Linking Material (23:1—25:18)

    B. Jacob Cycle (25:19—35:22)

        Linking Material (35:23—36:43)

    C. Joseph Cycle (37:1—50:26)[18]

Genesis 1:1 sets a cosmic frame of reference for the history that follows: "In the beginning, God created the heavens and the earth." The story of Genesis occurs on a global stage. Thus, Genesis does not consist of *mere* history but presents a theological history on the grandest of scales—the universe.[19] One cannot avoid the grand scale of the narrative

---

16. Das, *Paul and the Stories of Israel*, 23-28; cf. Longenecker, *Galatians*, 199-200.

17. Hays, *Echoes of Scripture*, 162.

18. The structural outline presented here is based on Waltke, *Genesis*, 19. See also Fishbane, "Composition and Structure," 15-38; Alexander, "Genealogies, Seed," 255-70; Arnold, *Genesis*, 4-7; DeRouchie, "Blessing-Commission," 219-47.

19. E. A. Speiser comments, "Primeval History seeks to give a universal setting for what is to be the early history of one particular people" (*Genesis*, liii). See also Westermann, *Genesis 1-11*, 65; Arnold, *Genesis*, 7. This scale makes the comparison of Genesis with ancient myth or epics is not entirely unwarranted. See Kikawada and Quinn,

in the primeval history of Gen 1–11. Not only does God create "the heavens and the earth" (Gen 1:1), he also destroys "all that is on the earth" with a flood (Gen 6:17). Even humanity, miniscule in comparison with the Creator and Judge, possesses a global purpose: to "fill the earth" (Gen 1:28; 9:1, 7). This grand history serves an eschatological purpose in the canon as the *Urzeit* to which the *Endzeit* corresponds, and as such, it is "backward-looking prophecy," forecasting the future in light of the past.[20]

When the story narrows to focus on Abram and his descendants, the context of Israelite history remains global and eschatological. The choice of Abram is the continuation of Yahweh's actions at Babel. At Babel, the families of the world were confused and scattered across the earth (Gen 11:8–9), but in Abram, Yahweh promised to bless "all the families of the earth" (Gen 12:3).[21] Even at the end of Genesis, Joseph rises as the savior of "all the earth" as "all the earth" come to him to buy grain (Gen 41:57).[22] Rather than signifying divine favoritism for a specific nation, the election of Abraham expresses Yahweh's intention to bless the whole world.[23]

This cosmic-oriented narrative centers on the conflict caused by human sin. The sin of humanity in the Garden is not a mere moral failure. It is a reversal of the divinely created cosmic order. God gave humanity dominion over the beasts of the field (Gen 1:26–30), but at the tree of the knowledge of good and evil, humanity submits to a beast in rebellion

---

Before Abraham Was, 47–48; Garrett, *Rethinking Genesis*, 127–45.

20. Sailhamer, "Creation, Genesis 1–11," 16. Sailhamer also identifies the correspondence of ראשית (Gen 1:1) to אחרית הימים (Gen 49:1; "Creation, Genesis 1–11," 96) See also Gunkel, *Schöpfung und Chaos*; Huddleston, *Eschatology in Genesis*, 45.

21. One obvious link between the two stories is the use of שם. The tower builders desired to "make a name" for themselves (Gen 11:4) while God promises to give Abram a "great name" (Gen 12:2). See von Rad, *Genesis*, 155; Hamilton, *Genesis 1–17*, 372; Dempster, *Dominion and Dynasty*, 76; Arnold, *Genesis*, 132. Peter J. Gentry writes, "Just as the divine word in Genesis 1:3 brings into being and existence things that are not, so in Genesis 12:3 it is the divine word that brings into existence a new order out of the chaos resulting from the confusion and curse of Babel" (Gentry and Wellum, *Kingdom through Covenant*, 225).

22. Joseph is a fulfillment of the promise that Abraham would be a blessing to the earth. See Waltke, *Genesis*, 536–37; Hamilton, "Was Joseph a Type?," 59–60; Emadi, "Covenant, Typology," 112. Joseph is also "an antitype of Noah," but unlike Noah, Joseph saves the earth (Hamilton, *Genesis 18–50*, 513).

23. Carol M. Kaminski writes, "The patriarchal narratives are an affirmation of the creation story and speak ultimately of God's faithfulness to his creation. Given that that promise of increase is a continuation of the primaeval blessing, its realization may be seen as a reaffirmation of the divine intentions for humankind. The patriarchs, therefore, take up the creation story as it is through them that the primaeval blessing is guaranteed and advancing" (*From Noah to Israel*, 110).

to God (Gen 3:1–13). God's ordered creation had been very good (Gen 1:31), but human rebellion results in cosmic disorder. Ultimately, the very earth that was created to sustain humanity will now consume them (Gen 3:17–19).[24] The conflict splits humanity into two groups: the seed of the serpent and the seed of the woman (Gen 3:15). While the seed of the woman must suffer at the fangs of the serpent, the seed of the woman will deliver a fatal blow to the head of the serpent in the future.[25]

The narrative of Cain and Abel in Gen 4:1–16 serves as the author's initial interpretation of the promise in Gen 3:15.[26] The story of fratricide demonstrates that the seeds of the serpent and the woman are not biologically determined. While the brothers share the same father and mother, they relate differently to Yahweh. Abel offers an offering pleasing to Yahweh, while Cain submits to the dominion of sin.[27] Abel thus is the seed of the woman while Cain is the seed of the serpent, each resembling their spiritual parent.[28] Since God gives Eve "another seed" in Seth (Gen 4:25), the cosmic conflict between these two types of humanity continues throughout the book of Genesis.[29]

The story continues when Abram and his descendants are chosen by Yahweh while individuals from other nations are marked by rebellion against Yahweh, especially in terms of sexual immorality.[30] A preview of the future blessing given to Abram's seed can be seen, though, in his defeat

---

24. Von Rad, *Genesis*, 91.

25. Wenham, *Genesis 1–15*, 79–81; Dempster, *Dominion and Dynasty*, 68–70; Hamilton, "Skull Crushing Seed," 30–54.

26. Waltke, *Genesis*, 93–94. For broader parallels between Gen 3 and 4, see Westermann, *Genesis 1–11*, 285–86; Arnold, *Genesis*, 79–80.

27. The animal-like crouching of sin at Cain's door in Gen 4:7 is a possible allusion to the serpent's striking of the heel in Gen 3:15. So Waltke, *Genesis*, 98.

28. Alexander, "Genealogies, Seed," 265; Waltke, *Genesis*, 17–22. Contra those who see the story as mythological of conflict between agricultural and pastoral lifestyles: Speiser, *Genesis*, 31; Gunkel, *Genesis*, 48–49. Rightly, Hamilton, *Genesis 1–17*, 222.

29. Huddleston, *Eschatology in Genesis*, 214–15.

30. The Egyptian Pharaoh takes Sarai into his harem (Gen 12:10–20). The Philistine kings of Gerar take both Sarah and Rebekah into their harems (20:1–18; 26:6–11). The Sodomites seek to defile Lot's visitors while Lot makes a counteroffer of his own daughters (Gen 19:4–11). Lot and his daughters produce the Moabites and the Ammonites through incest (Gen 19:30–38). The Canaanite Shechem rapes Dinah (Gen 34:1–4). Potiphar's Egyptian wife attempts to sleep with Joseph (Gen 39:7–20). Certainly, God's chosen people practiced sexual immorality as well. In these instances, sexual immorality identifies them with the sinfulness of humanity-at-large and magnifies God's electing grace (Gen 16:1–4; 29:30; 30:5, 9; 35:22; 38:1–30).

of the Mesopotamian kings.³¹ The aggressive gentile kings are defeated by the most unlikely of heroes—God's elect wanderer—while the victimized king of Sodom comes to Abram as a suppliant (Gen 14).³² While the election of a family creates an ethnic aspect to the seed of the woman, Genesis makes clear that spiritual identity cannot be equated with ethnicity. Quite surprisingly, Genesis portrays the cosmic struggle between the two seeds as manifesting itself within familial relations, especially between brothers. Genesis continues this theme of fraternal strife begun by Cain and Abel in the relationship between Isaac and Ishmael, Jacob and Esau, and Joseph and his brothers.³³

Nonetheless, the election of Abraham adds an additional layer to the eschatology of Genesis. Not only does it present an *Urzeit/Endzeit* eschatological schema but also a promise/fulfillment schema.³⁴ Despite this cosmic disorder, Yahweh promises to establish a kingdom through his elect.³⁵ To Abram, Yahweh promises to give a land, a people, and a great name—three essential ingredients for a great kingdom (Gen 12:1–2). Peter J. Gentry notes that God promises to make Abram into a great גוי. Typically, גוי describes non-Israelite nations, but Gentry posits that גוי is used in Gen 12:2 because it indicates "an *organised* community of people having *governmental*, *political*, and *social structure*" similar to the concept of a Greek πόλις.³⁶ By contrast, Yahweh uses משפחה to describe the other nations of the world, a word that "refers to an amorphous kin group larger than an extended family and smaller than a tribe."³⁷ From this, Gentry concludes that "the family of Abram is a real kingdom with eternal power and significance while the so-called kingdoms of this world are of no lasting power or significance. . . . God intends to establish

---

31. Dempster, *Dominion and Dynasty*, 79.

32. The king of Sodom must ask Abram for the return of his people, placing him in the position of a suppliant even though the lack of the particle נא in the request reveals a lack of gratitude on his part (Gen 14:21). See Wenham, *Genesis 1–15*, 32; Waltke, *Genesis*, 235; Arnold, *Genesis*, 149.

33. Cohen, "Two That Are One," 331–42; Petersen, "Genesis and Family Values," 5–23; Huddleston, *Eschatology in Genesis*, 202–3.

34. Jürgen Moltmann writes that "the eschatology of the prophets grew up on the soil of Israel's faith in the promise, and that in prophetic eschatology faith in the promise is wrestling with new experiences of God, of judgment and of history and thereby undergoing new, profound changes" (*Theology of Hope*, 126).

35. Hamilton, "Seed of the Woman," 253–73.

36. Waltke, *Genesis*, 17–22. Italics original. See also Cody, "Chosen People Called a Gôy?" 1–6; Hamilton, *Genesis 1–17*, 371–72.

37. Gentry and Wellum, *Kingdom through Covenant*, 244.

his rule over all his creation through his relationship with Abram and his family."[38] But Abram and Sarah are unable naturally to give birth to the promised descendant. Furthermore, Abram reveals himself to be infected with human sin like all humanity and thus incompetent to bring about Yahweh's promise (Gen 12:10-20; 16; 20). Only Yahweh's invasive action can bring about the fulfillment of his promises, as he demonstrates in the covenant-making ceremony of Gen 15.[39] But while Genesis gives previews of God's action (e.g., Gen 14; 41:57; 47:10), the covenant promise awaits a future fulfillment "in the latter days" (Gen 49:1).[40] The cosmic conflict that originates with the disordering of the cosmos by human sin and continues in the hostility between the seed of the serpent and the seed of the woman will come to an end when Yahweh establishes his kingdom through the seed of the woman and Abraham.

BOOK FIVE OF THE PSALMS

Three times Paul makes a clear allusion to the Psalter in Galatians: Gal 2:16 (Ps 143:2), 4:26 (Ps 87:5), and 6:16 (Pss 125:5; 128:6). One allusion comes from book four of the Psalms, and the others come from book five. Therefore, this section will examine the theme of cosmic conflict, first, broadly across the Psalter and, second, specifically in book five.

Psalms 1-2 stand as a thematic introduction to the entire collection.[41] While the two can be categorized as a wisdom psalm and a coronation psalm respectively, such categorization distracts from the essential unity of the two psalms.[42] Both psalms lack a superscription, making them unusual in book one.[43] Furthermore, the two psalms have significant lexical

---

38. Gentry and Wellum, *Kingdom through Covenant*, 244-45. See also Ruprecht, "Vorgegebene Tradition," 171-88; Ruprecht, "Traditionsgeschichtliche Hintergrund," 444-64; Wenham, *Genesis 1-15*, 274-78.

39. Gentry and Wellum, *Kingdom through Covenant*, 294-95.

40. Sailhamer, "Creation, Genesis 1-11."

41. Delitzsch, *Psalms*, 11; Childs, *Introduction to the Old Testament*, 516; Auffret, "Complements sur la structure littèraire," 7-13; Hossfeld and Zenger, *Psalmen I*, 45; Miller, "Beginning of the Psalter," 84-92; Mitchell, *Message of the Psalter*, 73-74; Grant, *King as Exemplar*, 41-70; Gillingham, *Journey of Two Psalms*; Brueggemann and Bellinger, *Psalms*, 32; McCann, "Shape and Shaping," 351-53.

42. For an example of this thematic categorization, see Craigie, *Psalms 1-50*, 56-69.

43. Pss 10 and 33 are the only other psalms lacking superscriptions in book one. In both instances, the missing superscription signals a close relationship with the preceding psalm. Psalm 10 continues an acrostic begun in Psalm 9 (Dahood, *Psalms 1-50*,

overlap.[44] Perhaps most important is the inclusio of benedictions using the verb אשר (Pss 1:1; 2:12).[45] Psalm 1 is the classic expression of two ways theology.[46] The psalmist declares the man who avoids the way of sinners and delights in God's Torah day and night to be אשר (Ps 1:1–2). Thus, he prospers (Ps 1:3). The wicked, however, will not stand in the judgment and will perish (Ps 1:4–6). Psalm 1 leaves no room for a mediating position. Either one is blessed or wicked. Patrick D. Miller writes, "These two categories of people dominate the psalms."[47] The righteous/wicked polarity reappears throughout the Psalter and features most prominently in psalms of lament in which the righteous are persecuted by the wicked (e.g., Pss 6, 22, 37).[48] Psalm 2 gives specific embodiment to these two categories of humanity. The kings of the earth are the wicked who will perish because they have rebelled against Yahweh and his Messiah (Ps 2:1–3). God scoffs at this flailing attempt at cosmic warfare by the earthly kings and preemptively declares his victory simply by stating that he has instituted his King on Zion (Ps 2:4–6). The Messiah then takes up the song. He tells that Yahweh declared him his Son and promised him global prosperity and dominance (Ps 2:7–8). The invitation is then issued to the rebellious kings to surrender and submit to the Royal Son and thus join in the Son's blessedness (אשרי; Ps 2:10–12).[49]

Gordon J. Wenham has argued that, as a collection of songs meant to be memorized and prayed, the Psalms encourage worshipers to adopt God's point of view and reject the point of view of the wicked.[50] As has been argued above, this divine worldview already appears in summary form in the first two psalms. Jamie A. Grant adds that the worldview

---

54; Craigie, *Psalms 1–50*, 123). Ps 33 continues Ps 32 through the linking verb רנן (Pss 32:11; 33:1; Hossfeld and Zenger, *Psalmen I*, 206).

44. הגה (Ps 1:2; 2:1); דרך (Ps 1:1, 6; 2:12); ישב (Ps 1:1; 2:4); תורה and חק (Ps 1:2; 2:7). See Auffret, *Literary Structure*; Auffret, "Essai sur la structure," 26–45; Auffret, "Complements sur la structure"; Grant, *King as Exemplar*, 61–63.

45. Dahood believes that "Blessed is the Man" serves as the title of book one (Dahood, *Psalms 1–50*, xxxi).

46. Weiser, *Psalms*, 103–105; Kidner, *Psalms 1–72*, 63; Brueggemann and Bellinger, *Psalms*, 30–31.

47. Miller, "Beginning of the Psalter," 85.

48. Miller, "Beginning of the Psalter," 85–86; Brueggemann and Bellinger, *Psalms*, 31.

49. Brueggemann and Bellinger, *Psalms*, 33.

50. Wenham, *Psalms as Torah*, 41–76. Wenham's work on memorization is largely based on Carr, *Writing on the Tablet*.

encouraged by Pss 1–2 reflects five Deuteronomic themes: (1) The individual must be devoted to Yahweh. (2) Torah is central to the life of a believer. (3) Yahweh reigns over all creation. (4) The king, Yahweh's co-regent, must rely completely on Yahweh. (5) Only two ways exist: to follow God or rebel.[51] Considering the post-exilic circumstances in which the Psalms were likely arranged, the pairing of these two psalms—one with its emphasis on Torah observance and the other with its messianic hope—"presents an eschatological hope for a new leader who would be the fulfillment of the Law of the King" in Deut 17:14–20.[52] Psalms 1–2 see the rebellious ambitions of the wicked and declare them futile. "The way of the wicked will perish" (Ps 1:6). Why? Because God has decreed blessing for his anointed Torah-devoted Son-King (Pss 1:1–3; 2:4–9). God's actions leave humanity with no other option: submit to God's king or die.[53] Psalms 1–2, therefore, serve as lenses through which all the other psalms are prayed.[54] David C. Mitchell writes, "The ensuing collection is to be about ultimate war between Yhwh's *mashiah* and his foes, his triumph and the establishment of his universal dominion, centred on Zion."[55]

Note, for example, how reading through the lenses of Pss 1–2 affects the interpretation of Ps 3. When the Psalter was arranged, the clarity of the worldview of Pss 1–2 faced the immediate challenge of Israel's post-exilic situation. The Jewish people were a minor ethnic group under the oppressive rule of other nations.[56] So also, Ps 3 highlights the discrepancy between the worldview declared in Pss 1–2 and daily life.[57] The

---

51. Grant, *King as Exemplar*, 65. See also Miller, "Deuteronomy and Psalms," 3–18.

52. Grant, *King as Exemplar*, 66–67. See also Miller, "Kingship, Torah Obedience," 127–42.

53. Brueggemann and Bellinger write, "Psalms 1 and 2 persuasively invite readers and hearers to basic decisions for living in relationship with or in opposition to YHWH" (*Psalms*, 35–36).

54. Grant calls the two psalms "hermeneutical spectacles" (*King as Exemplar*, 65). Gerald H. Wilson makes a similar argument for Psalm 1 alone, calling it a "hermeneutical introduction" ("Shaping the Psalter," 74).

55. Mitchell, *Message of the Psalter*, 87.

56. Waltke argues that the Psalms should be read in four stages: (1) the stage of the original author, (2) the stage of their usage in the first temple, (3) the stage of their arrangement in the post-exilic period, and (4) the stage of Christ's fulfillment ("Canonical Process Approach," 10–16).

57. In fact, Pss 3–7 are all laments. Brueggemann and Bellinger comment, "The location of this unit of five psalms of lament at the beginning of the Psalter is astonishing because this articulation of need and petition is jarringly in tension with the assurances

superscription sets Ps 3 within the context of David's flight—his personal exile—from Absalom. Absalom, despite being a genetic member of the Davidic line, finds himself on the side of the "wicked" nations who rebel against God's anointed (Ps 3:7). In the present era, the wicked triumph (Ps 3:1–2) but the worldview of Pss 1–2 calls forth faith in God's future deliverance (Ps 3:3–6). David thus cries out to God for salvation and expects the blessing promised in Pss 1–2 (Ps 3:7–8).

While each individual psalm can be read through the lenses of Pss 1–2, so also the collection itself reflect the two psalms that introduce it. By focusing on Pss 1 and 150, Walter Brueggemann argues that the Psalter moves from obedience to praise "by way of *candor about suffering* and *gratitude about hope*."[58] Brueggemann's suggestion, however, ignores the unity of Pss 1–2, and therefore fails to adequately represent the eschatological worldview of the psalms.[59] Praise will not come by Torah obedience alone, but specifically through God's anointed Torah-obedient King. Gerald H. Wilson more accurately describes the Psalter as moving from lament to praise.[60] But even more specifically, this general movement from lament to praise centers on the Davidic covenant.[61] James M. Hamilton Jr. attempts to summarizes the focus on the Davidic covenant as follows:

> Book 1 focuses on David's rise to power through affliction. Book 2 sings of David's reign down to the time of Solomon. Book 3 then reflects the time of Solomon to the exile from the land. Book 4 consists of exilic reflections on Yahweh's past deliverance of Israel. Then book 5 looks beyond exile and hopes for Yahweh's future deliverance of his people through the agency of the Davidic king.[62]

---

offered at the beginnings of Psalms 1 and 2. . . . But in these five psalms we hear the voice of the pious who have not received the promised prosperity" (*Psalms*, 36–37).

58. Brueggemann, "Bounded by Obedience," 72. Italics original.

59. Mitchell demonstrates that "the great majority of interpreters, historically speaking, regard the Psalms as foretelling eschatological events, interpreting them of Messiah, eschatological war, the ingathering of Israel, and so on" (*Message of the Psalter*, 64).

60. Wilson, "Shape of the Book of Psalms," 138–39. Wilson, however, overemphasizes the movement from "individual lamentation" to "public, communal proclamation of praise" ("Shaping the Psalter," 81). Because the individual is most often David, the principle of corporate solidarity is operative in these "individual" laments.

61. Several scholars have recognized the focus on the Davidic covenant. See, for example, Wilson, *Editing of the Hebrew Psalter*, 210–13; Walton, "Psalms," 21–31; Kleer, *Liebliche Sänger*; Wenham, "Towards a Canonical Reading," 343; Hamilton, *God's Glory*, 275–79.

62. Hamilton, *God's Glory*, 275. See also DeClaissé-Walford, "Meta-Narrative,"

Whether one agrees with this level of specificity on the significance of each book or not, Hamilton's summary does accurately reflect the focus on the Davidic covenant found throughout the Psalter.

For the purposes of this chapter, it is enough to say that book 5 stands as the culmination of the Psalter's Davidic covenant focus. Wilson claims that book five "is possibly the most diverse and difficult to sort out."[63] Three clear collections of Psalms stand out in the fifth book: the הלל psalms (111–17),[64] the songs of ascent (120–34), and the final הללו־יה chorus (146–50). Additionally, book five can be sorted into three divisions that begin with הדו ליהוה כי־טוב כי לעולם חסדו and end with הללו־יה: Pss 107–17, 118–35, 136–45.[65] If Pss 146–50 are meant to be the conclusion to the entire collection, book five can be subdivided into a chiastic structure centering on Pss 118–19:

  A Davidic Messiah Psalms (Pss 107–10)

    B Exodus הלל Psalms (Pss 111–17)

      C Deuteronomic King Psalms (Pss 118–19)

    B′ Ascent to Zion Psalms (Pss 120–35)

  C′ Davidic Messiah Psalms (Pss 136–45)[66]

As a whole, book five "is a commentary summarizing the preceding four books of psalms."[67] The two Davidic collections (Pss 105–10;

368–74.

63. Wilson, "Shaping the Psalter," 78.

64. Most interpreters include Ps 118 with the הלל psalms. Grant argues that while it historically came to function as part of the הלל psalms, it does not fit with the collection otherwise (*King as Exemplar*, 123–24). See also Wilson, "Shaping the Psalter," 78–79; Miller, "End of the Psalter," 104; Freedman, *Psalm 119*, 4.

65. Wilson, "Evidence of Editorial Division," 349–52; Kratz, "Tora Davids," 23–28; Allen, *Psalms 101–150*, 75. Klaus Koch similarly identifies these divisions but sees the conclusion of each section as groupings of הללו־יה psalms ("Psalter," 243–77).

66. This is largely adapted from Zenger's arrangement of book five. He argues that the three central sections corresponded to the feasts of Passover, Weeks, and Booths respectively ("Composition and Theology," 98–102). Zenger's arrangement, however, has been altered here to account for the textual markers הדו and הלל noted in the previous footnote as well as the argument of Grant that Pss 118–19 fit at the center of the collection, which will be discussed in more detail below (*King as Exemplar*, 122–25).

67. Zenger, "Fifth Book of Psalms," 88.

138–45) recapitulate the themes of the earlier Davidic collections (Pss 3–41; 51–72) with Pss 108 and 144 being rewritings of earlier psalms.[68]

More importantly, Pss 118–19 stand at the center of book five, being set apart between the הלל psalms (Pss 111–17) and the songs of ascent (Pss 120–34).[69] Psalm 118 echoes the contrast in Ps 2 between humanity and God. The psalmist trusts in God in his distress (Ps 118:5–7). He takes refuge (הסה) in God rather than in human princes, as is commanded in Ps 2:12 (Ps 118:8–9). The nations that raged in Ps 2:1 now surround the righteous psalmist (Ps 118:10). In Ps 2:8–9, God had promised the Messiah that he would give him possession of the nations and enable him to break them. In Ps 118:10–13, the righteous rejoices that God has fulfilled this promise. He sings repeatedly, "In the name of Yahweh I cut them off!" (Ps 118:10–12). Who is this one who fights and "comes in the name of Yahweh" (Ps 118:26)? While the speaker is nowhere identified explicitly as the Messiah, reading Ps 118 through the lenses of Pss 1–2 makes the resemblance between the righteous in Ps 118 and the Messiah in Ps 2 clear. But the parallels between Pss 1 and 119 are even clearer. Psalm 119:1 compliments the benediction of Ps 1:1.[70] While Ps 1:1 blessed the man "who does not walk in the counsel of the wicked," Ps 119:1 blesses those "who walk in the law of Yahweh." Just as Ps 118 contains the first-person narration of the Messiah in Ps 2, so also Ps 119 contains the first-person narration of the blessed man who delights in Torah in Ps 1. Grant concludes, "These juxtaposed psalms represent the zenith of the Deuteronomic kingship theology of the Psalter."[71]

Other psalms in book five support this kingship theme, even celebrating the militancy of the Divine Warrior and his Davidic Messiah. Psalms 108 and 144 are important examples of this. Psalm 108 explicitly names the enemies of Moab, Edom, and Philistia who God himself will tread upon (Ps 108:9, 13).[72] In Ps 144, God trains the Davidic king's hands

68. Zenger, "Fifth Book of Psalms," 82. Ps 108 comes from Pss 57:8–12 and 60:7–14. Ps 144 comes from Pss 8 and 18.

69. Grant also lists lexical and theological connections that make Pss 118–19 a unit (*King as Exemplar*, 176–87).

70. Eaton, *Psalms of the Way*, 46–52; Brueggemann and Bellinger, *Psalms*, 520. Westermann even argues that Ps 119 was the original conclusion of the Psalter due to its correspondence to Ps 1 (*Praise and Lament*).

71. Grant, *King as Exemplar*, 121.

72. Frank-Lothar Hossfeld and Erich Zenger comment that the psalmist "expects a return of the Davidic 'foundational era,' both territorially and by military means" (*Psalms 3*, 123).

for war (Ps 144:1).⁷³ In light of God's invasive actions, Ps 145 concludes the book with David's declaration of God's kingdom: "Your kingdom is an everlasting kingdom, and your dominion endures through all generations" (Ps 145:13).⁷⁴ This declaration then summons forth praise from all flesh (Ps 145:21). The הללו־יה chorus of Pss 146–50 is the final response to Yahweh's triumph through his appointed king.⁷⁵ While the Psalter begins with the polarity of the righteous and the wicked (Ps 1) and repeatedly revisits the dilemma of the righteous sufferer (e.g., Ps 3), it reaches its climax with the expectation of God's invasive action in establishing his kingdom through the Messianic King, introduced in Pss 1–2.

ISAIAH 40–66

Paul quotes Isa 54:1 in Gal 4:27. Many scholars identify an allusion to Isaiah in Gal 1:15 (Isa 49:1),⁷⁶ and the NA28 identifies an allusion in Gal 4:8 (Isa 37:19). Harmon argues that allusions and echoes to Isaiah in Galatians are so thorough that Paul's presentation of the gospel in Galatians could be described as Isaianic.⁷⁷ While one may not agree with every instance of Isaianic influence that Harmon proposes, Harmon's cumulative case remains strong for the immense influence of the prophet upon the apostle. In particular, as Harmon notes and the clearer quotes and allusions demonstrate, "Isaiah 40–66 appears to have been particularly significant for Paul's theology in general, and Galatians in particular."⁷⁸ Such influence justifies an investigation into the theme of cosmic conflict in Isa 40–66.

Isaiah 40–66 can be subdivided into two sections with each section organized as a chiasm:⁷⁹

73. Zakovitch, "Ordering of Psalms," 222; Brueggemann and Bellinger, *Psalms*, 599.

74. Bullock, "Double-Tracking," 482.

75. Brueggemann and Bellinger, *Psalms*, 605.

76. Sandnes, *Paul, One of the Prophets?*, 61–65; Martyn, *Galatians*, 157; Ciampa, *Presence and Function*, 111–12; Schreiner, *Galatians*, 101; Witherington, *Isaiah Old and New*, 17.

77. Harmon, *She Must and Shall Go Free*.

78. Harmon, *She Must and Shall Go Free*, 3.

79. Critical scholars have viewed these two sections as belonging to different authors, labeled Second and Third Isaiah respectively. Historically, Isaiah followed the Pentateuch in being dissected by higher criticism. For an overview, see Schultz, "Origins and Basic Arguments," 7–32. Critical scholars continue to grapple with the provenance of various sections of Isaiah and often regard the unity of the book as a mere redactional

I. Comfort and Redemption for Zion and the World (Isa 40–55)

    A Universal Consolation (Isa 40:1—42:17)

      B Promises of Redemption (Isa 42:18—44:23)

      B' Agents of Redemption (Isa 44:24—53:12)

    A' Universal Proclamation (Isa 54:1—55:13)

II. The Servants of Yahweh and the New Creation (Isa 56–66)

    A Universal Vision (Isa 56:1–8)

      B Problems (Isa 56:9—59:15a)

        C Divine Warrior (Isa 59:15b–21)

          D Nucleus (servant, Israel, Zion) (Isa 60–62)

        C' Divine Warrior (Isa 63:1–6)

      B' Problems (Isa 63:7—66:17)

    A' Universal Vision (Isa 66:18–24)[80]

After Hezekiah foolishly shows the Babylonian envoy all the riches of Jerusalem, Isaiah prophesies that Babylon will one day take all these riches along with the king's own sons into exile (Isa 39:1–8). Hezekiah responds by accepting the word of Yahweh in contrast with Ahaz's rejection of Isaiah earlier in the book (Isa 39:8; cf. 7:1—9:6).[81] Nonetheless, Hezekiah demonstrates only a short-sighted foundation for his comfort: "There will be peace and security in my days" (Isa 39:8b).[82] The prophecy that follows in Isa 40–55 offers a better consolation than Hezekiah's self-centered and temporary comfort.

---

unity. For recent contributions, see Berges, *Buch Jesaja*, 23–24; Tiemeyer, *For the Comfort of Zion*. Peter J. Gentry critiques this approach as leading to "atomistic exegesis." He argues that "as much as 50 percent of the 'meaning' of a text is communicated by the literary forms and micro- and macrostructures (i.e., arrangement) of the constituent parts" ("Literary Macrostructures," 227–28; cf. Routledge, "Is There a Narrative Substructure?," 183–204). This section will treat Isaiah as a literary unity in order to better understand the metanarrative of the book and the unified meaning of the section.

80. Gentry groups the Hezekiah narrative in Isa 38–39 with section one (Isa 40–66), whereas I see it as transitional between the two major parts of Isaiah. Otherwise, this outline is taken directly from Gentry ("Literary Macrostructures," 249–51). Gentry reproduces these two chiasms from Motyer (section one) and Boda (section two). See Motyer, *Prophecy of Isaiah*, 289; Boda, *Severe Mercy*, 213.

81. Dumbrell, *Faith of Israel*, 114–15; Hamilton, *God's Glory*, 201.

82. Oswalt, *Isaiah 1–39*, 697; Watts, *Isaiah 34–66*, 66.

Yahweh offers his people an eternal comfort by ending their "forced labor" through the pardoning of Israel's sins (Isa 40:1–2).[83] This liberating forgiveness will come when Yahweh himself returns to his people, revealing his glory to all flesh (Isa 40:3–5). Yahweh through his eternal word, therefore, offers his people a more substantial comfort than fading, grass-like humanity can produce (Isa 40:6–8). The comfort he offers is a revelation of himself as eternal and universally sovereign (Isa 40:9–31). By returning to his people, Yahweh accomplishes two goals: First, he seeks to display his supremacy. Second, he seeks to express his love for Israel.[84] Even though Israel will be overcome by Babylon, "the Holy One of Israel" will be their Redeemer and once again bring them through water and wilderness in a second Exodus (Isa 41:1–20). Then Israel will become "a light for the nations" so that the gentiles also might experience God's salvation (Isa 42:1–7). Yahweh describes these actions as a decree of חדשות that will result in universal praise to himself (Isa 42:8–17).[85] Whereas in "former" times Yahweh indicted Israel for trusting in foreign nations (e.g., Isa 7:9; 14:32), in the "new" times Yahweh's rescue of Israel will make Israel a beacon that enlightens the idolatrous nations to their need for him.[86] Yahweh declares this as an irrevocable עצה, which in Isa 40–55 designates his salvific plan (Isa 40:13; 44:26; 46:10–11).[87]

This redemptive plan will occur in two stages.[88] First, Yahweh will secure Israel's release from Babylon (Isa 42:18—43:21). God will execute this deliverance through his agent Cyrus, who will bring God's judgment upon Babylon and its gods (Isa 44:24—48:22).[89] Second, Yahweh will

83. צבא means "warfare" or "military service" and thus "forced labor" metaphorically (Isa 40:2). See HALOT, s.v. "צָבָא"; McKenzie, Second Isaiah, 17; Young, Isaiah, 3:22; Baltzer, Deutero-Isaiah, 51–52; Goldingay and Payne, Isaiah 40–55, 70.

84. Scheuer, Return of YHWH, 144. See also Blenkinsopp, Isaiah 40–55, 182.

85. The division of time into "former" (ראשון) and "new" (חדש) is a major eschatological feature in Isa 40–66 (cf. Isa 41:15, 22; 42:9–10; 43:9, 19; 48:3, 6; 61:4; 62:2; 65:7, 16–17; 66:22). See Bentzen, "Ideas of 'the Old' and 'the New,'" 183–87; Watts, Isaiah 34–66, 120.

86. Routledge, "Is There a Narrative Substructure?," 192–93. See also Oswalt, Isaiah 40–66, 45.

87. Jensen, "Yahweh's Plan," 443–55.

88. Scheuer, Return of YHWH, 133–36; Gentry, "Literary Macrostructures," 249–50.

89. The unity of Babylon with its gods transfers the political conflict between the Neo-Babylonian empire and Judah to the realm of cosmic conflict between Babylon and Yahweh. Interestingly, while Isa 19:23–25 foresees Assyria and Egypt as becoming part of God's people, Yahweh offers Babylon no such hope, which marks the city as the

atone for Israel's sins and will pour out his Spirit upon the nation (Isa 43:22—44:23). This act will be accomplished through the sacrificial work of Yahweh's Servant, who though righteous will die in the place of the wicked nation (Isa 49:1—53:12).[90] In response to Yahweh's actions, Zion is summoned to rejoice. Exile had made Zion barren but now she will abound with children (Isa 54).[91] This invitation to joy is then extended to all who are hungry and thirsty as Yahweh proclaims that the nations will run to his Davidic Servant and even the creation itself shall be transformed (Isa 55).

The replacement of thorns and briers by the cypress and myrtle (Isa 55:13) gives way to a fuller examination of this new creation in Isa 56–66.[92] This final section begins with a promise of Yahweh's interna-

---

archetypal enemy of Yahweh (e.g., Gen 11:1–9; 1 Pet 5:13; Rev 17–18). See Eidevall, *Prophecy and Propaganda*, 131–32.

90. The identity of Yahweh's servant(s) in Isa 40–55 is a matter of extensive debate. Many interpreters view most or all of the references to Yahweh's עֶבֶד as referring to the nation of Israel/Jerusalem corporately. E.g., Wilshire, "Servant-City," 356–67; Stern, "'Blind Servant' Imagery," 224–32; Blenkinsopp, *Isaiah 40–55*, 118–20. Isa 53, however, differentiates between the individual servant and the nation for whom he atones. This differentiation between the servant and the nation gave rise to the traditional Christian interpretation that the servant is the Messiah (Acts 8:26–40). E.g., Hugenberger, "Servant of the Lord," 105–40. Another option, however, fuses these two interpretations. The servant is indeed Israel, who has been unfaithful (Isa 44:1–5), but Yahweh promises the coming of a new Israel in the form of a representative Messiah (Isa 53). E.g., Dumbrell, "Role of the Servant," 105–13; Dempster, "Servant of the Lord," 154–60. For a historical overview of the issue from antiquity to the middle ages, see Laato, *Who Is the Servant of the Lord?* The theme of God's servant is so important that Charles H. H. Scobie identifies it as one of four elements that unites biblical theology (*Ways of Our God*, 301–468).

91. The name "Zion" is preferred over "Jerusalem" when the city is personified as a woman (Abma, "Travelling from Babylon to Zion," 3–28; *Bonds of Love*, 53–109; contra Reinoud Oosting, *Role of Zion/Jerusalem*, 190–94). That said, "Zion" also has a narrower theological semantic range than does the geo-political term "Jerusalem" since it "represents the final goal of God's salvific action" (Berges, "Personifications and Prophetic Voices," 54–82).

92. Hanson sees Third Isaiah (Isa 56–66) as an example of early apocalyptic eschatology but not quite yet exemplary of the apocalyptic genre, although the Divine Warrior myth comes close (Isa 59:15b–21; 63:1–6). He also takes note of "mythic material" in Second Isaiah (Isa 40–55) such as Yahweh's defeat of the dragon (Isa 51:9–11) and argues that, while the seeds of the apocalyptic genre are found here, the prophetic hope of Second Isaiah was too attached to real history in order to be truly apocalyptic (*Dawn of Apocalyptic*, 21–29). See also Cross, "Divine Warrior," 11–30; Cross, "New Directions"; Cross, *Canaanite Myth and Hebrew Epic*, 170; Brueggemann, *Isaiah 40–66*, 162–63; Blenkinsopp, *Isaiah 40–55*, 372–73; Ha, "Proto-Apocalyptic Worldviews." Oswalt has strongly refuted the view of Hanson and others on the reliance of myth in Divine Warrior texts. He writes, "To assert that every representation of [Yahweh] as [a warrior]

tional congregation of praise. Non-Israelites will "love the name of Yahweh" and will be brought into his house alongside Israel (Isa 56:1–8). Then Yahweh returns to a theme that began in Isaiah 1—the immorality and injustice practiced by Israel and especially by the Judean leadership (Isa 56:9—59:15a). Yahweh responds to this immorality and injustice as a warrior.[93] He straps on his armor to repay the wicked with his wrath, executing his justice globally from east to west (Isa 59:15b–21). While OT authors regularly depict Yahweh as a warrior (e.g., Exod 15:1–21; Judg 5; 2 Sam 22; Ps 68),[94] Isaiah 59 uniquely portrays his warfare as first against his own covenant people in retribution for their sin and then extending to the world.[95] This probably also explains Isaiah's second innovation of the Divine Warrior motif: In Isaiah, Yahweh's armor is metaphorical for his character.[96] The retributive justice, which Isaiah militaristically describes, overflows from Yahweh's holy character.[97] Yahweh's metaphorical armor, however, does not alleviate the violence suffered by his enemies. In the second rendition of the theme, Yahweh appears with crimson-stained garments, evocative of both blood and wine (Isa 63:1–2). He has trampled the wicked like grapes in a wine press (Isa 63:1–6).[98] With this terrifying vision still ringing in the ears, the prophet then turns to the present threat to Israel. Yahweh had shown Israel steadfast love, but Israel rebelled (Isa 63:7–14). The nation then is instructed to repent and pray for God's mercy and salvation (Isa 63:15—64:12).[99] Yahweh only partially

---

indicates borrowing of the Canaanite motif, especially when his warfare is of another nature (over ethical breaches) and on another plane (the spatio-temporal), is to find too much" ("Recent Studies," 297; see also Oswalt, "Myth of the Dragon," 163–72; Oswalt, *Bible among the Myths*).

93. Yoder Neufeld, *Put on the Armour*, 15.

94. Miller, *Divine Warrior*.

95. Yoder Neufeld, *Put on the Armour*, 23–24. See also Oswalt, *Isaiah 40–66*, 527.

96. While similarities exist with surviving myths, the differences remain strong. Yoder Neufeld claims that the "closest non-biblical parallel" is Enuma Elish 4 "where Marduk equips himself for battle with Tiamat," but Marduk's weapons are never identified as symbolizing virtues or character attributes (*Put on the Armour*, 28). See also Childs, *Isaiah*, 489–90; Goldingay, *Isaiah 56–66*, 221.

97. For an overview of the theme of holiness in Isaiah, see Routledge, "Is There a Narrative Substructure?" 194–95.

98. Brueggemann comments that "the theological point is that the God who comes in this violent mode is the God who will make things right in the midst of an abusive world" (*Isaiah 40–66*, 227). See also Goldingay, *Isaiah 56–66*, 372.

99. Scheuer writes, "Repentance is required because it is part of the reciprocity, of the essence of the relationship between YHWH and his people" (*Return of YHWH*, 142).

turns back from the impending warfare. He will judge Israel's idolatry (Isa 65:1–7), but he will not destroy all of Israel, preserving a remnant (Isa 65:8–16).

Gentry describes Isa 60–62 as the nucleus of the section.[100] God's glory will rise upon Zion replacing the light of sun and moon and will bring peace and prosperity upon the city (Isa 60). The Spirit-anointed servant then proclaims the good news of a new epoch—"the year of Yahweh's favor"—the age of justice and peace (Isa 61). The city that shall be ransacked by the Babylonians will one day be renamed: The Holy People, Yahweh's Redeemed, the Sought After, a City Not Forsaken (Isa 62:12). The conclusion of the book expands on this vision of a new epoch. Yahweh declares the coming of a new creation in which the sin and judgment of former times is no longer remembered and peace and prosperity will be eternally established (Isa 65:17–25). Thus, the joyful peace of Jerusalem will come in a new age and a new creation (Isa 66:7–24). In that new time and place, God's glorious presence shall return, and all nations will gather to worship him on Zion (Isa 66:18–23).[101] Childs writes,

> [T]he nature of Israel's salvation has been extended by Third Isaiah. . . . The promises of Second Isaiah of the glorious return from the Babylonian exile have not been repeated, but assumed as true and often rendered metaphorically to serve as background for Israel's final entrance into the transformed and glorified city.[102]

Childs's comment echoes what Oswalt has argued about the transition in Israelite eschatology. The pattern of development is not away from history but the organic extension of God's salvation to the entire cosmos.[103]

In Isaiah, the wicked—whether from rebellious Israel or the nations—oppose Yahweh's cosmic supremacy through their idolatry and immorality. Unthreatened by the rebellion of the wicked, Yahweh's holy character will be vindicated through his warrior-like judgment of Israel using Babylon, of Babylon using Cyrus, and ultimately of the whole world; but his holy character will also be demonstrated through the

---

100. Gentry, "Literary Macrostructures," 251. Childs writes, "The chapters that follow (60–62) portray the redeemed life experienced in the new and transformed Jerusalem, city of God" (*Isaiah*, 491). See also Westermann, *Isaiah 40–66*, 352–53; Oswalt, *Isaiah 40–66*, 534; Berges, *Book of Isaiah*, 401.

101. Oswalt, *Isaiah 40–66*, 687.

102. Childs, *Isaiah*, 545.

103. Oswalt, "Recent Studies," 293.

substitutionary death of his Servant, which will bring about the salvation of a remnant of Israel and make them a light to the nations. Hope can be found in Yahweh's promise of the coming kingdom, which, in Isaiah, is a renewed creation. The coming of a new creation will signify the commencement of a new age of Yahweh's favor, characterized by peace and prosperity.

HABAKKUK

Even though Paul quotes Habakkuk only once in Galatians, the quotation of Hab 2:4 in Gal 3:11 sits as the basis of much of Paul's argument in the central section of Galatians. J. Louis Martyn, for example, calls the quotation a "powerful climax" in Paul's argument.[104] He explains, "In Hab 2:4 Paul hears God promising the prophet that in the good news of Christ, the good news that has the power to elicit faith, God will one day make things right by creating eschatological life. That one day is the now of the Galatians."[105] The weight of this quotation from Habakkuk, therefore, justifies an investigation into the book of Habakkuk and an examination of the cosmic conflict theme in the prophet.

From very early in its history, Habakkuk has been read as a component of the larger collection of twelve prophets.[106] However, the nature of this unity of twelve diverse prophets remains a matter of debate among scholars. Paul R. House argues for unity based on a tripartite narrative: Sin (Hos–Mic), Punishment (Nah–Zeph), and Restoration (Hag–Mal).[107] More probably, as David L. Petersen argues, the unity of the Twelve is not literary but thematic.[108] Whether one sees the Twelve prophets as forming a precise narrative or a looser thematic anthology, the יום יהוה stands as the central theme of the Twelve.[109] While the term יום יהוה does not occur in all twelve prophets, the concept does.[110] The Twelve look ahead

---

104. Martyn, *Galatians*, 315.
105. Martyn, *Galatians*, 312.
106. E.g., Sir 49:10; Josephus, *Ag. Ap.* 1.8. See Redditt, "Formation of the Book," 1–26.
107. House, *Unity of the Twelve*, 71–108.
108. Petersen, "Book of the Twelve,?" 3–10.
109. Petersen, "Book of the Twelve?," 9–10; Rendtorff, "How to Read," 75–87; House, "Endings as New Beginnings," 313–38.
110. The term יום יהוה occurs in Joel 1:15; 2:1, 11; 3:4; 4:14; Amos 5:18, 20; Obad 15; Zeph 1:7, 14; Mal 3:23. But, as Rendtorff writes, "In many cases where the term 'day' appears, be it alone or in certain combinations, the reader of the Book of the Twelve

to "specific times" and "specific events" when Yahweh would intervene to judge the wicked and reestablish his rule on earth.[111] Therefore, the יום יהוה refers to repeatable instances of God's intervention in the regular history of Israel and the nations such as invasions, famines, and plagues while also referring to "a final, eschatological Day of the Lord" that "will eradicate sin for all eternity."[112] Describing the final יום יהוה, Aaron Schart writes,

> Die Propheten betonen die reale Zukünftigkeit dieses Tages. Es ist ein Tag, der ganz und gar Jahwe gehört. Ein Tag, der nicht wie alle anderen Tage bestimmt ist vom Dasein und den Handlungen der Natur und der Menschen, sondern direkt und eigentlich von Jahwe selbst.[113]

But discerning God's direct actions can be difficult in a chaotic world, "especially when innocent people were caught in war and devastation."[114] Habakkuk addresses "the dangers of despair and disillusionment" by confronting the problem of evil that arises from the יום יהוה theology of the Twelve.[115]

Habakkuk begins with an initial question from the prophet (Hab 1:2–4) followed by God's response (Hab 1:5–11). The prophet then issues a second complaint (Hab 1:12—2:1), which is also answered by Yahweh (Hab 2:2–20). The prophet then responds to Yahweh's declaration with a psalm that expresses the prophet's faith (Hab 3:1–19).[116]

In one sense, Habakkuk concerns himself with regional politics. Habakkuk's initial question indicts his own nation's unrighteousness.[117]

---

should associate it with something like the Day of the LORD" ("How to Read," 86).

111. House, "Day of the Lord," 181.

112. House, "Day of the Lord," 182.

113. Schart, *Entstehung des Zwölfprophetenbuchs*, 281.

114. Everson, "Canonical Location," 171.

115. Everson, "Canonical Location," 173.

116. Smith, *Micah–Malachi*, 97; Roberts, *Nahum, Habakkuk, and Zephaniah*, 82; Sweeney, "Structure, Genre," 63–83; Andersen, *Habakkuk*, 15; O'Neal, *Interpreting Habakkuk*, 78–79.

117. The prophet's initial complaint in Hab 1:2–4 has three possible targets: (1) the Assyrians, (2) the Judean leadership, or (3) the Egyptians. The Assyrian hypothesis does not easily explain Habakkuk's counter-protest in 1:13. Most interpreters opt for the second possibility, preferring to read Habakkuk through the lens of Mic 2–3 (e.g., Smith, *Micah–Malachi*, 99; Robertson, *Nahum, Habakkuk, and Zephaniah*, 139; Roberts, *Nahum, Habakkuk, and Zephaniah*, 88–90; Andersen, *Habakkuk*, 24–27). Everson proposes the third possibility, arguing that Habakkuk responds to the untimely death of

Those who should bring justice to Judean society instead destroy the nation with their violence resulting in the Torah's paralysis (Hab 1:2–4).[118] Yahweh's response expands the focus from domestic to regional politics (Hab 1:6). Shifting political fortunes created a time of regional uncertainty and chaos as the Assyrian Empire collapsed before Babylon's Nebuchadnezzar II joined by his Median and Scythian allies. Yahweh identifies this rising superpower as his tool of judgment upon his covenant people (Hab 1:12).[119] Human sin, however, unifies Judah and Babylon, placing them both under Yahweh's judgment. Yahweh characterizes the Babylonians as placing their confidence in their own power. "Their own strength is their god" (Hab 1:11). This arrogant self-worship intoxicates Babylon and drives them to seek universal domination (Hab 2:5). Yahweh pronounces a curse upon these builders of a city founded on iniquity (Hab 2:12–13).[120] By passing judgment upon Babylon, Yahweh affirms his universal sovereignty.[121] In contrast with Babylon's doomed ambitions, Yahweh announces what will certainly come to pass: "For the earth will be filled with the knowledge of the glory of Yahweh as the water covers the sea" (Hab 2:14). Both the Babylonians and their lifeless metal gods will be ineffective in executing their will (Hab 2:18–19). By contrast, Yahweh lives in "his holy temple" (Hab 2:20). Humans speak to mute idols, commanding them to "awake" and "arise" (Hab 2:19), but the

---

Josiah at Megiddo in 609 BC (2 Kgs 23:28–30; 2 Chr 35:20–27). If the MT order of the Twelve reflects chronology, then Habakkuk's placement between Nahum and Zephaniah would limit the prophet's date range at 612–598 BC ("Formation of the Book"). While this position possesses explanatory power for the composition of Habakkuk, it remains speculative. For the purposes of this examination of the cosmic conflict theme, the more common reading with Judah's unrighteousness in the prophet's crosshairs will be maintained.

118. Johnson, "Paralysis of Torah," 259–60; O'Neal, *Interpreting Habakkuk*, 81. Contra those who see the Torah's paralysis as an accusation against God (Roberts, *Nahum, Habakkuk, and Zephaniah*, 90; Andersen, *Habakkuk*, 118–19).

119. Smith, *Micah–Malachi*, 101–2; Robertson, *Nahum, Habakkuk, Zephaniah*, 148–49; Roberts, *Nahum, Habakkuk, and Zephaniah*, 95–96; Andersen, *Habakkuk*, 145–46.

120. By cursing arrogant Babylonians who build a city (בנה עיר) and using language echoing the description of Nimrod in Gen 10:9–10, Yahweh alludes to an earlier arrogant internationalist city-building agenda that arose on the plains of Shinar (Gen 11:4). See Robertson, *Nahum, Habakkuk, Zephaniah*, 195–96; Andersen, *Habakkuk*, 243.

121. Yahweh's universal sovereignty is also affirmed in the Book of the Twelve as a whole. The same God who judged Judah through the prophet Micah also judges Assyria in Nahum and Babylon in Habakkuk. See Nogalski, "Jerusalem, Samaria," 266; Porath, "'Stadt der Blutschuld,'" 334–35.

living God commands silence since no human can issue a command to him (Hab 2:20).[122] The message is as simple as it is clear: Human wickedness—whether it is found in Judah or in Babylon—will be defeated by Yahweh, and he will triumph over all the earth.

Habakkuk's closing psalm further affirms Yahweh's universal sovereignty. The psalm describes a "report" that Habakkuk has heard of a theophany (Hab 3:2).[123] Geographically, he locates the theophany as occurring in the south as God proceeds from Edomite territory (Hab 3:3).[124] The poetic descriptions of Yahweh's luminous appearance (Hab 3:3–4), use of plagues against his enemies (Hab 3:5), and wrath against rivers and sea (Hab 3:8) suggest that Habakkuk is poetically recounting the Exodus narrative as a divine military action.[125] God gloriously advances from Edom toward the enemy using the weapons of pestilence and plague (Hab 3:3–5). His actions not only terrify the nomadic peoples of Cushan and Midian, but even creation itself—the mountains, the deep, the sun and moon—react in terror to the sight of God with his unsheathed bow (Hab 3:6–11). In Hab 3:12, God goes on the attack against the nations, crushing "the head of the house of the wicked, laying bare from tail to neck" (Hab 3:13).[126] In doing so, Yahweh unilaterally brings salvation to his people and his Messiah (Hab 3:13).

At the beginning of the book, Habakkuk sees Yahweh's universal sovereignty as problematic. He cannot understand how God can use a wicked nation like the Neo-Babylonians to exercise justice upon "more righteous" Judah (Hab 1:13). He questions whether Yahweh will ever punish Babylon or will they continue "mercilessly slaughtering nations forever" (Hab 1:17)? Yet, the very attribute of Yahweh that arouses the complaint answers it as well. He will repay Babylon for their crimes. Only

---

122. Roberts, *Nahum, Habakkuk, and Zephaniah*, 128; Baker, *Nahum, Habakkuk and Zephaniah*, 66.

123. Cross argues that Hab 3 uses language from Canaanite myth like that in the Baal theophany found at Ugarit (*Canaanite Myth and Hebrew Epic*, 86, 102–3, 150). See also Anderson, "Awaiting an Answered Prayer," 57–71; Smith, "Concept of the 'City,'" 136–37; Smith, "Problem of the God," 240–41. While Habakkuk may have appropriated imagery from polytheistic sources, he did so for literary purposes not theological ones (Oswalt, *Bible among the Myths*, 93).

124. The coming of Yahweh from Edom appears also in Deut 33:2 and Judg 5:4. See Cross, *Canaanite Myth and Hebrew Epic*, 86.

125. O'Neal, *Interpreting Habakkuk*, 115–16.

126. The serpentine imagery echoes Gen 3:15. See Smith, *Micah–Malachi*, 116; Hamilton, *God's Glory*, 253.

Yahweh's dominance will be universal and everlasting.[127] This leaves Habakkuk and his hearers with a choice between two ways. The choice is either "puffed up" arrogance like the Babylonians or righteousness. Only the righteous will live, and they will do so by their faith in God's promised actions (Hab 2:4).[128] Habakkuk demonstrates such faith at the end of his psalm. He waits patiently for the יום צרה to come upon the Babylonians (Hab 3:16).[129] Because this Day of Yahweh will come, he will rejoice in the God who has made the promise, even when circumstances seem to indicate otherwise (Hab 3:17–19).

CONCLUSION

Genesis, Psalms, Isaiah, and Habakkuk share much in their understanding of cosmic conflict. First and most obviously, each of these books splits humanity into a polarity of spiritual groups: the righteous and the wicked. Although the language used alters, one either belongs to those who love God or those who rebel against God. The second locus builds on the first. Each book identifies the dual problem of human sin and suffering. In Genesis, human sin disrupted the cosmic order, and in Psalms, this disorder continues through the rebellious schemes of the wicked. Isaiah and Habakkuk address specifically the plight of Israel's own infection with human sin. Suffering exists because of human sin, although not in an entirely proportionate way. As all four books affirm, the righteous suffer at the hands of the wicked. From Abel to David to the suffering Servant, the present order of the world includes the unjust suffering of the righteous. This leads to a third observation: God's invasive action is seen as the solution to which the suffering righteous are directed to place their hope. He will restore justice and destroy the wicked. This intervention is consistently portrayed in martial terms. At times, God is portrayed as acting directly as Divine Warrior while in other instances he acts through his agent, the Seed of the woman or the Davidic Messiah. As Oswalt argues, the nature of this intervention grows organically in OT texts.[130] Genesis sees it as coming through a promised kingdom while Psalms expands

---

127. Whitehead, "Habakkuk," 265–81.

128. On אמונה as "faith," see Barr, *Semantics of Biblical Language*, 161–205; Roberts, *Nahum, Habakkuk, and Zephaniah*, 111–12; O'Neal, *Interpreting Habakkuk*, 95.

129. On יום צרה as a synonym of יום יהוה, see Rendtorff, "How to Read," 86.

130. Oswalt, "Recent Studies," 293.

that vision with its focus on the messianic king himself. To this, Isaiah adds the vision of the kingdom as a new creation. Habakkuk, although focusing less on the kingdom theme, nevertheless forecasts hope as the coming manifestation of God's glory, which fits well with the other three books. As Frank Thielman argues, these along with other OT texts share an "eschatological pattern" that moves "from plight to solution."[131]

Likewise, all three cosmic conflict loci—the polarity of the righteous/wicked, the problem of sin and suffering, and the solution of God's invasive action—can be easily found in Paul's own theology. By quoting or alluding to these earlier texts, Paul demonstrates his self-understanding of continuity with their theology. But comparison with earlier Scripture demonstrates that Paul's theology alters the thematic parallel of cosmic conflict in two primary ways. First, he reads all Scripture in light of the coming of the Son and the Spirit. As N. T. Wright has argued, Paul's theology stands in continuity with the central topics of Jewish thought, but he "rethought, reworked and reimagined them around Jesus the Messiah on the one hand and the spirit on the other."[132] Paul believes that God invasively acted through the sending of the Son and the Spirit. This action stands in continuity with God's promise, even while it represents an abrupt and surprising fulfillment of that promise.[133] Because of God's invasive actions, the polarity of the righteous/wicked has been reoriented around one's relation to the Son and Spirit. The determination of one's righteousness or justification comes on the basis of faith in the Son and is experienced through reception of the Spirit.

Second, because God's intervention has occurred in the Son and the Spirit, Paul believes that the new creation has already been inaugurated, although not yet fully realized, in the church.[134] Cosmic conflict, therefore, takes on a unique meaning for Paul. For Genesis, Psalms, and Habakkuk, conflict is cosmic in the sense that the truly significant struggle is for *global* domination between the wicked rebels and the Creator God. Isaiah adds to this understanding of cosmic conflict the idea that God's

---

131. Thielman, *From Plight to Solution*, 27–28.

132. Wright, *Paul and the Faithfulness of God*, 612.

133. John M. G. Barclay offers a helpful correction to those who oversimplify the continuity between the story of Israel and the coming of Christ (*Paul and the Gift*, 413–18).

134. Richard B. Hays rightly identifies Paul's hermeneutic as "ecclesiotelic" in that Scripture relates the activity of God in forming his people (*Conversion of the Imagination*, 171). Paul teaches his churches both "to think eschatologically" and to reshape their "identity in light of Israel's Scripture" (*Conversion of the Imagination*, 6).

victory will result in the coming of a new creation. In this development, one sees the organic growth of OT eschatology, as hypothesized by Oswalt. While initially expressed in terms of "human historical experience," that experience was eventually revealed to be "inadequate to reveal the whole scope of God's salvific intent."[135] Paul, however, goes even further. He believes that God's global victory has been achieved at the cross and the new creation has come through the Spirit. Nevertheless, there remains a time of overlap in which the present evil age continues for the sake of the global proclamation of God's victory to all nations.[136] For Paul, cosmic conflict involves the simultaneous existence of two ages and the opposition of each age's system of values. Those who have been justified are liberated already from the present evil age (Gal 1:4), even though they must continue to stand in this freedom (Gal 5:1).

---

135. Oswalt, "Recent Studies," 293.
136. Wright, *Paul and the Faithfulness of God*, 550–62.

4

Cosmic Conflict in Early Judaism

DESPITE THEIR DIVERSITY IN purpose and genre, the four OT books examined in the last chapter shared a theme of cosmic conflict. Three loci gave shape to that theme: (1) the polarity of the righteous/wicked, (2) the problem of sin and suffering, and (3) the solution of God's invasive action. While remaining self-consciously dependent upon earlier Scripture, Paul transformed the theme in two primary ways: (1) He read Scripture in light of the coming of the Son and the Spirit. (2) Because of the work of the Son and the Spirit, he believed that the new creation had already been inaugurated, although not yet fully realized, in the church.

This chapter will continue investigating Paul's intellectual context by examining other texts from early Judaism. Samples of texts will be taken from three categories: (1) the apocalyptic genre (Daniel; 1 Enoch; 4 Ezra; 2 Baruch),[1] (2) other Apocryphal and Pseudepigraphal writings (Jubilees; 1 Maccabees; 2 Maccabees; 4 Maccabees), and (3) the Dead Sea Scrolls (1QS; CD; 1QM). While Paul's quotations and allusions demonstrate his conscious dependence upon Genesis, Psalms, Isaiah, and Habakkuk, he does not demonstrate similar dependence upon these texts. Rather, these early Jewish texts, which are roughly contemporaneous with Paul,[2] be-

---

1. Daniel was regarded as a Scriptural prophet like Isaiah or Ezekiel during the Second Temple period. It belongs in this chapter rather than the previous one, however, because (1) Paul does not cite it in Galatians and (2) it is the foundational text of the apocalyptic genre. On the authority of Daniel in the period, see Steinmann, *Daniel*, 11–18.

2. Given an early date for Daniel and a late date for 4 Ezra and 2 Baruch, the period of the texts discussed in this chapter could stretch from the sixth century BC to the second century AD.

long to the intellectual milieu in which Paul wrote. None of these texts intentionally abandon earlier prophetic eschatology,[3] but like Paul, display conscious dependence upon earlier Israelite Scriptures while also developing the themes of Scripture in diverse ways. As in the previous chapter, this chapter has three modest goals: (1) to identify cosmic conflict as a thematic parallel between a sample of earlier Jewish documents, (2) to examine elements of continuity, discontinuity, and development on the theme without necessarily arguing for causation, and (3) to set Paul within his intellectual context and thus see his unique contributions to the theme. To paraphrase John M.G. Barclay, in early Judaism cosmic conflict was everywhere "but not everywhere the same."[4]

EXAMPLES OF COSMIC CONFLICT IN THE APOCALYPTIC GENRE

In 1979, John J. Collins proposed a definition of the apocalyptic genre based on a "common core of constant elements":

> "Apocalypse" is a genre of revelatory literature with a narrative framework, in which a revelation is mediated by an otherworldly being to a human recipient, disclosing a transcendent reality which is both temporal, insofar as it envisages eschatological salvation, and spatial insofar as it involves another, supernatural world.[5]

This definition focuses on the common form of the apocalyptic genre, but the genre also shares a common function. Collins writes, "The function of the apocalyptic literature is to shape one's imaginative perception of a situation and so lay the basis for whatever course of action it exhorts."[6] One way that apocalyptic texts accomplish this function is by placing the circumstances confronted by the text within the broad context of a cosmic conflict. Four significant apocalyptic texts will demonstrate this: Daniel, 1 Enoch, 4 Ezra, and 2 Baruch.

---

3. Hanson, *Dawn of Apocalyptic*, 7–8. Contra von Rad, *Old Testament Theology*, 301–15.
4. Barclay, *Paul and the Gift*, 6.
5. Collins, "Towards the Morphology," 9; Collins, *Apocalyptic Imagination*, 4–6.
6. Collins, *Apocalyptic Imagination*, 42. See also Collins, "Early Christian Apocalypticism," 7.

Daniel

The book of Daniel begins with a bold assertion concerning the cosmic conflict in which Judah and Babylon are participants.[7] Daniel 1:1–2 relates how Nebuchadnezzar besieged and captured Jerusalem during the reign of Jehoiakim. Victorious Nebuchadnezzar looted "some of the vessels from the house of God" and stored them in "the treasury of the house of his god" in "the land of Shinar" (Dan 1:2).[8] To Nebuchadnezzar, his military supremacy corresponded to the theological supremacy of his god over the God of Judah. However, the author of Daniel subverts Nebuchadnezzar's theological claim with a simple statement: "The Lord gave Jehoiakim the king of Judah into his hand" (Dan 1:2). Nebuchadnezzar did not achieve victory over Judah and its God. Instead, Nebuchadnezzar was given the victory according to the plan of the Lord.[9]

The theme of divine sovereignty continues in the macrostructure of the book, which consists of two interlocking chiasms:

Hebrew Introduction to Aramaic Narrative: God rules kings (Dan 1).

   A A rock destroys four kingdoms filling the earth (Dan 2).

      B God delivers his three servants (Dan 3:1–30).

         C God humbles Nebuchadnezzar (Dan 3:31—4:34).

         C' God humbles Belshazzar (Dan 5:1—6:1).

      B' God delivers his servant Daniel (Dan 6:2–29).

   A' Aramaic Introduction to Hebrew Visions: The Son of Man destroys four beasts, subjecting all nations (Dan 7).

      D Little horn of Greece will desolate holy place and people (Dan 8).

---

7. For the sake of simplicity, this overview of the cosmic conflict theme in Daniel will limit itself to the Hebrew/Aramaic text, which constitutes a structural unit. Since the Greek additions to Daniel (Sus; Bel; Pr Azar; Sg Three) were likely attempts "to enhance theological themes in the Hebrew and Aramaic Daniel," a detailed examination of the additions would likely further demonstrate the importance of the theme to Greek Daniel (Steinmann, *Daniel*, 67). All verse references correspond to the MT, which at points differs from English versification.

8. ארץ־שנער alludes to Gen 11:2, emphasizing Babylon's pride and antagonism against God. See Goldingay, *Daniel*, 15; Lucas, *Daniel*, 52; Steinmann, *Daniel*, 80; Newsom, *Daniel*, 36.

9. Goldingay, *Daniel*, 22; Steinmann, *Daniel*, 84–85; Newsom, *Daniel*, 33–34.

E Daniel prays for holy place and people (Dan 9).

D' King of Greece will desolate holy place and people (Dan 10–12).[10]

God repeatedly delivers Daniel and his friends from the crises created by foolish despots, and by doing so, he makes their lives illustrative of the salvation he promises to the Jewish people. In both Nebuchadnezzar's dream in chapter 2 and Daniel's vision in chapter 7, God reveals the mystery of his plan for the world, which gives his people the "wisdom and strength" to persevere through trials (Dan 2:17–23).[11] Both visions foresee a succession of four human kingdoms that are eventually destroyed and replaced by an eternal, heavenly kingdom (Dan 2:31–45; 7). When Nebuchadnezzar and Darius set themselves in the place of God (Dan 3:1–7; 6:7–10), the revelation of God's eternal kingdom strengthens Daniel and his friends to act according to divine wisdom, and God delivers each of them from certain death (Dan 3:8–30; 6:11–29). The triumph of God's kingdom over all human kingdoms is foreshadowed in God's humbling of both Nebuchadnezzar and Belshazzar who arrogantly exalt themselves over the God of Judah (Dan 3:31—6:1).[12]

"Daniel 7 is the pivot around which the entire book turns," both structurally and theologically.[13] In Dan 7:13–14, "one like a son of man" comes "with the clouds of heaven" to stand before God, "the Ancient of Days." This Son of Man receives an indestructible kingdom that will encompass "every people, nation, and language" and will last forever. Daniel asks an angel to interpret this vision (Dan 7:15–16). The angel responds with a strong contrast between two types of kingdoms: The four kingdoms shall "arise out of the earth," but the God of heaven will give a kingdom to his "holy people" (7:17–18). The angelic interpretation emphasizes three contrasting elements of the two types of kingdoms: (1)

---

10. This interlocking structure is based on the work of Andrew E. Steinmann ("Shape of Things," 38–42; *Daniel*, 21–23). For variations on a chiastic structure for the book, see Lenglet, "Structure littéraire," 169–90; Collins, *Apocalyptic Vision*, 11; Collins, *Daniel*, 30; LaCocque, *Daniel in His Time*, 11; Pierce, "Spiritual Failure," 221; van Deventer, "End of the End," 73.

11. Collins, *Daniel*, 51; Goldingay, *Daniel*, 48; Steinmann, *Daniel*, 124; Newsom, *Daniel*, 72; Beale and Gladd, *Hidden but Now Revealed*, 29–46.

12. James M. Hamilton Jr. calls this foreshadowing of the deliverance of the saints and the judgment of God's enemies "proleptic proof" and "anticipatory evidences" (*God's Glory*, 326).

13. Steinmann, *Daniel*, 332.

a locative contrast: the human kingdoms come from the earth, but the kingdom of the Most High is revealed from heaven;[14] (2) a temporal contrast: the human kingdoms are temporary, but God's kingdom is "forever, forever, and ever" (Dan 7:18); (3) a moral contrast: the human kingdoms are marked by chaos, violence, and pride, whereas God's kingdom comes from the Judge himself and is given to the "holy people" (Dan 7:9–10; 18; 22).[15]

The visions found in Dan 8–12 expand upon the vision of Dan 7. One aspect of these visions worth noting is the periodization of history. Besides the four kingdoms found in Dan 2 and 7, the final chapters of Daniel cite specific values of time: "2,300 evenings and mornings" (Dan 8:14), "seventy years" (Dan 9:2), "seventy weeks" that is divided into two periods of seven and sixty-two weeks (Dan 9:24–26), "a time, times, and half a time" (Dan 7:25; 12:7), "1,290 days" (Dan 12:11), and "1,335 days" (Dan 12:12). Collins argues that the periodization of history in apocalyptic literature performs two functions: (1) It demonstrates that history is determined and therefore under God's control. (2) It enables the reader "to locate his own generation near the end of the sequence."[16] In addition to specific divisions of time, Daniel contains generalized temporal phrases, which indicate that the time of the end has been definitively planned by God.[17] In Dan 12, Daniel sees that this appointed time of the end involves the ultimate deliverance of Israel by means of resurrection— the righteous to everlasting life and the wicked to everlasting contempt (Dan 12:2).[18] Daniel's readers are thus encouraged to endure persecution by placing their hope in God's end-time invasive action.

---

14. Since God's kingdom comes from heaven, the vision does not summon militant resistance against empire. Contra Frend, *Martyrdom and Persecution*, 48.

15. Newsom, *Daniel*, 237.

16. Collins, *Daniel*, 11–12.

17. עת קץ (Dan 8:17; 11:35, 40; 12:4, 9); קץ למועד (Dan 8:19; 11:27); אחרית הימים (Dan 10:14); הימים (Dan 10:14); המועד (Dan 11:29, 35); העת (Dan 12:1); הקץ (Dan 12:13); קץ הימין (Dan 12:13).

18. Scholars disagree on whether this resurrection is universal for all humanity (Steinmann, *Daniel*, 560–61) or partial for Israel or another portion of humanity (Alfrink, "L'idée de résurrection," 355–71; Hartman and Di Lella, *Daniel*, 308; Collins, *Daniel*, 392; Lucas, *Daniel*, 295). For more on resurrection in Dan 12:2, see Chase, "Resurrection Hope." On the importance of resurrection to the tradition of the suffering righteous, see Kleinknecht, *Leidende Gerechtfertigte*, 88–92.

1 Enoch

The text of 1 Enoch or Ethiopian Enoch comes from the Ge'ez translation of possible Greek, Hebrew, and Aramaic texts. Michael A. Knibb claims that the Ge'ez text was, however, more than a simple translation but included "editorial intervention."[19] This editorial intervention occurred in the fourth century at the earliest—after the Ethiopian kingdom of Axum adopted Christianity—but more likely occurred in the fifth or sixth centuries.[20] In its present form, Ethiopian Enoch imitates the Pentateuch in consisting of five books. While Greek manuscript evidence confirms the existence of four books in Greek, the Akhmim manuscripts and Charles Beatty-Michigan papyrus demonstrates that two sections, the Book of Watchers (1 En. 1–36) and the Epistle of Enoch (1 En. 91–108), circulated independently.[21] Knibb concludes that "the Aramaic text of the *Book of Enoch* known from the Dead Sea fragments, the Greek translation, and the Ethiopic version cannot simply be equated, but represent different stages in the development of a text that underwent an extended process of evolution."[22] Despite this, Knibb maintains that 1 Enoch "remains one of the most important sources we possess for our knowledge of Judaism in the late Second Temple period, but in discussing its significance for the Judaism of this period it is important that we keep in mind the precise textual status, and time of origin, of the passages on which we rely."[23]

The Book of the Watchers (1 En. 1–36) exists in an Aramaic fragment as well as complete Greek and Ge'ez translations. It likely represents the second oldest section of 1 Enoch after the Astronomical Book (1 En. 72–82), dating to the third century BC.[24] Chapter 1 presents a militaristic theophany that serves as the introduction to the central theme of 1 Enoch.[25] God—extolled as ὁ θεὸς τοῦ αἰῶνος— will arise from his dwelling place, march upon Sinai, and appear from heaven in "the power of his strength" (1 En. 1:2–4).[26] At his appearing, all—including the Watchers

---

19. Knibb, *Essays*, 44.
20. Knibb, *Essays*, 43–44.
21. Knibb, *Essays*, 50.
22. Knibb, *Essays*, 54.
23. Knibb, *Essays*, 55.
24. Nickelsburg, "Enoch," 2:509; Docherty, *Jewish Pseudepigrapha*, 127.
25. Black, *1 Enoch*, 13; Nickelsburg, *1 Enoch 1*, 129.
26. All translations from 1 Enoch, 4 Ezra, 2 Baruch, and Jubilees are from Charlesworth, *Old Testament Pseudepigrapha*.

and creation itself—will tremble in fear before God (1 En. 1:5–7). At this time, the great judgment will commence by which God will condemn the wicked and grant peace to the righteous (1 En. 1:8–9).

The Book of Watchers explains the necessity of this great judgment by finding the origin of evil's increase upon the earth in an elaboration of Gen 6:1–4.[27] Two hundred angels, led by Semyaz, take human wives for themselves and through their union produce a race of giants (1 En. 6–7). These giants terrorize the earth and eat people (1 En. 7:4–6).[28] The terror unleashed by angelic fornication signifies the greater terror of sin that the Watchers reproduce on the earth. The Watchers introduce to humanity the arts of weapon forgery, jewelry craftmanship, magic, and astrology (1 En. 8).[29] Those suffering under this injustice unleashed upon the earth cry out, and three holy angels—Michael, Surafel, and Gabriel—bring the cry for justice before God (1 En. 9). God responds by instructing the angels to preserve Enoch's family but to bind Azazel, the fallen angel (1 En. 10:1–8). The judgment of the giants, however, does not annihilate their threat, but turns them into evil spirits who will corrupt humanity until the end of the age (1 En. 15:8—16:3).[30] The spirits of the Watchers also continue to lead humanity into idolatry, teaching them "to offer sacrifices to demons" until the day of judgment (1 En. 19:1).

The Parables of Enoch (1 En. 37–71) are likely the latest component of 1 Enoch, composed in the first century BC or first century AD and preserved only in Ge'ez.[31] The Parables, nonetheless, continue the militaristic vision set forth in 1 En. 1. In the second parable, God's judgment will fall upon both the human kings of the earth as well as the demon Azazel and his demonic army (1 En. 55:4). Enoch sees "an army of the angels of punishment marching, holding nets of iron and bronze" (1 En. 56:1).[32] In the third parable, these demonic angels even possess military titles

---

27. Matthew Goff argues that the author of the Book of the Watchers is driven by exegetical concerns over Genesis ("Warriors, Cannibals," 83–89; cf. Nickelsburg, *1 Enoch 1*, 166–68). Contra Philip R. Davies who argues that both depend upon an earlier narrative that is preserved more fully in 1 Enoch ("Enoch Was Not," 97–107).

28. Nickelsburg argues that the giants represent the destructive power of Alexander's armies (*1 Enoch 1*, 184).

29. Nickelsburg, "Enoch," 509–10; Collins, *Seers, Sibyls*, 49; Reed, *Fallen Angels*, 29–44; Goff, "Warriors, Cannibals," 85.

30. Henryk Drawnel argues that the equation of the giants with demons comes from a Mesopotamian background ("Mesopotamian Background," 14–38).

31. Black, *1 Enoch*, 18, 181–88; Docherty, *Jewish Pseudepigrapha*, 127.

32. Nickelsburg and VanderKam, *1 Enoch 2*, 206.

including "centurions," "chiefs over fifties," and "chiefs over tens" (1 En. 69:3).[33] Through the agency of this angelic army, "death proceeds against the people who dwell upon the earth" (1 En. 69:7). Death therefore constitutes the greatest threat to humanity since it "destroys everything" (1 En. 69:11). God's deliverance will come through the Danielic Son of Man who will remove the kings of the earth from their thrones (1 En. 46; cf. Dan 7:13-14).[34] When this Chosen One sits on the Davidic throne, God will force Sheol to return the dead and will save the resurrected righteous (1 En. 51:1-3). Then the earth also will be renewed and fruitful (1 En. 51:4-5). Just as the Son of Man abides in heaven, so also the divine plan itself secures the future of God's people.[35]

The Apocalypse of Weeks, found in the Epistle of Enoch (1 En. 91-108; ca. second century BC),[36] provides the timeframe for these Messianic actions (1 En. 93:1-10; 91:11-17). In the apocalypse, all of human history is divided into ten weeks that represent eras of time. Weeks 1-3 span from creation to the flood while weeks 4-6 include the giving of the law, the building of the temple of Solomon, the destruction of the temple, and exile (1 En. 93:1-8).[37] While Enoch says he was born in the first week, the actual author places his own generation in the seventh week characterized by "an apostate generation" (1 En. 93:9-10).[38] The great judgment comes in the imminent ninth and tenth weeks (1 En. 91:12-15). Then "the first heaven will depart and pass away," and "a new heaven will appear" (1 En. 91:16). In this new heaven, the eternal age will commence (1 En. 91:17). As Collins comments, "The overview of history and the cosmic judgment provide encouragement for the 'chosen righteous' and, more basically, confirm their special status in the design of God."[39]

---

33. Nickelsburg and VanderKam, *1 Enoch 2*, 299.

34. Black argues that "there is nothing specifically Christian" in the portrayal of the Son of Man in the book (*1 Enoch*, 188). Contra Milik, *Ten Years*, 33. On the use of Dan 7 in 1 Enoch, see VanderKam, "Daniel 7," 291-307.

35. Collins, *Apocalyptic Imagination*, 191.

36. Dexinger, *Henochs Zehnwochenapokalypse*, 137-40; Stuckenbruck, *1 Enoch 91-108*, 9-13; Docherty, *Jewish Pseudepigrapha*, 128.

37. Nickelsburg, *1 Enoch 1*, 439-40; Stuckenbruck, *1 Enoch 91-108*, 57-60.

38. Dexinger, *Henochs Zehnwochenapokalypse*, 133; Nickelsburg, *1 Enoch 1*, 447-48; Stuckenbruck, *1 Enoch 91-108*, 56-57.

39. Collins, *Apocalyptic Imagination*, 65.

4 Ezra

Fourth Ezra, along with its sister text 2 Baruch, dates to the period following the fall of Jerusalem in AD 70.[40] Since the text only exists in various versions (Latin, Syriac, Ge'ez, Arabic, Georgian, and Armenian) and neither a Greek translation nor a Hebrew/Aramaic original has been found, a level of uncertainty remains around the text. Nevertheless, many scholars today assert that the seven visions of the book constitute a literary unity.[41] The issue of divine justice unifies the book. The presenting problem of the book is the seeming injustice of the fall of Jerusalem, which the book pseudonymously presents as being to Babylon but in the author's own context was to Rome. Ezra asks why Babylon has been given dominion over Zion? Could Babylon really be more righteous than Israel (4 Ezra 3:28–35)? The angelic guide, Uriel, bluntly identifies Ezra's questions as erroneous, telling Ezra that his understanding has "utterly failed" (4 Ezra 4:2).[42] The visions that follow record Ezra's journey from questioning to deeper faith.[43]

A central component of the book's conception of divine justice revolves around the human condition after Adam.[44] Adam disobeyed, and thus death spread from him to his offspring—all nations (4 Ezra 3:7–8; cf. 6:54). Adam's sin was like "a grain of evil seed" that has produced immense ungodliness (4 Ezra 4:30–32; cf. 7:11–12). Ezra laments the human condition, "For an evil heart has grown up in us, which has alienated us from God, and has brought us into corruption and the ways of death, and has shown us the paths of perdition and removed us far from life" (4

---

40. Myers, *I and II Esdras*, 129–31; Schreiner, *4. Buch Esra*, 291–306; Stone, *Fourth Ezra*, 9–10; Docherty, *Jewish Pseudepigrapha*, 137. On the relationship of 4 Ezra and 2 Baruch, see Lied, "Current Scholarship," 247. Charlesworth argues that 2 Baruch is a response to 4 Ezra ("4 Ezra and 2 Baruch," 155–72). Matthias Henze proposes that both texts originated in apocalyptic oral performances, which were later written down ("'4 Ezra' and '2 Baruch,'" 181–200).

41. Brandenburger, *Verborgenheit Gottes*, 91–147; Stone, *Fourth Ezra*, 14–23; Barclay, *Paul and the Gift*, 281. For an overview of the debate concerning the literary unity of 4 Ezra, see Collins, *Apocalyptic Imagination*, 196–200.

42. Ezra's failure is due to human limitation. See Myers, *I and II Esdras*, 181; Stone, *Fourth Ezra*, 83.

43. Collins describes it as a transition "from skeptic to believer," but the word "skeptic" is too associated with atheism and agnosticism in our present context to be helpful (*Apocalyptic Imagination*, 199). Ezra never questions theism, but he does begin at a point of confusion about the character of God.

44. Myers, *I and II Esdras*, 124–25; Stone, *Fourth Ezra*, 63–66.

Ezra 7:48).⁴⁵ "O Adam," Ezra cries, "what have you done? For though it was you who sinned, the fall was not yours alone, but ours also who are your descendants" (4 Ezra 7:118). While 4 Ezra remains confident that the way to life can be found through the Mosaic law, Israel's Adamic bent toward evil makes it almost impossible for them to follow the way to life.⁴⁶ Nevertheless, in the last times, God will justly distinguish between two groups of humanity: those who despised the law and those who trust the covenants (4 Ezra 7:76-87).

In light of the coming judgment, Ezra must reorient his perception of current events. He must regard present tribulations with reference to the coming of a new age. Just as Esau entered the world first with Jacob grasping at his heel, so also the present age will be followed by a new one (4 Ezra 6:8-10; cf. Gen 25:26). The present age will end with the day of judgment, and then the "immortal age to come" will commence (4 Ezra 7:113). As Uriel explains to Ezra, the present age is aging and will soon die (4 Ezra 4:26-27; 5:50-55; 6:20; 14:10-12, 17), and since the present age is growing old, then Ezra should know "that it is the very time when the Most High is about to visit the world which he has made" (4 Ezra 9:1-2).⁴⁷ This visitation occurs through the agency of the Messiah who will judge the ungodly and save the remnant of Israel (4 Ezra 12:31-34).⁴⁸ The nations will gather to fight the Messiah, but he will destroy them with a stream of fire pouring from his mouth (4 Ezra 13:8-45). Then a hidden city and land will be revealed, which is identified as Paradise where the tree of life grows (4 Ezra 7:26; 8:52).

These twin components of 4 Ezra—the sinful human condition and the coming new age—shape the instructions for Ezra and his community. God commands Ezra to reprove and instruct his people that they might repent before the end comes (4 Ezra 14:13-18). The hope of God's people

---

45. Gabriele Boccaccini unsuccessfully tries to differentiate between Paul's focus on Adam and 4 Ezra's focus on the corrupt heart ("Evilness of Human Nature," 71-72).

46. Burkes, "'Life' Redefined," 57; Stewart, "Narrative World," 388-90.

47. Koch, "Esras erste Vision," 46-75; Coggins and Knibb, *First and Second Books of Esdras*, 125; Stone, *Fourth Ezra*, 92-93.

48. Collins explains, "[The Messiah's] appearance is accompanied by the traditional signs of a theophany. His powers are supernatural, and he represents far more than a restoration of the Davidic kingdom. In short, the messiah has not simply displaced the expectation of a heavenly savior. The two strands of tradition have been fused so that both have been transformed" (*Apocalyptic Imagination*, 209). Even so, the Messiah's kingdom is transitional rather than eternal in 4 Ezra. See Myers, *I and II Esdras*, 126-29; Stone, *Fourth Ezra*, 207-13.

lies outside of this age in the age to come.[49] Nevertheless, throughout 4 Ezra, the tone remains pessimistic that the people will in fact repent and enter into eternal life. Uriel declares, "Many have been created, but few will be saved" (4 Ezra 8:3; cf. 7:20, 48, 51; 8:1; 9:18–22).[50] To become one of the few who will be saved, Ezra's readers must pursue obedience to the law as the way to life.[51]

2 Baruch

Second Baruch, which is only extant in corrupted Syriac manuscripts, confronts the same theological dilemma as 4 Ezra—the destruction of Jerusalem by the Romans. Through the course of his seven visions, Baruch moves from distress to comfort through the renewal of his confidence in God's promise to Israel. To comfort Baruch, God must first correct Baruch's this-worldly concept of God's promise. God does this by interpreting Isa 49:16. Although God only quotes the first line, "On the palms of my hands I have carved you" (2 Bar. 4:2), the discussion that follows relies heavily on the following line: "your walls are continually before me" (Isa 49:16). While Baruch understood the statement to refer to the earthly Jerusalem, God reveals that it refers to the heavenly temple that will one day be revealed (2 Bar. 4:3).[52] This initial redirection from this world to the world to come is expanded in the three apocalyptic revelations that follow.[53] The visions demonstrate that the new world will possess continuity with Israel's history (2 Bar. 53–74), but it will nonetheless come as a promise that will be fulfilled from beyond this world by God's intervention in the sending of Messiah and the judgment of the wicked (2 Bar. 29–30; 36–39). Present circumstances may cause some to question God's sincerity in making the promise (2 Bar. 22:4), but God makes clear that he will fulfill his promise in his own timing, which is imminent since the world is growing old (2 Bar. 23:7; 82:2; 85:10). In the approaching time

---

49. Harnisch, *Verhängnis und Verheissung*, 89–178; Barclay, *Paul and the Gift*, 285.

50. Myers, *I and II Esdras*, 257–58; Coggins and Knibb, *First and Second Books of Esdras*, 194; Stone, *Fourth Ezra*, 280–81; Collins, *Apocalyptic Imagination*, 211–12; Burkes, "'Life' Redefined," 62–63.

51. Kleinknecht, *Leidende Gerechtfertigten*, 102; Stewart, "Narrative World," 391.

52. Murphy argues that "it is likely that the author knew the context of this verse and expected his readers to know it as well" (*Structure and Meaning*, 86).

53. See Henze, *Jewish Apocalypticism*, 78–83; Murphy, *Structure and Meaning*, 71–116; Murphy, "Temple," 671–83; Sulzbach, "Fate of Jerusalem," 138–52.

of fulfillment, the Messiah will "uproot" the armies of Israel's enemies (2 Bar. 39:7). Those nations who have oppressed Israel "will be delivered up to the sword" (2 Bar. 72:6).

In Baruch, God's promise is a function of the Mosaic law.[54] Moses received "the lamp of the eternal law" (2 Bar. 59:2). The Mosaic law performs two functions: "This (lamp) will announce to those who believe the promise of their reward and to those who deny the punishment of the fire that is kept for them" (2 Bar. 59:2). Since the promise is a function of the law, the promise will be given to those who keep the law. Reflecting deuteronomistic theology, Baruch admonishes the elders of Israel to sow the law in their mind so that they would be protected from the final cosmic judgment (2 Bar. 32:1). Such protection is needed because, similar to 4 Ezra, humanity has followed the rebellious example of Adam (2 Bar. 23:4; 48:42, 46; 54:15, 19; 56:5). Therefore, Baruch tells his family and friends to "not forget his Law" since by obeying the law, they will participate in the glorious and eternal consolation of Zion (2 Bar. 44). When he addresses the nation, he says, "If you, therefore, look upon the Law and are intent upon wisdom, then the lamp will not be wanting and the shepherd will not give way and the fountain will not dry up" (2 Bar. 77:16). Still Baruch recognizes that apart from God's grace there is no hope of salvation: "For if he judges us not according to the multitude of his grace, woe to all us who are born" (2 Bar. 84:11; cf. 48:18; 51:7; 75:2-8; 77:11). Obedience to the law does not make one worthy of salvation. Rather, it is an expression of faith or trust in God. The righteous subject themselves to the law "in faith" (2 Bar. 54:5), and those who are "faithful" will be glorified "in accordance with their faith" (2 Bar. 54:21; cf. 54:16). "The good that was mentioned before will be to those who have believed" (2 Bar. 42:2). In fact, the law itself enables and strengthens this faith since it orients faith toward the future fulfillment of the promise.[55] The righteous put their trust in God "because, behold, your Law is with us" (2 Bar. 48:22a). The law speaks a promise to those who obey: "we know that we do not fall as long as we keep your statutes" (2 Bar. 48:22b).

The destruction of Jerusalem, therefore, should be viewed as discipline (2 Bar. 1:5; 4:1; 78:3-5; 79:3).[56] Since Israel has failed to keep the

---

54. For similar accounts of 2 Baruch's theology of the law, see Burkes, "'Life' Redefined"; Gurtner, "Eschatological Rewards," 107-15; Henze, *Jewish Apocalypticism*, 206-27; Lied, *Other Lands*, 2-3; 136-40; Murphy, *Structure and Meaning*, 117-33.

55. Murphy, *Structure and Meaning*, 64-6; Gurtner, "Eschatological Rewards."

56. Willett appeals to Lev 26:14-18 and Prov 3:11-12 for OT background to divine

law and thus attain the promise, God has intervened to correct Israel. Now Israel must respond rightly to God's discipline.[57] Baruch calls on the nation to respond, "Therefore, if you think about the things you have suffered now for your good so that you may not be condemned at the end and be tormented, you shall receive hope which lasts forever and ever, particularly if you remove from your hearts the idle error for which you went away from here" (2 Bar. 78:6).[58] If they do this, then the God who made the promise to their forefathers will not forget them (2 Bar. 78:7).

Cosmic Conflict in the Apocalyptic Genre

All four apocalypses examined above utilize militaristic language to describe God's invasive action at the end of time. In Daniel, God's eternal kingdom will triumph over the violent kingdoms of humanity (e.g., Dan 7). First Enoch begins with the Divine Warrior theme as God sets out to execute justice against demonic armies (e.g., 1 En. 1:2-4). Both 4 Ezra and 2 Baruch foresee an apocalyptic battle between the Messiah and the nations (e.g., 4 Ezra 13:8-45; 2 Bar. 72:6). These militaristic actions are justified on the basis of the polarity of the righteous and wicked, which all four texts assume. While they differ on the origin of human sin—1 Enoch credits the Watchers while 4 Ezra emphasizes Adam's culpability—all four texts place human sin at the center of humanity's plight in general and Israel's in particular. But God's invasive action will bring a solution to this plight.[59] While much has been written about the influence

---

discipline (*Eschatology*, 22-23). Willett delineates seven types of Jewish theodicy: retribution, disciplinary, probationary (testing of the righteous), redemptive, future retribution, theophany, and "everything is good" (*Eschatology*, 11-33). Second Baruch's theodicy is not entirely disciplinary. It also notably features examples of future retribution against God's enemies (e.g., 2 Bar. 12:2-4).

57. Rightly, Henze: "But historical predetermination does not imply the predestination of the individual. . . . To the contrary, [2 Baruch] never fails to stress the central importance of human free will and uses the inevitability of the end as an additional incentive for the reader to act" (*Jewish Apocalypticism*, 280). It is not clear, however, as Murphy claims, that this response entailed an acceptance of pacifism against the Romans ("2 Baruch," 663-69). Concerning apocalyptic eschatology as motivation for obedience, see Leuenberger, "Ort und Funktion," 206-46; Willett, *Eschatology*.

58. Kleinknecht comments on 2 Baruch, "So ist das Leiden hier nicht mehr nur ein Kennzeichen der Gerechten, sondern geradezu *das* Kennzeichen geworden, so daß es für die Gerechten die Gewißheit des himmlischen Lohns impliziert" (*Leidende Gerechtfertigte*, 103).

59. Thielman, *Theology of the New Testament*, 41-45.

of the apocalyptic genre and/or the apocalyptic worldview upon Paul, this much should be clear: (1) Paul, like these apocalyptic texts, believed that Israel's hope lay in God's invasive action that would end the evil of this age and establish God's eternal kingdom. (2) But unlike these texts, Paul believed that God's invasive action had already been accomplished through the sending of the Son and the Spirit and the new creation had been inaugurated.[60]

EXAMPLES OF COSMIC CONFLICT IN OTHER APOCRYPHAL AND PSEUDEPIGRAPHAL WRITINGS

The next four texts do not constitute a unified genre. Jubilees may be labeled as "rewritten Bible," but it also shares qualities common to apocalyptic texts.[61] First and 2 Maccabees are similar to the historical narrative found in earlier OT books while 4 Maccabees presents itself as philosophical treatise.[62] Despite this diversity, these texts share the thematic parallel of cosmic conflict.

Jubilees

Composed in the second century BC in Hebrew, the book of Jubilees comes to us in a Ge'ez version and Hebrew fragments from Qumran.[63] Jubilees shares characteristics with apocalyptic literature, featuring both angel-mediated revelation (Jub. 1:1–2:1) and the periodization of history (e.g., Jub. 1:0, 26, 29; 3:1, 8, 11, 15; 4:1).[64] But unlike apocalyptic literature, Jubilees features a retelling of Genesis and part of Exodus. Through this combination of revelatory authority and biblical retelling, Jubilees asserts itself as the divine interpretation of earlier Scripture.[65]

---

60. These two points reflect the conclusion of Martinus C. de Boer in a recent essay, but his continued defense of a cosmological versus forensic division between apocalyptic texts should be rejected ("Apocalyptic," 63).

61. Docherty, *Jewish Pseudepigrapha*, 17.

62. deSilva, *Introducing the Apocrypha*, 248–50, 270–72, 356–58.

63. VanderKam, *Jubilees*, ix–xvi; Docherty, *Jewish Pseudepigrapha*, 14.

64. Collins, *Apocalyptic Imagination*, 83–84; Docherty, *Jewish Pseudepigrapha*, 17. Todd Russell Hanneken argues that Jubilees uses the form of apocalypse to subvert apocalyptic theology, but the theology of Jubilees does not differ significantly enough from other apocalypses to warrant his claim (*Subversion of the Apocalypses*).

65. Segal, *Jubilees*, 4–5; Hanneken, *Subversion of the Apocalypses*, 235. On the

One important aspect of this authoritative interpretation is the inclusion of angelic spirits in narratives that previously lacked them.[66] God creates the angels on the first day of creation (Jub. 2:2), and like in 1 Enoch, the "sons of God" in Gen 6:1–4 are identified as the angelic Watchers (Jub. 4:21–22; 7:21–25).[67] Despite being destroyed by the flood, the Watchers continued to influence humanity through an astrological text they left behind (Jub. 8:1–4).[68] Furthermore, the offspring of the Watchers (although possibly a different offspring from the Nephilim) are demons who lead astray the posterity of Noah (Jub. 5:1, 9; 10:1–6).[69] Yahweh responds by instructing the angels to bind the demons, but the chief of demons, Mastema, successfully appeals to God for the freedom of a tenth of the demons (Jub. 10:7–9). Jaques T. A. G. M. van Ruiten explains that this event "implies that Mastema has a function in the divine order."[70] In the narrative that follows, this demonic force, although reduced by 90 percent, subjugates the nations.[71] In Ur, Mastema and his demons lead humanity into idolatry (Jub. 11:4–5; cf. 1:11; 22:17). But by rejecting the idolatry of his native city and family, Abram receives God's revelation, which liberates him from demonic power (Jub. 12:1–27).[72] In the text, a power struggle develops between Mastema and God's elect, Abram. Mastema afflicts humanity with a plague of ravens, but Abram turns back the plague (Jub. 11:9–22).[73] Mastema, however, provokes Yahweh to test Abraham through the sacrifice of Isaac. Instead, Abraham's faith puts Mastema to shame (Jub. 17:16; 18:12).[74] This ongoing conflict between Abraham's line and Mastema prompts Abraham to bless Jacob, saying, "And may the spirit of Mastema not rule over you or over your seed in

---

methods of interpretation in Jubilees, see Ruiten, *Primaeval History Interpreted*, 365–75.

66. VanderKam, *Jubilees*, 126–31; Segal, *Jubilees*, 9–10; Kugel, *Walk through Jubilees*, 73.

67. Segal, *Jubilees*, 103–43.

68. Stuckenbruck, "Book of Jubilees," 303–6. Jubilees demonstrates a concern that Israel abide by a solar calendar rather than a lunar one (e.g., Jub. 4:21; 6:36–37). See VanderKam, *Calendars*, 21–25; Scott, *On Earth as in Heaven*, 86–88.

69. Scott, *On Earth as in Heaven*, 7; Segal, *Jubilees*, 152.

70. Ruiten, *Abraham*, 161. See also VanderKam, *Jubilees* (2001), 128–29; Segal, *Jubilees*, 176–80.

71. Ruiten, *Abraham*, 162; Kugel, *Walk through Jubilees*, 83–84.

72. Ruiten, *Abraham*, 44.

73. Segal, *Jubilees*, 186–87; Ruiten, *Abraham*, 28–29. On the origin of the narrative, see Brock, "Abraham and the Ravens," 135–52; Crawford, "Exegetical Function," 91–97.

74. On similarities and differences with Job, see Ruiten, *Abraham*, 212–14.

order to remove you from following the Lord" (Jub. 19:28).[75] The blessing seems to have been effectual since Mastema does not appear again in the narrative until Moses visits the court of Pharaoh, where Mastema is seen as the spiritual power behind Egypt (Jub. 48). Nevertheless, God exercises authority over Mastema, sending "all the powers of Mastema" to kill the firstborn of Egypt (Jub. 49:2).[76]

These origin stories present two polarities that explicate the uniqueness of Israel and the condition of the world. The horizontal polarity consists of the opposition between Israel and the nations. This polarity, however, finds its source in the vertical polarity between the divine and the demonic. While other nations are ruled by spirits, Israel is ruled by God himself (Jub. 15:31-32).[77] Therefore, the struggle of Israel is to resist the attempts of Belial to rule over them (Jub. 1:20; 15:33).[78] The angel who mediates Jubilees, however, tells Moses that Israel will eventually fall prey to Belial and will pollute the promised land with sin (Jub. 23:11-21). Then God will send the nation into captivity, to which the nation will respond with repentance (Jub. 1:13-18; 23:22-26). The result will be the reestablishment of the nation in peace and blessing (Jub 23:27-32).[79] The restoration of Israel, however, is only the beginning of the final era of history that will culminate in a new creation. There will be a "day of the great judgment" at the end of history (Jub. 23:11), and then "the day of the new creation when the heaven and earth and all of their creatures shall be renewed according to the powers of heaven and according to the whole nature of earth" (Jub. 1:29; cf. 4:26). For Jubilees, all of world history fits into three epochs spanning from creation to new creation: (1) The Era of the Patriarchs (50 jubilee cycles), (2) The Era of Israel's Sin and Exile (20 jubilee cycles), and (3) The Era of Restoration of the Nation and the Creation (50 jubilee cycles).[80] Only in this final invasive act of judgment and new creation will God resolve the conflict between himself and the demonic rulers that influence world events. To Paul, however,

---

75. Ruiten, *Abraham*, 250.

76. Segal, *Jubilees*, 210-14, 223-27.

77. Reed, "Enochic and Mosaic Traditions," 357-58; Kugel, *Walk through Jubilees*, 5-9.

78. Segal, *Jubilees*, 251-56.

79. Scott, *On Earth as in Heaven*, 77-79; Endres, "Eschatological Impulses," 323-37.

80. Scott, *On Earth as in Heaven*, 152. For more on eschatology in Jubilees, although based on a redactional theory that has not gained wide-spread support, see Davenport, *Eschatology*.

God had already defeated evil and inaugurated the new creation through the crucifixion of the Messiah.

1, 2, and 4 Maccabees

In 1, 2, and 4 Maccabees, the concept of cosmic conflict is central to explaining the historical events detailed in the three books. Nonetheless, each book possesses its own emphases.[81] First Maccabees presents the early history of the Hasmonean dynasty in a style reminiscent of 1–2 Samuel or 1–2 Kings and thus functions as propaganda to legitimize the dynasty.[82] The author identifies two groups of antagonists: (1) the Hellenistic rulers that oppress Israel, especially Antiochus IV (e.g., 1 Macc 1:10); (2) the Jews who capitulate to Hellenization (e.g., 1 Macc 1:11–15). These antagonists oppress both the holy remnant of the people and the holy city (e.g., 1 Macc 3:59). The holy city is portrayed as violated by the stationing of troops, stockpiling of weapons, and desecration of the temple (1 Macc 1:33–40), while the faithful remnant suffers death for resisting the Hellenization policy (1 Macc 1:63–64). This dual oppression of city and people are symptoms of the antagonists' hatred of God and his law, which is physically enacted through their destruction of the books of the law (1 Macc 1:56–57). By contrast, the elderly Mattathias exhibits Phinehas-like zeal for the law and thus for God (1 Macc 2:24–28, 49–50, 54; cf. Num 25:10–18). After Mattathias's death, the mantle of Phinehan-zeal passes to Judas Maccaebeus, who strapped on his weapons of war to execute justice against both Hellenistic oppressors and apostate Jews (1 Macc 3:1–9).

Although the narrative of 1 Maccabees is not generally supernatural, the author utilizes repeated narrative signals to identify God as the one who destroys the enemies.[83] These narrative signals include accounts of speeches, prayers, and worship before or after battle (1 Macc 3:60;

---

81. It is not clear that these different emphases point to opposing propagandists in the case of 1 and 2 Maccabees. Contra Goldstein, *I Maccabees*, 4.

82. Goldstein, *I Maccabees*, 21; Harrington, *Maccabean Revolt*, 57; deSilva, *Introducing the Apocrypha*, 248–49. Contra Pfeiffer, *History of New Testament Times*, 493; Bartlett, *1 Maccabees*, 30.

83. Two exceptions are the earthquake in 1 Macc 9:13 and the paralyzation of Alcimus in 1 Macc 9:54–57, but the exceptions prove the rule. Not only is it unusual in 1 Maccabees to credit victory to a supernatural event, but the nature of these more "natural" supernatural events contrasts sharply with the angelic armies found in 2 Maccabees.

4:9–11, 24–25, 30–33; 5:33; 7:36–38, 40–42; 9:46). The double agency of the war is summarized in 1 Macc 3:21–22: "But we fight for our lives and our laws, and God himself will crush them before us."[84] Ironically, however, while Isaiah rebuked the kings of Judah for appealing to foreign protection rather than trusting in God alone (Isa 7–12; 39), 1 Maccabees appeals to the Hasmoneans' alliances with Rome and Sparta to legitimize the Judean state (1 Macc 8; 12:1–23).[85] This suggests that the inclusion of these diplomatic letters serves the central purpose of dynastic legitimization, demonstrating that the Hasmoneans were regarded by foreign powers as *bona fide* rulers. The depiction of double agency in battle serves this same purpose by demonstrating God's recognition of Hasmonean authority and showcasing the zealousness of the Hasmoneans.[86]

By contrast, 2 Maccabees has a much greater emphasis on God's invasive actions. While prayer remains a central theme in 2 Maccabees as in 1 Maccabees (2 Macc 3:22; 8:2–4, 29; 10:4, 16, 27, 38; 12:6, 15–16, 28, 36, 41–42; 14:34–36, 46; 15:21–24, 27),[87] 2 Maccabees uniquely identifies the angelic cavalry as God's means of delivering Israel.[88] In the first episode of the narrative, Seleucus IV sends Heliodorus to Jerusalem to confiscate the temple treasury, but when the priests pray, God responds by sending three angelic riders who strike Heliodorus (2 Macc 3:22–34; cf. 4 Macc 4:10–12).[89] Heliodorus, whose life is spared, then gives testimony that God watches over the temple and will destroy any who desecrate it (2 Macc 3:39). The striking of Heliodorus, therefore, foreshadows the greater desecrations of Antiochus IV and the divine justice that will avenge the temple.[90] Prior to Antiochus's plundering of the temple, for

---

84. Tilly, *1 Makkabäer*, 116.

85. Goldstein, *I Maccabees*, 346; Bartlett, *1 Maccabees*, 95; deSilva, *Introducing the Apocrypha*, 264.

86. Middleton, *Radical Martyrdom*, 130.

87. Lichtenberger, "Gottes Nähe," 135–49.

88. The author mentions the angel of the Lord striking the army of Sennacherib (2 Macc 8:19; 15:22; cf. 2 Kings 19:35; 2 Chron 32:20–21; Isa 37:36; Farmer, *Maccabees, Zealots*, 97–111), but he may also conflate this event with 2 Kings 6:17 and 7:6 (Goldstein, *II Maccabees*, 211). The Heliodorus incident also alludes to Dan 11:20 (Goldstein, *II Maccabees*, 196–97). Additional influence comes from Greek sources that relate similar omens of the gods appearing before battle (Goldstein, *II Maccabees*, 211; Schwartz, *2 Maccabees*, 251–52).

89. In the two letters to the Egyptian diaspora that introduce the book, the author highlights God's deliverance of Israel in both its history and more recent events (2 Macc 1:11, 17, 24–29; 2:17–18).

90. Abel, *Livres*, 233; Bartlett, *1–2 Maccabees*, 41–42; Dommershausen, *1 Makkabäer*;

about forty days, an angelic cavalry appeared above Jerusalem as an omen of God's protection (2 Macc 5:2-4), and twice more the angelic cavalry would deliver God's people (2 Macc 10:29-31; 11:8-14). Second Maccabees gives greater emphasis, therefore, to divine intervention than does 1 Maccabees. While Israel's enemies trust in "arms and human courage," Israel trusts in "the Almighty God who is able to strike down those coming against us—even the whole world—with a single nod" (2 Macc 8:18).[91] The two watchwords given to Israel before battle also emphasize divine activity: θεοῦ βοηθείας (2 Macc 8:23) and θεοῦ νίκης (2 Macc 13:15).[92] While in a vision Jeremiah gives Judas a holy golden sword to strike down his enemies (2 Macc 15:16), God alone strikes down Antiochus IV (2 Macc 9:5-12).

Even though 2 Maccabees envisions Israel's deliverance as coming from God, the book also identifies God as the source of the people's suffering. God ordained the suffering of the nation as discipline (2 Macc 6:10-17, 32-33).[93] In the midst of the nation's discipline, the author highlights two episodes of the suffering righteous: the martyrdom of Eleazer (2 Macc 6:18-31) and the martyrdom of the seven brothers and their mother (2 Macc 7:1-42). While in Daniel the saints are delivered from suffering, in 2 Maccabees the saints die.[94] Eleazer's death exemplifies fear of God and noble courage (2 Macc 6:28, 30-31).[95] The seven brothers and their mother go to their death confident in the resurrection of the righteous (2 Macc 7:9, 11, 14, 23, 29, 36).[96] While these martyrs suffer for the sins of the nation (2 Macc 7:18, 38), the disciplinary nature of the suffering allows them to simultaneously affirm that Israel has not been forsaken (2 Macc 7:16) and that their persecutors will face justice in the

---

2 *Makkabäer*, 117; Donaldson, *Judaism and the Gentiles*, 53-54; Schwartz, *2 Maccabees*, 201; Doran, *2 Maccabees*, 89-90.

91. 2 Macc 8:18 alludes to Ps 20:8 (Abel, *Livres*, 270; Goldstein, *II Maccabees*, 331; Schwartz, *2 Maccabees*, 336).

92. Abel, *Livres*, 271; Schwartz, *2 Maccabees*, 340; Doran, *2 Maccabees*, 177.

93. Schwartz, *2 Maccabees*, 21-22; Doran, *2 Maccabees*, 150.

94. Middleton, *Radical Martyrdom*, 131.

95. Henten, *Maccabean Martyrs*, 210-32.

96. Kleinknecht, *Leidende Gerechtfertigte*, 126. For this contrast between the two episodes, see Schwartz, *2 Maccabees*, 299. In 4 Maccabees, the martyrs do not hope for physical resurrection but immediate spiritual life in the presence of God with their faithful ancestors (4 Macc 7:3, 19; 9;8; 13:17). The difference is likely due to the influence of Hellenistic philosophy on 4 Maccabees. See Dupont-Sommer, *Quatrième*, 44-47.

end (2 Macc 7:17, 19, 31).[97] Middleton, taking note of both the themes of heavenly warfare and the suffering righteous, comments:

> The traditional Holy War ideology has been combined in 2 Maccabees with developing eschatological promise, creating a potent apocalyptic matrix within which to interpret the deaths of the faithful. They have affected the cosmos by turning God's anger away from the people and in 2 Maccabees, for the first time, a military struggle is placed in an apocalyptic framework.[98]

Middleton perhaps goes too far by suggesting that 2 Maccabees is unique in placing an historical military struggle "in an apocalyptic framework."[99] In 2 Kgs 6:17, Elijah sees the angelic cavalry, and in 2 Kgs 7:8, the Syrian army hears the sounds of a great army. Nonetheless, 2 Maccabees has taken the theme of cosmic conflict from earlier Scripture and mixed it with historical narrative for the specific purpose of giving clarity and emphasis to heaven's involvement in the earthly struggle between Israel and her persecutors. By doing so, the deaths of the righteous martyrs become contributions to Israel's victory in the cosmic war by reconciling Israel to God.[100]

While 2 Maccabees focuses on this external struggle of the martyrs against their persecutors, 4 Maccabees philosophically analyzes the internal "contest of the heart" (4 Macc 15:29). Demonstrating the influence of Hellenistic philosophy, 4 Maccabees seeks to prove that "reason is sovereign over the passions" (4 Macc 1:7).[101] After carefully defining the terms of the discourse (4 Macc 1:13–35), 4 Maccabees attempts to prove the supremacy of reason through three martyr examples: Eleazer, the seven brothers, and their mother. In each case, reason conquered passion, enabling each martyr to remain faithful to the law until death (4 Macc 6:31–35; 13:1–18; 17:7–16). Therefore, each martyr is extolled

---

97. Jarvis J. Williams argues that "the text of 2 Macc 7:32–38 teaches that the martyrs function in the martyrological narratives as representatives of and as substitutes for sinful Israel and that they function as the nation's Yom Kippur" (*Christ Died*, 95.). See also Kleinknecht, *Leidende Gerechtfertigte*, 125; Henten, *Maccabean Martyrs*, 135–56.

98. Middleton, *Radical Martyrdom*, 131.

99. Middleton, *Radical Martyrdom*, 131.

100. Middleton, *Radical Martyrdom*, 131–32.

101. On the author's possible educational background, see deSilva, "Author of 4 Maccabees," 501–31. On the author's use of Hellenistic philosophy as a tool of resistance, see deSilva, "Using the Master's Tools," 99–127.

for enduring the struggle like an athlete or a soldier (4 Macc 6:9–10; 9:8, 24).¹⁰² But in each of these instances, 4 Maccabees demonstrates an escalation in the struggle against the passions.¹⁰³ The seven brothers not only die nobly, like Eleazer did, but also do so by overcoming "the passions of brotherly love" (4 Macc 14:1; 15:13). The mother must overcome the passions of maternal instinct, which 4 Maccabees regards as greater torture than that endured by Daniel and his friends (4 Macc 14:11—17:6). Thus, the mother is extolled as a "champion of the law, defender of true religion, and winner of the prize in the inward contest of the heart" (4 Macc 15:29), as well as a "soldier of God in the cause of piety" (4 Macc 16:14). The magnitude of the suffering of the righteous martyrs makes their deaths substitutionary atonement for the sins of the nation (4 Macc 6:28–29; 17:21–22).¹⁰⁴ This mastery over the passions comes through the four cardinal virtues: φρόνησις (prudence), ἀνδρεία (courage), δικαιοσύνη (justice), and σωφροσύνη (self-control; 4 Macc 1:18).¹⁰⁵ The author thus demonstrates that the "barbaric" law of the Jews is the source of these "civilized" virtues (4 Macc 5:22–24; 18:10–19).¹⁰⁶ Thus the internal conflict that each human experiences must be won by dependence upon God's revealed wisdom in the law.

Each of these three books places the struggle of the Jewish people during the Maccabean revolt within the context of a cosmic conflict. The battle—whether actual military warfare or the battle of martyrdom—is between the righteous and the unrighteous. God must intervene to bring about victory and justice. While 1 Maccabees sees God's intervention as occurring through the aid of human effort, 2 Maccabees portrays God's actions as occurring through angelic cavalry for Israel's armies and resurrection of the nation's martyrs. Fourth Maccabees sees God's intervention as coming through a moral strengthening mediated by the law. Second and 4 Maccabees, in particular, see this cosmic conflict as being manifested in the martyrdom of righteous Jews. As Middleton argues, "Their

---

102. David A. deSilva comments, "Athletic imagery was a potent resource for transforming an experience of victimization into a moral victory" (4 *Maccabees*, 144; cf. Henten, *Maccabean Martyrs*, 238).

103. The escalation also appears in the manner of death. Both the final son and his mother throw themselves into the fire (4 Macc 12:19; 17:1). On this self-immolation, see deSilva, *4 Maccabees*, 202.

104. Williams, *Christ Died*, 95–103.

105. E.g., Plato, *Rep.* 4.426–35.

106. deSilva, "Using the Master's Tools," 110–12. See also deSilva, "Human Ideal," 61–64.

deaths are cosmic in scope. So whereas their deaths do not directly bring about victory (although 4 Maccabees comes close), they do create the cosmic conditions for God once again to intervene on the side of the Israelites in the deuteronomistic Holy War tradition."[107] Jarvis J. Williams has demonstrated that Paul utilized these martyrological traditions as "an intentional missiological move on his part to contextualize the death of Jesus for Jewish and gentile sinners to highlight the efficacious nature of Jesus' death for them."[108] Yet, as Williams points out, Paul differs significantly from the Maccabean texts. For Paul, the death of Christ, unlike the martyrs, brought a full and final liberation to God's people, and it did so for *both* Jews and gentiles.[109] But even more than that, the cross brought forth a new creation.

EXAMPLES OF COSMIC CONFLICT IN THE DEAD SEA SCROLLS

Sectarians define themselves by conflict. Therefore, it is not surprising to see cosmic conflict in the writings of the sectarian community at Qumran. Frank Moore Cross and John J. Collins have labeled the sectarians an "apocalyptic community," even though none of their writings fit neatly within the apocalyptic genre.[110] The Qumran sect possessed an apocalyptic worldview that sharply distinguished between the righteous and the unrighteous and expected God to invade human history in order to execute justice and establish Israel's rule over the world.

The Community Rule

Among the sectarian documents found in the caves near Qumran, the Community Rule records the sect's theology in its purest and clearest form. The Community Rule divides humanity into two categories: "the sons of light" and "the sons of darkness" (e.g., 1QS I, 9–10). The identity of each group emerges from the spirit that primarily rules them, either the spirit of truth/light or the spirit of injustice/falsehood/darkness (1QS III, 17–24). God himself "created the spirits of Light and Darkness" (1QS

---

107. Middleton, *Radical Martyrdom*, 132.
108. Williams, *Christ Died*, 187.
109. Williams, *Christ Died*, 188.
110. Cross, *Ancient Library*, 76–78; Collins, *Apocalypticism*, 10.

III, 25) and "established the spirits in equal measure until the final age" (1QS IV, 15-17). Every man possesses both spirits and thus at times performs the vices of the spirit of darkness and at other times the virtues of the spirit of light (1QS IV, 2-14). But constitutionally, one is either a child of righteousness or a child of injustice, ruled by "the Prince of Light" or by "the Angel of Darkness" (1QS III, 20-23). These two spirits—residing within each human being but also ruling different segments of humanity—engage in a fierce struggle within the present time (1QS IV, 17-18).[111] Only at "the time of the visitation" will God destroy the spirit of darkness forever and will cleanse humanity with "the spirit of holiness," restoring humanity to "all the glory of Adam" (1QS IV, 18-26). The time of visitation relates in some way to the coming of "the Prophet and the Messiahs of Aaron and Israel" rather than a theophany (1QS IX, 11). Until that Messianic time, the sectarian community must endure "the dominion of Belial" (1QS I, 18; II, 19). To walk by the spirit of light in this dark period required separating from the wicked and residing in the wilderness to study and obey the Torah (1QS VIII, 13-16). In this way, sectarians sought to separate themselves from both those ruled by the Angel of Darkness and the spirit of Belial that seeks to reside in their own hearts (1QS X, 21).

This theology of cosmic conflict resembles Zoroastrian dualism in some significant ways. In Zoroastrian myth, the supreme God Ahura Mazda, the Wise Lord, begets twin children: Spenta Mainyu, who is associated with truth and light, and Angra Mainyu, who is associated with deception and darkness.[112] Like the Community Rule, Zoroastrianism teaches that humanity must choose between these two spirits. Nonetheless, there remains a significant difference. In the Community Rule, God creates the two spirits rather than begets them. This difference introduces a significant theological problem. Whereas Zoroastrian dualism emphasizes the free choice of Angra Mainyu to become evil, the Community Rule makes God the creator and upholder of evil.[113] Whether or

---

111. Elaine H. Pagels demonstrates this internal struggle to be a theological difference between Qumran and Jubilees or 1 Enoch, writing that the Essenes "place at the very center of their theology, cosmology, and *anthropology* the cosmic war between God with his allies and Satan or Belial along with its allies, both angelic and human" ("Social History," 127; italics added).

112. *Yasna* 30-31; cf. Plutarch, *Is. Os.* 46-47 (369D-370C).

113. The sectarians could have found justification for this view in passages like Isa 45:7 or 2 Sam 19:9 (Collins, *Seers, Sibyls*, 293-94); or resemblances to Zoroastrianism could be merely coincidental with the doctrine of the two spirits arising from Jewish

not this resemblance to Zoroastrianism signifies dependence on Persian sources remains uncertain, but the comparison of the two traditions does accentuate the particular dualism of the Qumran sect.[114]

Despite the possibility of Persian influence, this dualism comes "mediated through Jewish apocalypticism."[115] The sectarians awaited the day that God would put an end to the struggle between good and evil by judging the wicked and perfecting the righteous. The Community Rule gives little detail about this expectation, which it labels "His visitation" (1QS III, 18). The Community Rule does teach that the sect will prepare the way for God's visitation by moving to the wilderness (1QS VIII, 14; cf. Isa 40:3). This divine visitation would in some way be preceded by or coincide with the coming of three figures: The Prophet, the Messiah of Aaron, and the Messiah of Israel (1QS IX, 11). The sparsity of information on the ultimate eschatological event in the Community Rule suggests that sectarians were well informed about the community's eschatology through other verbal or written sources like the War Scroll.

The Damascus Document

The Damascus Document, discovered in the Ben Ezra synagogue of Cairo in 1896, was initially credited to an unknown sect labeled the Zadokites by scholars, but after the discovery of the Dead Sea Scrolls in the mid-twentieth century, it became apparent that the Damascus Document was a product of the sect that lived at Qumran.[116] While the Community

---

Scripture itself (Heger, "Another Look," 39–101). This difference from Mazdaist Zoroastrianism led some French scholars to argue for influence from the Zoroastrian sect Zurvanism (Michaud, "Mythe Zervanite," 137–47; Duchesne-Guillemin, "Zervanisme," 96–99; Philolenko, "Doctrine," 163–211). Zurvanism, however, did not come to prominence until the Sassanid period beginning in the third century AD, and it remains unclear when Zurvanism originated or even if it was ever considered distinct from Mazdaism. See Zaehner, *Zurvan*; Iyer, *Faith and Philosophy*, 213–15.

114. Collins writes that "the question of Zoroastrian influence has seldom received the attention it deserves" because the Zoroastrian sources are relatively late and most scholars of early Judaism lack competency in the Avestan language (*Dead Sea Scrolls*, 155–56). See also Levison, "Two Spirits," 2:169–94.

115. Goff, "Looking for Sapiential Dualism," 21.

116. Reif, "Damascus Document," 109–31; Collins, *Dead Sea Scrolls*, 14–15. Ben Zion Wacholder has argued that CD was authored by a single author against the earlier consensus that the document was a composite of diverse sources (*New Damascus Document*). Philip R. Davies similarly concludes that CD is "a coherent composition" (*Damascus Covenant*, 202). Contra Schechter, *Fragments*, xxv–xxvi; Campbell, "Essene-Qumran Origins," 143–56.

Rule describes the struggle between the two spirits in more universalist terms, the Damascus Document connects the cosmic conflict more closely with the political turmoil that likely gave rise to the sect in the first or second century BC. The Damascus Document asserts that 390 years after Nebuchadnezzar conquered Jerusalem, God visited and blessed his people (CD I, 5–8). However, for an additional twenty years, "they were like blind men groping for the way" (CD I, 9–10).[117] Therefore, God "raised for them a Teacher of Righteousness to guide them in the way of His heart," but a Scoffer—a Wicked Priest—also arose who led the nation away from the path of righteousness and blessing (CD I, 11–18; cf. 1QpHab VIII, 8–9). These "seekers after smooth things" persecuted the righteous (CD I, 18). Scholars continue to disagree on the historical events referenced in the Damascus Document, but most interpretations rely on one of three possible identifications of the "Wicked Priest": (1) Jonathan Maccabee, appointed to the high priesthood over the legitimate line (152 BC);[118] (2) Hyrcanus II, appointed by Queen Salome Alexandra who empowered the Pharisees (ca. 70–40 BC);[119] (3) a series of high priests from Judas Maccabee to Alexander Jannaeus.[120]

Whatever hypothesis might be correct, the function of the Damascus Document remains the same. It sets the recent history of the sectarian community within its eschatological context.[121] The Damascus Document sees the rejection and persecution of the Teacher of Righteousness as typified in earlier Israelite history, both in the calling of Abraham from Ur and the rebellion at Kadesh (CD III, 1–11). Events in the past serve as the pattern that will be escalated in the future. The Prince of Light raised up Moses and Aaron, but Belial raised up Jannes and his brother (CD V,

---

117. For a discussion of this chronology, see Laato, "Chronology in the Damascus Document," 605–7.

118. Milik, *Ten Years*, 65–71; Jeremias, *Lehrer*, 36–78; Murphy-O'Connor, "Essenes and Their History," 229–30; Vermes, *Dead Sea Scrolls*, 60–66. Other minority proposals from the same period include Onias III (Freedman and Geoghegan, "Another Stab," 17–24) and Simon Maccabee (Cross, *Ancient Library*, 109–60).

119. Dupont-Sommer, *Écrits esséniens*, 274; Collins, *Dead Sea Scrolls*, 170–72.

120. This theory is known as the Groningen Hypothesis. See van der Woude, "Wicked Priest," 349–59; García Martínez, "Qumran Origins," 113–36; García Martínez and van der Woude, "'Groningen' Hypothesis," 521–41. For a critique, see Lim, "Wicked Priests," 415–25.

121. Albert I. Baumgarten writes, "What was important about the past for a sectarian was not some antiquarian interest, but the relevance of the past for present and future, establishing that sectarian's link with previous and future generations" ("Perception of the Past," 12). See also Campbell, *Use of Scripture*, 206–8.

18–19). So too "at the end of days," another Teacher of Righteousness will arise. The community awaits that future day when God will visit again, destroying Belial forever (CD VII, 20—VIII, 3). Until then, the community must follow the current Teacher's interpretation of Torah (CD VI, 4–21).[122] These patterns reveal that the community lives at a crucial point in the history of Israel and the world. The period between the initial Teacher of Righteousness and "the Messiah out of Aaron and Israel" is the age of the New Covenant foreseen by Jeremiah (CD B I–II; cf. Jer 31:31).[123] But in this age, Belial has been unleashed against Israel (CD IV, 13). He seeks to snare Israel in his three nets: fornication, riches, and profanation of the temple (CD IV, 14–18). The Damascus Document quantifies this period as "about forty years" (CD XX, 15). By enduring persecution and following the Teacher of Righteousness' interpretation of Torah (CD IX–XVI), the sectarians will "live forever" and possess "all the glory of Adam" (CD III, 20).

The War Scroll

By contrast with the Community Rule and the Damascus Document, the War Scroll, as the name suggests, is much more militaristic. George J. Brooke writes, "That there should be a composition in the sectarian collection from the eleven caves at and near Qumran as militaristic as the *War Scroll* has been recognized as intriguing, even problematic, from the outset."[124] Scholars have found it difficult to reconcile the War Scroll with Philo's description of the Essenes as pacifists.[125] But Collins argues, "Eschatological militancy is not necessarily incompatible with apparent pacifism in the present. . . . [V]iolence is only deferred to the proper time. It is not disavowed."[126] The increased militarism in the scroll may also reflect the crisis in which it was composed, like the Maccabean revolt or the Roman occupation of Judea.[127] Nevertheless, the militancy of the War

---

122. Contra Wacholder who reads every reference to the Teacher of Righteousness as a future forerunner of the Messiah ("Teacher of Righteousness," 75–92).

123. Davies, *Damascus Covenant*, 180–81.

124. Brooke, "Text, Timing," 61.

125. Philo, *Prob.* 87. See Zerbe, *Non-Retaliation*, 129–33.

126. Collins, *Dead Sea Scrolls*, 61; see also Jassen, "Dead Sea Scrolls and Violence," 12–44; Kampen, "Wisdom, Poverty," 215–36.

127. Duhaime, *War Texts*, 62–102; Schultz, *Conquering the World*, 31–39.

Scroll remains firmly eschatological.[128] The war it depicts is at the end of the age, and the military tactics it espouses, although similar to Roman warfare, is highly stylized and unrealistic.[129]

The war of the scroll is the ultimate expression of the struggle between the two spirits of light and darkness simultaneously involving human forces and supernatural powers (1QM XIII). "At that time, the assembly of gods and the hosts of men shall battle" (1QM I, 10), and the battle "shall be a time of salvation for the people of God, an age of dominion for all the members of His company, and of everlasting destruction for all the company of Belial" (1QM I, 5). Reflecting the prophecies of Daniel 11, the War Scroll foresees an attack on Israel from the south by the king of the Kittim (1QM I, 4).[130] Allied to the Kittim are the ancient Israelite enemies of Edom, Moab, and Ammon (1QM I, 1).[131] For six rounds of battle, each side will gain the upper hand, but in the seventh round, God will intervene with a mighty hand to give Israel victory (1QM I, 14). This deliverance will commence a forty-year period of war — the final trial for Israel before it enters the eschatological promised land (1QM II, 6).[132] For six years, Israel will prepare for the fighting, and then for twenty-nine years Israel will fight against multiple nations (1QM II, 6-14).[133] The na-

128. Pagels, "Social History,'" 127; Vermes, *Dead Sea Scrolls*, 165.

129. Duhaime, "War Scroll," 133-51; Duhaime, *War Texts*, 83-94; Jassen, "Violent Imaginaries," 182. Despite its shortcomings as a military manual, 1QM serves to "manipulate troop psychology" (Weitzman, "Warring against Terror," 213-41).

130. For the relationship of 1QM to Dan 11:40-45, see Flusser, *Qumran and Apocalypticism*, 138-58; Duhaime, *War Texts*, 65-70. Concerning the unified Israel of the text, Martin G. Abegg Jr. comments that in the eschatological battle, "Israel would finally become coincident with the sectarian community" ("Covenant of Qumran," 97). See also Schultz, *Conquering the World*, 363-65. For the identification of the Kittim of Assyria as the Romans, see Yadin, *Scroll of the War*, 22-26; Brooke, "Kittim in the Qumran Pesharim," 135-59; Eshel, "Kittim in the *War Scroll*," 29-44; Schultz, "Kittim of Assyria," 63-77; Schultz, *Conquering the World*, 127-57; Jassen, "Violent Imaginaries," 187-91.

131. Jassen comments, "The identification of 'Edom, Moab, Amon, and Philistia' as among the armies of Belial rehearses the many times that these nations have oppressed Israel in the past and waged war against Israel. The end-time armies of the Sons of Light therefore have an opportunity to reverse centuries of Israelite/Jewish disempowerment" ("Violent Imaginaries," 186).

132. Jassen, "Violent Imaginaries," 194-95.

133. The five remaining years are accounted for by breaks in the fighting to observe sabbatical years (1QM II, 8). See Schultz, *Conquering the World*, 171-83. For alternative chronologies of the forty years war, see Carmignac, *Règle de la Guerre*, 35; Yadin, *Scroll of the War*, 20-21; Jongeling, *Rouleau de la guerre*, 92-93; Ibba, "*Rotolo Della Guerra*," 86; Flusser, *Qumran and Apocalypticism*, 146-47; 153-54.

tions mentioned in the twenty-nine-year conflict come from the Table of Nations in Gen 10 and thus symbolize a truly international war.[134]

Behind both Kittim in the first war and the international alliance in the second war stands the powers of darkness, the angels of Belial's kingdom (1QM I, 1; XI, 8). But in the end, God's intervention with a "mighty hand" rather than Israel's own military might will bring about victory (1QM I, 14; XII, 7-9).[135] Raija Sollamo explains that "the supreme leader and hero of the eschatological war is Yahweh himself."[136] The theme of divine intervention receives further emphasis through the messages that the War Scroll commands to be inscribed on the trumpets and banners of Israel, messages like "The Mighty Hand of God in War Shall Cause all the Ungodly Slain to Fall" and "From God comes the Might of War against All Sinful Flesh" (1QM III-IV).[137] Like in the Damascus Document, the ultimate divine victory is seen as an escalation of the pattern from Israel's past. Israel like David will slay the Goliath-like Kittim (1QM XI, 1-5). Just as God destroyed Pharaoh's army in the Red Sea, so too shall he destroy the Kittim (1QM XI, 9-10).[138]

The text reveals something important about the worldview of the sectarians, at least during the period in which it was authored: The holy war theme from ancient Israelite Scripture was not spiritualized at Qumran.[139] Rather the sectarians escalated the theme, expecting to one day be involved in the ultimate apocalyptic battle.[140] Alex P. Jassen, focusing on the rhetorical function of the text with reference to social anthropology, argues that the War Scroll functioned "as a propagandistic tool to prepare the sectarians for this war."[141] By reading or even reciting the text in the period before the eschaton, the sectarians reinforced the dualism of their

---

134. Schultz, *Conquering the World*, 184-204; Jassen, "Violent Imaginaries," 193.

135. This divine intervention is sometimes described as a theophany and at other times as occurring through angelic agents. See Schultz, *Conquering the World*, 97. Surprisingly for a militant eschatological text, the Davidic Messiah receives no mention (unless 4Q285, fr. 7 belongs to the main text), and the high priest plays a leading role instead. See Abegg, "Covenant of Qumran," 83.

136. Sollamo, "War and Violence," 351. See also Brooke, "Text, Timing," 59-60.

137. Yadin, *Scroll of the War*, 43; Jassen, "Violent Imaginaries," 199-202.

138. Duhaime, *War Texts*, 104-15.

139. In the Temple Scroll also, the sectarians fail to downplay, reinterpret, or spiritualize the holy war theme (11QT II).

140. Duhaime, "Règle de la Guerre," 67-88.

141. Jassen, "Violent Imaginaries," 203.

apocalyptic worldview and legitimated the violence they expected to participate in during the eschatological future.[142]

Cosmic Conflict at Qumran

Of all the texts examined here, the texts from Qumran feature the theme of cosmic conflict most conspicuously. The polarity between the righteous and the wicked is nowhere contrasted more sharply than at Qumran, as seen through comparison with Zoroastrian dualism. Likewise, the sectarians developed the locus of God's invasive action to a degree of militarism unparalleled by the other texts examined here. At Qumran, the sectarians expected war to break forth, God to invade, and Israel to be rescued. By contrast, Paul believed God's people had already been liberated through the death of God's Son and that the new age had already been inaugurated.

CONCLUSION

The Jewish texts examined in this chapter share a theme of cosmic conflict as well as the three loci that give shape to the theme: (1) the polarity of the righteous/wicked, (2) the problem of sin and suffering, and (3) the solution of God's invasive action. These texts largely follow the influence of earlier Scripture by splitting humanity into two polar groups: the righteous and the wicked. Some of these books give greater attention to the spiritual forces behind these human groups. In those texts, heavenly beings are polarized between angels and demons and exercise influence over human events (e.g., Dan 10; 1 En. 8; Jub. 10:1–6; 2 Macc 10:29–31). In the case of Qumran, the correspondence between spiritual influence and human identity is absolute. Either one is ruled by the Prince of Light or the Angel of Darkness (e.g., 1QS III, 20–23). Each book also identifies the dual problem of human sin and suffering. Those texts that address the origin of sin differ on the issue. First Enoch and Jubilees emphasize the sin of the Watchers (e.g., 1 En. 6–8; Jub. 4:21–22). Fourth Ezra and 2 Baruch trace humanity's sinful condition back to Adam (e.g., 4 Ezra 3:7–8; 2 Bar. 48:42). Qumran claims that God himself created the opposing spirits of light and darkness (e.g., 1QS III, 25). On the topic of suffering, the historical context of these books directs their focus to the

---

142. Jassen, "Violent Imaginaries," 203.

specific suffering of the Jewish people for their sin, whether that suffering occurred in the Babylonian exile (e.g., Dan 9:3–19; Jub. 1:13–18), the Hellenization scheme of Antiochus IV (e.g., 2 Macc 6:10–17), or the destruction of Jerusalem by the Romans (e.g., 4 Ezra 3:28–35; 2 Bar. 1:5). Each text encourages the Jewish people to hope in God's invasive actions. Most texts point in some way to God's invasive actions in the past, such as his care for the Patriarchs (Jubilees), the exilic generation (Dan 1–6), or the Maccabean warriors and martyrs (1 Maccabees; 2 Maccabees; 4 Maccabees). Qumran exemplifies a form of typology, applying patterns from God's actions in the past to events in the future (e.g., CD V, 18–19; 1QM XI, 9–10). But most of these texts also look forward to God's future invasive actions. Almost all anticipate the establishment of God's eternal kingdom and/or new creation (e.g., Dan 7; 1 En. 51; 4 Ezra 7:26; 2 Bar. 39:7; Jub. 1:29; 1QM I, 5). Because of their focus on relatively current events, 1, 2, and 4 Maccabees pay less attention to the future. Nevertheless, 2 Maccabees highlights belief in the resurrection while 4 Maccabees focuses on immediate spiritual life with God (e.g., 2 Macc 7:9; 4 Macc 7:3). Militaristic language is prominent across the board to describe the actions of God, his agents, and his people, even though that language serves varying functions. The apocalypses reveal the triumph of God over the kingdoms of the world and often portray the Messiah as a victorious king (e.g., Dan 7; 1 En. 1:2–4; 4 Ezra 13:8–45; 2 Bar. 72:6). Jubilees focuses on the demonic domination over humanity and Israel's resistance against these forces (e.g., Jub 15:31–32). First Maccabees identifies God's hand in the historic battles of the Hasmoneans (e.g., 1 Macc 3:21–22). In 2 Maccabees, God intervenes through angelic cavalry (e.g., 2 Macc 5:2–4), and in both 2 and 4 Maccabees, the death of the martyrs is described as contributing to the cosmic conflict (e.g., 2 Macc 6:31; 4 Macc 9:8). The War Scroll develops militaristic language to the fullest in its account of the final apocalyptic war.

In the previous chapter, it was demonstrated that the nature of God's invasive actions grew organically in OT texts.[143] This diverse collection of texts does not demonstrate the same organic growth. Instead, there is a general unity on an important theme—cosmic conflict—and on the loci that give shape to that theme. Middleton claims that the theme of cosmic conflict in early Judaism grew from Israel's holy war tradition. According to Middleton, "the concepts of apocalypticism and the dualism of Holy

---

143. Oswalt, "Recent Studies," 293.

War" combined in the period to elevate Israel's conflict with the gentiles onto the cosmic stage of God's conflict with his demonic enemies, and in light of this development, "the final hope of victory still lay in God fighting through the might of Israel's conventional military forces as in classical Holy War tradition."[144] This explanation gives only a partial representation of the evidence. In his examination of the period, Middleton only examines Daniel, 1 Maccabees, and 2 Maccabees in any detail.[145] As a result, he fails to appreciate the diverse ways that texts from the Second Temple period utilized the theme. Indeed, a significant degree of unity on the theme exists, coming largely from the common sources shared by all Jewish texts: the history of the Jewish people and earlier Scripture. But, as has been demonstrated above, beyond this thematic unity comes immense diversity concerning the nature of God's future invasive actions.

The pen of Paul enters into this diverse atmosphere with what could be considered outlandish innovations. As discussed in the previous chapter, Paul altered the theme of cosmic conflict in two primary ways: (1) He read all Scripture in light of the coming of the Son and the Spirit. (2) Because God's intervention has occurred in the Son and the Spirit, Paul believes that the new creation has already been inaugurated, although not yet fully realized, in the church. Even after examining additional texts in this chapter, these two innovations retain their groundbreaking character. Note the outlandishness of Paul's proposal: Paul asserts that a Jew named Jesus from a village called Nazareth in Galilee is in fact the Davidic Messiah. This Jesus has brought liberation from the present evil age and inaugurated the new creation through execution by the Romans. As a result, God has sent his Holy Spirit and justified those who believe in this good news. For Paul, therefore, the future is now, and the new creation is here. The cosmic conflict in which the Galatians are engaged exists because of the overlap of the present age with the new creation. That said, a third innovation becomes especially apparent in comparison with the other texts examined in this chapter: Paul believed that the gentile nations were to be included in the people of God through faith in the gospel of Christ apart from the law (e.g., Gal 1:16; 2:7–10; 3:7–9). Terrence L. Donaldson's monumental study on the period demonstrates that Jewish attitudes toward non-Jews were diverse rather than monolithic.[146] So, the caricature of particularistic Judaism versus universalistic

---

144. Middleton, *Radical Martyrdom*, 132.
145. Middleton, *Radical Martyrdom*, 130–32.
146. Donaldson, *Judaism and the Gentiles*, 507–13.

Christianity should be discarded. The texts examined above range in attitudes toward the gentiles from belief that they are under demonic dominion (Jub. 15:31–32), to expectation that the nations will fight Israel in an international war (1QM II, 6–14), to the hope of eschatological salvation for some non-Jewish nations (2 Bar. 76:2–3). Even in view of such diversity, Paul innovates in preaching that the gentiles can be justified *by faith in Christ apart from the law*. As Michael F. Bird writes,

> This marginal place was fraught with peril, since it threatened the cultural norms and institutional structures overseen by leaders who were no doubt alarmed at Paul's dismantling of social boundaries and the consequences of his eschatological enthusiasm for Christ's lordship.[147]

These Pauline innovations would indeed get Paul and his churches into trouble, but they also provided the framework in which Paul taught his churches to understand persecution as well as the support they needed to endure suffering. The local events they experienced were in fact part of a cosmic conflict between God and the present evil age.

To summarize, chapters 2–4 have examined a theme of cosmic conflict, first in Galatians and then in texts that give clues to Paul's intellectual context. Chapter 5 will shift toward the topic of persecution in Galatia. In order to understand how Paul connects persecution to the theme of cosmic conflict, the historical situation at Galatia must first be examined. What do Paul's references to persecution in Galatians indicate about the circumstances of the Galatian churches? Was persecution even happening? Who was being persecuted or was vulnerable to persecution? Who were the persecutors? What types of persecution were occurring or likely to occur?

---

147. Bird, *Anomalous Jew*, 29.

5

Persecution in Galatians

IN *THE MYTH OF Persecution: How Early Christians Invented a Story of Martyrdom*, Candida R. Moss writes, "There's almost no evidence from the period before Constantine, or the Age of the Martyrs, to support the idea that Christians were continually persecuted."[1] Early Christians "invented martyrdom stories and saw their history as a history of persecution" because myths of martyrdom served both apologetic and devotional purposes.[2] Certainly martyr stories served these and other identity-formation purposes, but is it justified to label persecution as a "myth"? Certainly, few would defend the authenticity of hagiographic narratives or even the notion of constant and continual persecution in the early centuries of the Christian church. Not until the edict of Decius in AD 249, which required persons to sacrifice to the Roman gods, did an empire-wide persecution of Christians initiate, but even this edict was not directed specifically at Christians. Instead, it was an attempt by Decius to bring religious homogeneity to the empire and thus give greater security to the empire's political integrity.[3] Prior to the edict of Decius, "there were only isolated, local persecutions."[4] Nevertheless, such isolated

---

1. Moss, *Myth of Persecution*, 32. See also Moss, *Other Christs*; Moss, *Ancient Christian Martyrdom*.

2. Moss, *Myth of Persecution*, 33–36. Similarly Hopkins, "Christian Number," 198.

3. J. B. Rives explains, "It is thus not surprising that before Decius' decree on universal sacrifice, there has been no centrally organized persecutions of Christians: it was only when a 'religion of the Empire' had been defined and its boundaries set that there could be a systematic persecution of people who transgressed those boundaries" ("Decree of Decius," 153).

4. Ste. Croix, "Why Were the Early Christians Persecuted?," 7. See also Sherwin-

and local persecutions actually occurred and served a significant role in the formation of early Christian identity, especially in relation to Christianity's self-understanding of its history.

Questions concerning the extent and authenticity of persecution in early Christian history extend to the interpretation of passages that refer to persecution in Galatians. The minimization and neglect of the theme prompted Ernst Baasland's article in 1984.[5] While Baasland brought attention to the theme, the historical background to this theme remains problematic, being one aspect of the broader debate about the identity of Paul's opponents. In the most thorough examination of persecution in Galatians to date, John Anthony Dunne attempts to sidestep the issue of historical reconstruction, instead focusing on "Paul's depictions, interpretations, and evaluations of the situation and his opponents."[6] History, however, cannot be easily bifurcated from theology. Therefore, before examining persecution as a manifestation of cosmic conflict in the letter, the historical questions about persecution in Galatia must be addressed. This chapter will reconstruct the historical background to the instances of persecution mentioned in Galatians. This historical reconstruction will serve as a basis of the examination of Paul's theology in chapter 6. This chapter will begin with a review of possible references to persecution in Galatians. After examining each instance of persecution identified in Galatians, the individual pieces will be put together to offer a unified portrait of the historical background to Paul's letter.

POSSIBLE REFERENCES TO PERSECUTION IN GALATIANS

Paul primarily utilizes διώκω to express the persecution theme in Galatians. Διώκω occurs five times in the letter (1:13, 23; 4:29; 5:11; 6:12).[7]

White, "Amendment," 23–27; Ste. Croix, "Rejoinder," 28–33; Barnes, "Legislation," 32–50; Barnes, "Pre-Decian Acta Martyrum," 509–31; Bisbee, *Pre-Decian Acts*; Middleton, *Radical Martyrdom*, 1–3.

5. Baasland, "Persecution," 135–50.

6. Dunne, *Persecution and Participation*, 50.

7. Διώκω means "to pursue" or "to run toward." Paul uses it in this sense in Phil 3:14, writing, "I run toward (διώκω) the goal for the prize of the upward call of God in Christ Jesus." But more often in the NT it means "to pursue someone in order to harass them or do them harm" or "to persecute" (e.g., Matt 5:11; Acts 7:52; Rom 12:14; 1 Cor 4:9, 12; 15:9; Phil 3:6; Rev 12:13). The five uses of the verb in Galatians clearly carry the meaning "to persecute." See BDAG, s.v. "διώκω"; L&N, 15.158, 223; 39.45; 68.66; 89.56;

The first instance in 1:13 refers to Paul's "former life in Judaism" when he "persecuted the church of God intensely." Galatians 1:23 refers to the same instance of persecution by recalling how the churches in Judea marveled that "he who formerly persecuted us now preaches the faith that he once tried to destroy." The verb does not appear again until 4:29 when Paul identifies the Galatian churches with Isaac who was also "persecuted." In 5:11, Paul asks, "But, brothers, if I still preach circumcision, then why am I still being persecuted?" Then finally in 6:12 he accuses his opponents of avoiding being "persecuted for the cross of Christ."

In addition to these occurrences of διώκω, six other possible references to persecution may be identified in the book:[8] (1) In 3:1, Paul describes the early preaching of the gospel in Galatia as Christ being "publicly portrayed as crucified." Does this refer to the persecution that accompanied gospel proclamation? (2) In 3:4, Paul asks, "Did you suffer/experience (ἐπάθετε) so much in vain—if indeed it was in vain?" (3) In 4:13, Paul makes reference to "a weakness of the flesh" (ἀσθένειαν τῆς σαρκός), which may refer to his own persecution. (4) In 4:17–18, Paul points to the zeal that his opponents have for the Galatian Christians. Given the background of Phinehan zeal in Second Temple Judaism, this may be a reference to hostile pressure.[9] (5) In 4:19, Paul speaks of "again suffering labor pains." Is this a reference to his persecution? (6) In 6:17, Paul boasts that he bears on his body "the marks of Jesus" (τὰ στίγματα τοῦ Ἰησοῦ), which has largely been interpreted as referring to Paul's scars from persecution. Each of these possible references to persecution must be critically examined in order to reconstruct the situation in Galatia.

This overview of occurrences of διώκω and other possible references to persecution identifies four possible instances of persecution or likely persecution referenced in Galatians: (1) Paul's persecution of the church before the revelation of Christ (1:13, 23), (2) the persecution that

---

Baasland, "Persecution," 136–39.

8. Some interpreters also identify the following passages as referring to persecution: (1) the curse motif (1:8–9; 3:10–14; e.g., Baasland, "Persecution," 141–44). (2) the Abba-cry (4:6; cf. Rom 8:15; e.g., Keesmaat, *Paul and His Story*, 179–81; Dunne, *Persecution and Participation*, 78–86). (3) the vice and virtue lists (5:13–26; Dunne, *Persecution and Participation*, 58–59). Since these passages say little about the historical circumstances themselves, they will not be examined in this chapter. One other possible reference, 2:19–21, will be examined in relation to 3:1 below (e.g., Baasland, "Persecution," 145).

9. On the association of zeal with violence, see 1 Macc 2:26; Dunn, *New Perspective*, 11–13; Wright, *Paul and the Faithfulness of God*, 84–87.

Paul endured after the revelation of Christ (3:1; 4:13, 19; 5:11; 6:17), (3) the potential persecution that Paul's opponents avoid (6:12), and (4) the persecution of the Galatian Christians (3:4; 4:17-18, 29).

INSTANCE 1: PAUL THE PERSECUTOR (1:13, 23)

In his former life, Paul "persecuted the church of God intensely and tried to destroy it" (1:13; cf. 1:23). No significant scholar—ancient or modern—has ever questioned Paul's account of his early life as a persecutor of Jewish Christians. In fact, Craig S. Keener calls the fact "undisputed."[10] Paul's own testimony in other letters consistently affirms that he was a former persecutor of the church (1 Cor 15:9; Phil 3:6; 1 Tim 1:13), and the account of Luke—Paul's missionary teammate—serves only to give greater detail about Paul's activities as a persecutor, consistent with Paul's own testimony.[11] In Acts 7:58 and 8:1, Saul of Tarsus is introduced as a witness to Stephen's execution and possibly even as the leader of those who instigated Stephen's trial and subsequent death.[12] At any rate, Saul did eventually assume the role of lead persecutor (Acts 8:3). Acts affirms Paul's characterization of his persecutions as "intense" or "violent" (ὑπερβολή; Gal 1:13), depicting him as dragging off not only men but also women to prison.[13] In Acts 9:1-2, an enraged Saul asks the high priest for letters of recommendation to the synagogues of Damascus in order to extend arrests to the Diaspora.[14] During Paul's defense before Agrippa, Luke portrays him as recounting the escalation of his activities. First, he opposed "the name of Jesus of Nazareth," which then drove him to imprison Christians in Jerusalem, and finally he expanded his activities to "foreign cities" (Acts 26:9-12).

---

10. Keener, *Acts*, 1446.

11. On the historical value of Acts, see Keener, *Acts*, 166-220; Schnabel, *Acts*, 28-41.

12. By laying their garments at Saul's feet, the witnesses may be recognizing Saul's authority (cf. Acts 4:35, 37; 5:2). See Peterson, *Acts*, 268; Keener, *Acts*, 1445.

13. Women were less likely to suffer punishment in the Roman empire. Valerius Maximus characterizes Sulla as extremely wicked on the basis that he slew women as well as men (Val. Max. 9.2.1). See Keener, *Acts*, 1482-83.

14. Bruce, *Acts*, 180-81; Keener, *Acts*, 1618-30; Schnabel, *Acts*, 442-43. Saul's mission of persecution seems to have been well-known enough that both Ananias and those who attended the Damascus synagogues already knew about it (Acts 9:13-14, 21). See Schnabel, *Acts*, 448.

Galatians 1:14 provides a plausible motive for Paul's activities. His rapid advance "in the Jewish way of life" was motivated by "extreme zeal" for Jewish traditions.[15] Richard N. Longenecker represents a common interpretation of ζηλωτής when he writes that "ζηλωτής here should be taken only as 'an ardent observer of Torah.'"[16] Thus Longenecker rejects the conclusion of J. B. Lightfoot in a previous generation of scholarship, who linked ζηλωτής to an extreme wing of the Pharisees that later became known as Zealots.[17] The research of James D. G. Dunn and N. T. Wright however into Second Temple Judaism has turned the tide once again toward connecting zeal with violence, although not necessarily with a well-defined party or sect.[18] Wright goes as far as to claim that "zeal" was "an obvious code word for revolutionary aspiration," denoting "a ready willingness to take the law into one's own hands."[19] The connection of zeal with violence emerges primarily from 1 Maccabees, which presents the violent actions of Phinehas in Numbers 25 as exemplary for later generations of Israelites (1 Macc 2:24–27, 50–60). While not every instance of ζηλωτής in the NT refers to violence,[20] when zeal is connected by the context to a central aspect of Jewish identity it often entails violence (e.g., John 2:17; Acts 5:17; 13:45; 22:3–4). As Dane C. Ortlund has shown, however, such zeal motivated violence, not as mere nationalism, but as an "intense devotion to live out the way of life prescribed by Torah."[21] So, in Gal 1:13–14, Paul gives a glimpse into his motivations as a persecutor: Before God revealed his Son to Paul, Paul was so devoted to Jewish traditions that he violently persecuted the church of God with the goal of destroying it.

---

15. On ἐν τῷ Ἰουδαϊσμῷ, see Sänger, "Ἰουδαϊσμός," 150–85. Cf. Das, *Galatians*, 147–52; Oakes, *Galatians*, 52–54. Contra Mason, "Jews, Judaeans," 457–512.

16. Longenecker, *Galatians*, 30. Similarly Martyn, *Galatians*, 155.

17. Lightfoot, *Galatians*, 81–82.

18. Dunn, *New Perspective*, 11–13; Wright, *Paul and the Faithfulness of God*, 84–87; Fairchild, "Paul's Pre-Christian Zealot Associations," 514–32. On the ubiquity of zeal in Palestinian Judaism beyond the Zealot sect, see Hengel, *Zealots*, 177–83.

19. Wright, *Paul and the Faithfulness of God*, 84–85.

20. Ζῆλος, ζηλόω, and ζηλωτής may indicate "eagerness" (e.g., 1 Cor 14:12; Titus 2:14; 1 Pet 3:13) or "jealousy" (e.g., Acts 17:5; Rom 13:13; 1 Cor 13:14; Jas 4:2). See BDAG, s.v. "ζῆλος; ζηλόω; ζηλωτής."

21. Ortlund, *Zeal without Knowledge*, 148. Cf. Ortlund, "Phinehan Zeal," 299–315; Bruce, *Acts*, 180. Contra Dunn, *New Perspective*, 148.

INSTANCE 2: PAUL THE PERSECUTED
(3:1; 4:13, 19; 5:11; 6:17)

Once Paul began "preaching the faith that he once tried to destroy" (1:23), he also began suffering for that faith at the hands of those who, like his former self, were zealous for Jewish traditions.

Galatians 5:11

In 5:11, Paul clearly refers to himself as the victim of persecution. Paul asks, "But, brothers, if I still proclaim circumcision, why am I still being persecuted?" Connecting his persecutions with the revealed gospel of Christ, Paul infers that to preach circumcision and thus avoid persecution would mean to eradicate the scandal of the cross.[22] Thus, he argues that "the preaching of circumcision is antithetical to and entirely nullifies the preaching of Christ crucified."[23] The book of Acts affirms both that Paul was in fact persecuted and that his persecution arose from his preaching. In Luke's record, the account of Pisidian Antioch serves as typical of Paul's missionary activities.[24] Paul enters the city and preaches Christ in the synagogue from the Law and Prophets (Acts 13:14-41). Angered at the positive reception Paul received among the Gentiles, the Jewish community in the city incited the Gentile leaders to persecute Paul and his missionary team (Acts 13:44-52). Luke identifies the same general pattern as occurring at Iconium and Lystra: Paul preaches, and the Jews are angered and incite the Gentile leaders to persecute Paul and his team (Acts 14:1-23).[25] Assuming the validity of the south Galatia hypothesis,[26]

---

22. Dieter Mitternacht rightly comments, "The real issue of 5:11, however, is the immovable bond between persecution and the cross" ("Foolish Galatians?," 428).

23. Longenecker, *Galatians*, 233.

24. On the exemplary nature of the episode at Pisidian Antioch in Luke's narrative, see Marshall, *Acts*, 236; Schnabel, *Acts*, 564. Contra Matera who writes that in 5:11 "persecution should be understood as persecution from the agitators, not persecution from Jews" who Paul polemically accuses of persecuting him "by opposing the circumcision-free Gospel he preaches to the Gentiles" (*Galatians*, 190).

25. Parsons, *Acts*, 197.

26. Stephen Mitchell in his monumental work on Anatolia concludes that "there is virtually nothing to be said for the north Galatian theory" (*Anatolia*, 2:3-4). See also Breytenbach, *Paulus und Barnabas*; Riesner, *Paul's Early Period*, 286-91; Witulski, *Adressaten des Galaterbriefes*; John, *Galaterbrief im Kontext*, 133-53.

this pattern of events—the movement from preaching to persecution—had been witnessed first-hand by the Galatian Christians.

Galatians 3:1

Does this connection between preaching and persecution also then appear in Paul's earlier assertion that "Jesus Christ was publicly portrayed as crucified" before the eyes of the Galatians (3:1)? Basil S. Davis has argued that Paul portrayed Christ crucified through his own suffering.[27] Most commentators, however, think that Paul describes the vivid preaching of the gospel.[28] But might the phrase κατ' ὀφθαλμούς suggest more than verbal proclamation alone?[29] Davis believes so and argues that 2:19–21 sheds light on Paul's expression in 3:1.[30] This suggestion, however, only shifts the problem to different ground. The question now becomes: When Paul speaks of having been crucified with Christ does he reference his persecution?[31] This suggestion is problematic since the death Paul speaks of is, as he states explicitly in 2:19, death "to the law." Galatians 2:19–21, then, speaks of an eschatological transition that Paul has *personally* experienced and that, gnomically, every "I" who is united to Christ through faith experiences (6:14–15).[32] So the immediate context of 2:19–21 lends

---

27. Davis, "Meaning of ΠΡΟΕΓΡΑΦΗ," 194–212. Some interpretations of προγράφω merit little consideration. It seems unlikely that Paul references the "writing beforehand" of the Scriptures (Hays, "Galatians," 250–51) or that Paul utilized visual aids in his preaching (Duncan, *Galatians*, 77–79; Balch, "Suffering of Isis/Io," 27–28; Lopez, *Apostle to the Conquered*, 163).

28. Schlier, *Brief an die Galater*, 80; Mußner, *Galaterbrief*, 205; Betz, *Galatians*, 131; Fung, *Galatians*, 129; Longenecker, *Galatians*, 100–101; Matera, *Galatians*, 112; Dunn, *Galatians*, 152; George, *Galatians*, 209; Martyn, *Galatians*, 283; Schreiner, *Galatians*, 182; de Boer, *Galatians*, 171–72; Moo, *Galatians*, 182.

29. Davis, "Meaning of ΠΡΟΕΓΡΑΦΗ," 205.

30. Davis, "Meaning of ΠΡΟΕΓΡΑΦΗ," 206–10.

31. Davis never states explicitly that 2:19–21 refers to persecution, but he suggests this by conflating two lines of argument: (1) Paul "proudly endured persecution for the sake of his Law-free gospel," and (2) Paul "lived in union with the crucified Christ" ("Meaning of ΠΡΟΕΓΡΑΦΗ," 212). The suggestion that anytime Paul speaks of union he also refers to persecution cannot be sustained.

32. Although the word "rectification" is problematic, de Boer, otherwise rightly, explains, "Christ's crucifixion was an event on the stage of human history that Paul regards as the central moment in God's apocalyptic-eschatological act of cosmic rectification through the person and work of Christ, his Son. In Paul's understanding of the gospel, everyone who 'has come to believe in Christ Jesus' (v. 16a) participates in, is joined to or taken up into, this all-embracing cosmic, apocalyptic event that spells the end of the

no support for understanding προγράφω as referring directly to Paul's persecution.³³

Nevertheless, 2:19-21 does possibly clarify how Paul vividly preached the cross. Davis comments, "So when 3.1 is read as directly following the preceding verses it becomes quite evident that Paul is describing himself as the canvas upon which the crucified Christ was publicly displayed."³⁴ But if 2:19-21 clarifies the nature of Paul's display of Christ crucified in 3:1, then this display did not occur specifically through persecution, but through Paul's personal transformation and eschatological transition—Christ living in him (2:20). So, while Paul certainly speaks of his vivid proclamation of the gospel, he may also reference his own embodiment of that message through his own life. Considering that Paul commonly connected preaching and persecution in his letters, persecution may be one aspect of this embodiment of the gospel *indirectly* referred to in 3:1 (cf. Col 1:24-29; 1 Thess 2:1-12). But, most importantly, sufficient evidence does not exist to read 3:1 as a *direct* reference to Paul's persecutions.³⁵

Galatians 6:17

A more probable appeal to persecution occurs in 6:17 where Paul claims to bear on his body τὰ στίγματα τοῦ Ἰησοῦ. Στίγμα refers to the brand of a slave or religious tattooing.³⁶ In both these examples of στίγμα, the marks indicate human or divine ownership over the one so marked. Paul does not appeal to an actual branding or tattoo since such would violate Jewish

---

old age, where malevolent powers hold sway over God's creation.... Crucifixion with Christ represents for the individual believer the destruction of one's participation in the old age, where the law functions as an oppressive, enslaving power" (*Galatians*, 161). See also Seifrid, "Paul, Luther, and Justification," 221; Schreiner, *Galatians*, 171-72; Das, *Galatians*, 267-73; Barclay, *Paul and the Gift*, 384-87.

33. Mitternacht argues for reading persecution in 3:1 on the basis of correspondence between 3:1-5 and 4:12-15 ("Foolish Galatians?," 424). But as will be discussed below, 4:12-15 does not directly relate to persecution.

34. Davis, "Meaning of ΠΡΟΕΓΡΑΦΗ," 208.

35. Although recognizing the influence of Davis, Das presents a mediating position similar to the one argued here. He writes, "Paul *in some way* embodied Christ to the Galatians" (*Galatians*, 287-88; italics added). See also Keener, *Galatians*, 213-14.

36. Betz, "στίγμα," 7:657-64; BDAG, s.v. "στίγμα"; L&N, 8.55, 33.481, 90.84; Longenecker, *Galatians*, 299. Keener, however, questions the ubiquity of slave branding during the period (*Galatians*, 584-85).

law and practice (e.g., Lev 19:28).³⁷ Rather, as Jeffrey A. D. Weima writes, "the 'marks of Jesus' here primarily serve to contrast the persecution willingly experienced by Paul with the persecution deliberately avoided by his 'mark-less' opponents."³⁸ According to Paul, his opponents boast in the fleshly mark of circumcision in order to avoid the bodily (ἐν τῷ σώματί) marks that actually count—the marks of persecution (Gal 6:12–13).³⁹ Paul, on the other hand, shows that he is owned by Jesus through scars that imitate the suffering of Jesus himself.⁴⁰ Paul makes a similar claim about his physical scars in 2 Cor 4:10 where he writes that he is "always carrying the death of Jesus in the body" through persecution.⁴¹ The verb βαστάζω in Gal 6:17 may also allude to the Jesus-tradition recorded in Luke and John of "bearing" the cross (Luke 14:27; John 19:17).⁴² But even if βαστάζω does not allude to the Jesus-tradition, the contrast between 6:12–13 and 6:17 sufficiently demonstrates that Paul refers to the scars of persecution he had experienced while the meaning of the word στίγμα adds that these scars marked Paul out as owned by Jesus. As Eastman vividly paraphrases, "You want something to brag about? You want identity markers? I'll give you identity markers! You see these scars? I'm branded for Jesus. Become like me!"⁴³

Galatians 4:13

Another possible reference to Paul as a victim of persecution involves the difficult phrase ἀσθένειαν τῆς σαρκός in 4:13. A. J. Goddard and Stephen Anthony Cummins argue that Paul's "weakness" refers to "a context of

---

37. Weima, "Gal 6.11–18," 98; Schreiner, *Galatians*, 384. Contra Dinkler, "Jesu Wort Vom Kreuztragen," 125–26. It is also unlikely that Paul refers to eye problems (Hirsch, "Zwei Fragen zu Galater 6," 196–97) or his future martyrdom (O'Neill, *Recovery of Paul's Letter*, 82).

38. Weima, "Gal 6.11–18," 99.

39. Paul does not likely speak figuratively since the types of ordeals that he catalogs in 2 Cor 11:23–33 would have certainly left actual physical scars on his body. While we cannot know for certain how many of these ordeals he had undergone when writing Galatians, he certainly had undergone enough to have sufficient scars. So Burton, *Galatians*, 360; Dunn, *Galatians*, 347.

40. Burton, *Galatians*, 361; Schlier, *Brief an die Galater*, 210–11; Hays, "Galatians," 347; Keener, *Galatians*, 585.

41. Moo, *Galatians*, 404; Das, *Galatians*, 654.

42. Betz, *Galatians*, 325; Schreiner, *Galatians*, 384.

43. Eastman, *Recovering Paul's Mother Tongue*, 109. See also deSilva, *Galatians*, 514–15.

conflict and persecution which attended Paul's original mission among the Galatians."[44] Paul's appeal evokes the Maccabean martyr tradition and identifies persecution as "the burden of the suffering righteous" that exemplifies the suffering of Christ himself.[45] The Galatian Christians did not initially despise Paul for his suffering but accepted him as God's righteous messenger; yet after experiencing the blessedness of suffering, they now reject him and his gospel.[46] Goddard and Cummins stress that such an interpretation of Paul's ἀσθένεια unifies the section in an "intelligible way" with what comes before and after and thus makes the appeal a substantial part of Paul's argument.[47] Furthermore, they claim that their interpretation fits both with the historical evidence of Acts as well as with Paul's other letters (e.g., Acts 14:8–20; 2 Cor 11:23–33; 1 Thess 3:3–5).[48] In conclusion, they write, "Finally, this passage provides further evidence of the almost normative correlation between faithfulness to the crucified Christ and experience of persecution and suffering."[49] Despite the internal consistency of their view, the natural meaning of ἀσθένεια is problematic for Goddard and Cummins since the noun usually refers to sickness.[50]

Scott J. Hafemann offers an alternative interpretation that reads ἀσθένεια naturally as sickness but nonetheless relates Paul's sickness to his apostolic suffering.[51] Hafemann rightly argues that attempting to in-

44. Goddard and Cummins, "Ill or Ill-Treated?," 94. Followed by Hays, "Galatians," 293–94; Mitternacht, "Foolish Galatians?," 421–23; Eastman, *Recovering Paul's Mother Tongue*, 100–109; Dunne, *Persecution and Participation*, 161–69.

45. Goddard and Cummins, "Ill or Ill-Treated?," 103.

46. Goddard and Cummins, "Ill or Ill-Treated?," 114.

47. Goddard and Cummins, "Ill or Ill-Treated?," 116.

48. Goddard and Cummins, "Ill or Ill-Treated?," 121.

49. Goddard and Cummins, "Ill or Ill-Treated?," 122.

50. Black, "Weakness Language," 15–36; BDAG, s.v. "ἀσθένεια." See also the critique of Longenecker, "Until Christ," 106.

51. Hafemann, "Because of Weakness," 131–46. Followed by Schreiner, *Galatians*, 285–86; Das, *Galatians*, 460. Troy W. Martin rejects both sickness and persecution as the referent for ἀσθένεια. Since ἀσθένειαν τῆς σαρκός lacks any possessive pronouns, Martin contends that the "flesh" in question is not Paul's flesh but the flesh of the Galatians. The sinful weakness of their flesh motivated Paul to evangelize them. As Gentiles, however, the Galatians were tempted to despise Paul's circumcised flesh (4:14), but while they originally resisted that temptation, the pressure of Paul's opponents to undergo circumcision risks pushing them back into paganism ("Whose Flesh?," 65–91). Martin's view is unlikely, however, since Paul is the subject of the verb εὐηγγελισάμην and thus the absence of a possessive pronoun means that the "flesh" belongs to the subject, Paul. See Das, *Galatians*, 457.

terpret ἀσθένεια as persecution fails to account for the fact that in 4:13 ἀσθένεια is the *cause* of his preaching, while elsewhere persecution is the *consequence* of his preaching (5:11; 6:12, 17).[52] Rather, Paul's weakness must indicate physical sickness.[53] But that does not mean that Paul is simply referring to the providential circumstances that brought him to Galatia.[54] Rather Paul's sickness was "instrumental" in his proclamation of the gospel.[55] Hafemann makes this point as an extension of his earlier work on 2 Cor 2:14—3:3 in which he claims that Paul's apostolic suffering served a revelatory function.[56] In 2 Corinthians, Paul's sufferings are "not mere circumstance, but instead are the outworking of God's plan to spread the gospel."[57] Therefore, rather than pitting Paul's suffering and possession of the Spirit against one another, as the super-apostles had done, Paul glories in weakness. Hafemann explains, "Paul is weak and suffers as an embodiment of the cross of Christ, but he is also a pneumatic through whom the power and Spirit of God are being manifested and poured out."[58] Since "Paul's suffering and his ministry of the Spirit are, in fact, convincing evidence for the validity of his apostolic authority and ministry," to reject Paul is to reject God as well.[59] In Galatians also, Paul's bodily sickness was "the vehicle through which the saving power of God, climactically revealed in Christ, was being made known in the world."[60] While the principle of God's power being revealed through human weakness does apply generally to Paul's theology of persecution, Hafemann convincingly and significantly demonstrates that 4:13 does not refer to Paul's persecutions.

---

52. Hafemann, "'Because of Weakness,'" 133. Keener suggests that Paul's weakness could refer to injuries from persecution (*Galatians*, 376).

53. Hafemann, "'Because of Weakness,'" 133.

54. Hafemann, "'Because of Weakness,'" 134. Some suggest that Paul may have left the marshy coasts of Pamphylia for the higher elevation of Pisidian Antioch in order to recover from malaria. See Ramsay, *St. Paul the Traveller*, 94–97; Das, *Galatians*, 455. Keener rightly calls the hypothesis "possible but speculative" (*Acts*, 2032).

55. Hafemann, "'Because of Weakness,'" 136.

56. Hafemann, *Suffering and the Spirit*, 67, 174.

57. Hafemann, *Suffering and the Spirit*, 72.

58. Hafemann, *Suffering and the Spirit*, 220.

59. Hafemann, *Suffering and the Spirit*, 221.

60. Hafemann, "'Because of Weakness,'" 140.

Galatians 4:19

If 4:13 does not refer to persecution, what then of 4:19? Paul tells the Galatian Christians that he is "again suffering labor pains." Do these labor pains refer to Paul's initial persecution in Galatia?[61] Beverly Roberts Gaventa has rightly identified "apocalyptic expectation" in Paul's language.[62] Even so, Gaventa goes too far when suggesting that the labor pains are "of the cosmos itself" and not "of an individual apostle."[63] Rather Paul's labor as an apostle relates to the labor of the "barren one" in Isaiah 54:1, where ὠδίνω occurs again (4:27).[64] The promise of children in Isaiah 54:1 grounds Paul's statement that believers have the heavenly Jerusalem as their mother (4:25-26). Paul has become an agent of this birth process through his call to preach Christ among the Gentiles (1:16), and thus his apostolic labor is an apocalyptic labor of bearing the children for the heavenly Jerusalem.

In 4:19, Paul's labor has a temporal limit: "until Christ is formed in you." Once this goal is established, then his labor pains will have ended.[65] Paul's complaint, however, is that there has been an unnecessary repetition of these pains. He is suffering "again" (4:19). Through Paul's preaching, the Galatian Christians have already been delivered from the present evil age, but through the preaching of a false gospel, the Galatian Christians are being tempted to return to their former slavery (1:4; 5:1). This threat has forced Paul to undergo these labor pains anew.[66] Paul's present labor pains cannot be equated with physical persecution since his anguish concerns the possible reversion of the Galatian Christians to an enslaved state under the present evil age. So, Paul's metaphor of labor pains primarily possesses an emotional referent—the agonizing, motherly love he has for his spiritual children.[67] Certainly, as has been

---

61. So Martyn, *Galatians*, 430; Eastman, *Recovering Paul's Mother Tongue*, 97-126; Schreiner, *Galatians*, 289; Dunne, *Persecution and Participation*, 175-77.

62. Gaventa, "Maternity of Paul," 191-94. See Isa 13:6-8; Jer 6:24; Mic 4:10; 1 En. 62:4; 2 Bar. 56:6; 4 Ezra 4:42. Gal 4:19 does not allude to Isa 45:10. Rightly Eastman, *Recovering Paul's Mother Tongue*, 117-19; Das, *Galatians*, 472. Contra Martyn, *Galatians*, 428-29; Harmon, *She Must and Shall Go Free*, 171-73.

63. Gaventa, *Our Mother Saint Paul*, 37. Rightly Oakes, *Galatians*, 150-51.

64. Rightly Dunne, *Persecution and Participation*, 175.

65. Gaventa, "Maternity of Paul," 196; Dunn, *Galatians*, 240; Moo, *Galatians*, 289; Das, *Galatians*, 474.

66. Gaventa, "Maternity of Paul," 196; Das, *Galatians*, 474.

67. Rightly, Burton, *Galatians*, 249; Longenecker, *Galatians*, 194; Dunn, *Galatians*,

argued above, the initial period of evangelization included physical pain endured by Paul, but the correspondence between the past and the present in Paul's appeal suggests that he has his emotional distress primarily in view here, not his physical suffering.

To summarize, in 5:11 and 6:17, Paul identifies himself as the victim of persecution. The narrative of Acts 13:13–14:23 records Paul undergoing such persecution during his initial evangelization of Galatia, and in agreement with Paul's words in 5:11, connects this persecution to Paul's preaching. Galatians 3:1, however, does not refer to Paul's persecution. Neither does 4:13 or 4:19 refer to Paul's persecution but instead reference Paul's physical illness (4:13) and emotional anguish (4:19).

INSTANCE 3: THE OPPONENTS AS POTENTIAL TARGETS (6:12)

In 6:12, Paul asserts that his opponents promote circumcision in order to avoid being "persecuted for the cross of Christ." The statement is a corollary of what he had already stated in 5:11 about himself: He is persecuted because he does not preach circumcision, refusing to abandon the scandal of the cross. Paul's reference to his opponents as potential targets of persecution, if they choose to abandon the preaching of circumcision, potentially serves as one of the most revealing allusions to the situation in Galatia. Two primary questions arise from the verse: Who would have potentially persecuted Paul's opponents? And how where these people appeased by the preaching of circumcision? Three possible persecutors have been identified by scholars: (1) Zealot or zealous Jews, (2) Roman authorities, and (3) local Jewish synagogues.

Zealot Jews

Robert Jewett has identified the potential persecutors as the Zealots. He begins by arguing that Paul's opponents were "Jerusalem-oriented" Jewish Christians who had come into Galatia from the outside.[68] This explains "Paul's polemic against Jerusalem (4:25–31) and his reference

---

239; Moo, *Galatians*, 288–89.

68. Jewett, "Agitators," 339. The following favor Jewett: Bruce, *Epistle to the Galatians*, 269; Longenecker, *Galatians*, 291; Dunn, *Galatians*, 123; Weima, "Gal 6.11–18," 97; Martyn, *Galatians*, 562; Witherington, *Grace in Galatia*, 446; Moo, *Galatians*, 393.

to the Judean churches (1:22)."[69] Jewett explains that the period from the late forties AD until the outbreak of the Jewish War saw a growing Zealot campaign in Judea and Galilee with the twin goals of undermining Roman control and purifying Israel.[70] Due to this political reality, "Jewish Christians in Judea were stimulated by Zealotic pressure into a nomistic campaign among their fellow Christians in the late forties and early fifties."[71] To avoid persecution from the Zealots, Jewish Christians compelled gentile Christians to become fully Jewish through circumcision and Torah-obedience. As Paul's autobiography demonstrates, the Judean church was indeed threatened with destruction by zealous persecutors (1:13–14). Furthermore, the Zealot threat may also explain Peter's fear in 2:12. Did the men who came from James bear a message about Zealotic persecution against the Judean churches?[72]

Jewett's thesis, however, is not without its problems. Jewett's appeal to the Zealots as a party that exercised immense influence during the period may be anachronistic.[73] This issue may be solved, however, simply by shifting the blame to zealous (lowercase) Jews, of which Paul counts himself in 1:13–14, rather than a more formal Zealot (uppercase) sect.[74] More troubling for Jewett's reconstruction, however, is the geographical distance involved. Why would Judean Christians worry themselves with Galatian gentiles who were far removed from the political situation in Judea and Galilee?[75] Or to put it differently, would the circumcision of Galatian gentiles really serve as sufficient proof of the loyalty of the Judean churches to the agenda of the Zealots and thus save them from persecution? John M. G. Barclay even-handedly concludes, "It is not impossible that the opponents were acting under Zealot pressure in Palestine (so

---

69. Jewett, "Agitators," 339.

70. Jewett, "Agitators," 340. See Josephus, *Ant.* 20.113, 118; Josephus, *J.W.* 2.254–57, 264–65; 4.335–44.

71. Jewett, "Agitators," 341.

72. Dunn, "Incident at Antioch," 45, n. 36; Dunn, *Galatians*, 123.

73. Fung, *Galatians*, 6–7; Muddiman, "Anatomy of Galatians," 259–60; Esler, *Galatians*, 74.

74. This is essentially the position held by Felix John, who arrives at this position because he is unconvinced that the crisis would have arisen directly from local Galatian concerns (*Galaterbrief im Kontext*, 211). J. Louis Martyn makes an even more conservative assessment, writing only that the opponents were motivated "to keep on good terms with persons of considerable power" ("Law-Observant Mission," 354).

75. Matera, *Galatians*, 230; Das, *Galatians*, 635.

Jewett), but such a thesis hangs rather precariously from the single thread of Paul's comment in 6:12."[76]

Roman Prosecution

Instead of a Zealot threat, Bruce W. Winter points to potential prosecution against the Christian community arising from Roman authorities. He identifies the phrase θέλουσιν εὐπροσωπῆσαι in 6:12 as legal language that situates the conflict in Galatia within the public square.[77] Winter argues that gentile Christians would have been required to participate in the imperial cult. Jewish Christians would have pressured gentile Christians to fully identify with the *religio licita* of Judaism through circumcision and thus protect themselves from persecution as well as the larger community.[78] Winter writes, "Galatian Christianity had to be seen to be Jewish if Jewish Christians and the movement as a whole were to survive in this particular province."[79]

Justin K. Hardin modifies Winter's proposal. As Hardin acknowledges, the *religio licita* status of Judaism is a myth of history.[80] It is unlikely then that the persecution in Galatia came *directly* from Roman authorities. Instead, Hardin hypothesizes, the persecution experienced by the Galatians and feared by Paul's opponents came from the Jewish community, and like in Acts 13–14, "the Jewish community had turned over this nascent group to the civic authorities."[81] The gentile Christians in Galatia were both "attempting to negotiate their new status as the people of God" and "were under pressure to continue with their pagan practices."[82] Following Troy W. Martin, Hardin believes that Gal 4:10 refers to the imperial cult calendar.[83] Paul, therefore, is addressing two fronts in Galatians. Hardin writes, "Although some of the Galatian Jesus-believers were seriously considering the option of circumcision,

---

76. Barclay, "Mirror-Reading," 88.
77. Winter, *Seek the Welfare*, 137–39.
78. Winter, *Seek the Welfare*, 139–41. Similarly Oepke, *Brief des Paulus*, 201.
79. Winter, *Seek the Welfare*, 141.
80. Hardin, *Galatians and the Imperial Cult*, 102–14. See also Das, *Paul and the Stories of Israel*, 189–200.
81. Hardin, *Galatians and the Imperial Cult*, 150.
82. Hardin, *Galatians and the Imperial Cult*, 150.
83. Hardin, *Galatians and the Imperial Cult*, 116–47; Martin, "Apostasy to Paganism," 437–61; Martin, "Time-Keeping Schemes," 105–19.

the churches as a whole had taken a step back and had begun to observe the emperor's festal calendar in order to assuage their precarious social status as believers in Jesus."[84] Hardin's proposal, however, ultimately fails because it requires one to interpret 4:10 in a way contrary to its literary context, which is a discussion of the efficacy of the Mosaic law.[85]

Alexander V. Prokhorov offers an alternative modification of Winter's work. Prokhorov claims that Paul's opponents were gentiles who had already undergone circumcision, and having saved themselves from persecution, they sought to save others as well.[86] He concludes, "Surprisingly, the Jews and the synagogue might have been completely unaware of any of this.... The Jews were not part of the Galatian problem."[87] Prokhorov's argument remains possible but lacks evidence. How might one identify Paul's opponents as Jews through proselytization rather than by birth without Paul's explicit statement that such was the case?

Two decades after making his original proposal, Winter has confronted the issue again, ultimately rejecting both Hardin and Prokhorov's modifications and doubling down on his thesis with little modification. Citing Mitchell's description of imperial cultic sites discovered in Pisidian Antioch and Iconium, Winter claims that the imperial cult exercised immense influence over Galatia during the period.[88] Furthermore, circumcision was so repugnant to gentiles that only a considerable threat could explain the motivation for gentile Christians to undergo the rite.[89] In addition to the legal language of θέλουσιν εὐπροσωπῆσαι in 6:12, Winter now argues that "the verb διώκω used in the forensic semantic domain meant to 'prosecute.'"[90] Paul's opponents specifically feared

---

84. Hardin, *Galatians and the Imperial Cult*, 146.

85. Schreiner, *Galatians*, 37; John, *Galaterbrief im Kontext*, 169–77.

86. Prokhorov, "Taking the Jews Out," 182.

87. Prokhorov, "Taking the Jews Out," 183. Brigitte Kahl offers another attempt at an imperial interpretation of Galatians. She begins with the cultural imagery evoked by "Galatia" and displayed on the Great Altar of Pergamon, which portrays the triumph of the gods over the giants. The scene, however, represents the triumph of civilized Rome over the barbarian Gauls. In Galatians, Kahl claims, Paul combats this imperial order. Paul confronts this imperial law of servitude by adopting a self-giving and nonviolent posture ("Reading Galatians and Empire," 21–43; Kahl, *Galatians Reimagined*).

88. Winter, *Divine Honours*, 226–27; Mitchell, *Anatolia*, 1:104.

89. Winter, *Divine Honours*, 228–32. Winter primarily cites the research of Hodges, "Ideal Prepuce," 375–405.

90. Winter, *Divine Honours*, 243.

prosecution for forming illegal *collegia*.⁹¹ In order to escape such prosecution, the Galatian churches had "to show they qualified as a legitimate Jewish 'association.'"⁹² In order to identify as Jewish, it was necessary that all male gentile Christians undergo circumcision.⁹³ Winter summarizes,

> If only all Gentile Christians would observe the Jewish rites and operate within the parameters in daily life, the Christian communities as a whole would not be put in jeopardy, but could gather to meet weekly and personally be exempt from performing imperial cultic honours.⁹⁴

Winter's updated reconstruction continues to be problematic. First, his proposal depends too heavily on a legal interpretation of θέλω, εὐπροσωπέω, and διώκω. While these words occasionally do occur within a legal semantic domain, they also regularly occur without legal meanings.⁹⁵ The repetitive use of διώκω in Galatians presents a particular problem. Why should διώκω mean "prosecute" in 6:12 when it more naturally indicates persecution elsewhere (1:13, 23; 4:29; 5:11)? Second, while many problems exist for imperial readings of Paul in general,⁹⁶ Galatians in particular resists such a reading because of its emphasis on Jewish categories and Scripture.⁹⁷ If Paul's opponents *merely* saw circumcision as a means to escape prosecution under Roman law, why does Paul spend so much space arguing that "by works of the law no one will be justified" (2:16)? It seems that Paul's opponents, even if they were concerned about justification in Roman courts, were much more concerned about

---

91. Like many scholars, Winter has abandoned the terminology of *religio licita*. Instead, he bases his argument on the specific Roman laws concerning *collegia*. Citing the work of O. F. Robinson, he claims that *collegia* were limited to monthly meetings under Roman law, but the Jews were specifically exempted in order to allow weekly worship in synagogues (Winter, *Divine Honours*, 243; Robinson, *Criminal Law*, 80).

92. Winter, *Divine Honours*, 243.

93. Winter argues that ἀναγκάζω means to "contend that such a thing is necessarily so" (cf. LSJ, s.v. "ἀναγκάζω"). For Winter, the verb indicates that circumcision was an essential part of adopting Jewish identity (*Divine Honours*, 237–43).

94. Winter, *Divine Honours*, 244.

95. Das writes, "The problem with Winter's analysis is that these terms may also be used in *non*-political contexts. The word itself does not convey a political sense, and Paul's context does not identify concerns with governing authorities" (*Galatians*, 634; italics original; cf. Das, *Paul and the Stories of Israel*, 210–14).

96. See Burk, "Is Paul's Gospel Counterimperial?," 309–37; Kim, *Christ and Caesar*.

97. Witherington writes, "Paul is basically silent on the Emperor cult in this letter. The issues he raises and problems he deals with are Jewish in character" (*Grace in Galatia*, 448).

justification before the God of Abraham.⁹⁸ Finally, Winter's proposal suffers from lack of historical support. While the imperial cult may have had significant influence in the region from the reign of Augustus onward, as Mitchell's research seems to demonstrate,⁹⁹ it does not necessarily follow that Roman authorities prosecuted Christians for lack of observance or churches as illegal *collegia*.¹⁰⁰ As is well-known, the correspondence between Trajan and Pliny the Younger are the earliest first-person testimony in our possession of Roman hostility toward Christians as Christians, but it was written half a century after Galatians.¹⁰¹ On the other hand, the expulsion of the Jews from Rome by Claudius is more contemporary with Paul and thus more likely to be similar to the situation surrounding Paul's missionary activity. Suetonius records the expulsion of the Jews from Rome due to rioting over someone name *Chrestus*.¹⁰² This is almost certainly a misunderstanding of Χριστός.¹⁰³ Jews in Rome were rioting over the proclamation of Jesus of Nazareth as Messiah, and Emperor Claudius, failing to understand the religious issues at stake, exiled the entire Jewish population from the city. Even Suetonius, whether due to flawed sources or his own misunderstanding, fails to accurately report the event. Ultimately, the evidence for Roman prosecution simply does not convince. As John concludes, "Soziale Probleme, die den Gemeinden aus vermeintlichen Ansprüchen der kultischen Verehrung des Σεβαστός/ Augustus erwuchsen, kommen als Entstehungsfaktoren der galatischen Krise nicht in Betracht."¹⁰⁴

---

98. John rightly writes, "Historisch erscheint der galatische Konflikt des Paulus *primär* als auf einer theologischen—nicht sozialen—Ebene angesiedelt" (*Galaterbrief im Kontext*, 211). Contra Mitternacht, "Foolish Galatians?," 433.

99. Mitchell, *Anatolia*, 1:104. Das concludes from his reading of Mitchell that "participation in the imperial cult was enforced not through imperial intervention but through enticements from the urban elite and through neighborly peer pressure" (*Paul and the Stories of Israel*, 200). See also Fishwick, *Imperial Cult*, 529–32.

100. La Piana, "Foreign Groups," 275–76; Ste. Croix, "Why Were the Early Christians Persecuted?," 17; Harland, *Associations*, 164–73; Das, *Paul and the Stories of Israel*, 186–89. John claims that the structures necessary to enforce required cult observance did not exist (*Galaterbrief im Kontext*, 176–77).

101. Pliny, *Ep.* 10.96–97. Moss rightly emphasizes that Pliny's concern was primarily the economic effect that Christianity had on Roman religion and that Romans were not apt to target Christians specifically prior to AD 250 (*Myth of Persecution*, 139–45).

102. Suetonius, *Claud.* 25. See Das, *Paul and the Stories of Israel*, 203.

103. Das, *Solving the Romans Debate*, 150–58.

104. John, *Galaterbrief im Kontext*, 177.

Local Synagogues

Perhaps a simpler explanation of the evidence is best. A. Andrew Das writes, "Hypotheses such as Jewett's and Winter's are unnecessary. The concerns at Galatia were more immediate."[105] Local Jewish synagogues—apart from any Zealot threat or possible Roman prosecution—were doubtlessly troubled by one primary issue: The fellowship of Jews with uncircumcised gentiles on the basis of the gospel of a crucified Messiah.[106] In the minds of the local Jewish communities, the issue represented abandonment of "the fundamental convictions of their ancient religion."[107]

This is in fact how Luke presents the local situation during the initial period of evangelization in Galatia.[108] Interestingly in Luke's account, the Jews of Pisidian Antioch do not demonstrate any alarm over Paul's initial proclamation of the gospel but instead beg for further explanation on the following Sabbath (Acts 13:42). Only when gentiles flooded the synagogue to hear Paul did the Jewish community begin arguing against Paul (Acts 13:45), and only when Paul declared that the message was going to the gentiles did the Jewish community incite persecution against Paul and the missionary team (Acts 13:46–50).[109] At Iconium also, the problem seems to be that "a great number of both Jews and Greeks believed" (Acts 14:1). Because of this equal standing between Jews and Greeks, the

---

105. Das, *Galatians*, 636.

106. Mark D. Nanos has made a similar argument, although in his reconstruction Paul's opponents (which he calls "the influencers") are Jews who do not accept a crucified Messiah. These influencers are synagogue officials who are tasked with assimilating Gentiles into Jewish life. If they fail in this task, then they will face criticism and loss of status, which Paul rhetorically labels "persecution" (*Irony of Galatians*, 257–77; cf. Walter, "Paul and the Opponents," 362–66). The content of Galatians, however, makes it extremely unlikely that Paul's opponents were non-Christian Jews. See John, *Galaterbrief im Kontext*, 187–91. Keener prefers to see the issue as a combination of influences from Jerusalem and local Jewish activity (*Galatians*, 566–67).

107. Das, *Galatians*, 636. Similarly Burton, *Galatians*, 350; Betz, *Galatians*, 315–16; Cousar, *Galatians*, 149; de Boer, *Galatians*, 398.

108. John rejects the position held here because he relegates Acts to a secondary source due to its later date (*Galaterbrief im Kontext*, 137).

109. Kilgallen concludes, "In short, the Gentiles are asked to embrace the salvation Yahweh offers to His People, which is faith in Jesus, and the blessings promised to Abraham and his offspring will follow; it is this offer which 'the Jews' do not believe is 'from Yahweh,' but it is what makes Paul a credible Christian Apostle to the Gentiles" ("Hostility to Paul," 15). See also Bruce, *Acts*, 265–69; Keener, *Acts*, 2092; Schnabel, *Acts*, 586.

Jewish community "stirred up the Gentiles and poisoned their minds" (Acts 14:2). Even at Lystra, Jews from Pisidian Antioch and Iconium arrived to incite the gentile mob to stone Paul (Acts 14:19). While the record of persecutions at Pisidian Antioch, Iconium, and Lystra focuses on the suffering of Paul and his team, Luke also records Paul's expectation that these new Galatian disciples would suffer similar persecution. Paul strengthened and encouraged the disciples, saying, "It is necessary to go through many tribulations in order to enter the kingdom of God" (Acts 14:22).[110] In light of such a volatile local situation, Jewett's hypothesis of Zealot activity is, as Das labels it, "unnecessary."[111] Neither is it necessary to hypothesize that the inciting issue was prosecution as illegal *collegia* or failure to worship Caesar.[112]

Rather Jewish Christians found themselves in the impossible position of being rejected by their ethnic and religious communities for their association with uncircumcised gentiles. This rejection may have been expressed in mere social and economic pressure, or it may have also taken the form of violence similar to what had occurred when Paul first visited the region. Either way, some Jewish Christians sought a *rapprochement* with local Jewish communities by compelling gentile Christians to undergo circumcision and observe Torah.[113] Certainly, they saw themselves

---

110. Bruce, *Acts*, 280; Parsons, *Acts*, 203.

111. Das, *Galatians*, 636.

112. While the NT presents the Jewish community as adept at influencing Roman authorities to accomplish their own ends (e.g., Luke 23:2; John 19:12–16; Acts 17:6–8; 23:2–9), this is different from Winter's proposal that Roman law was the inciting issue (*Divine Honours*, 244).

113. Were Paul's Jewish Christian opponents from Galatia, or were they outsiders? As Gal 2 demonstrates, this strategy was not limited to the Galatian churches but affected Jerusalem and Antioch as well. From this, Francis Watson concluded that Paul's opponents in Galatia were the "men from James" who previously came to Antioch (2:12; Watson, *Paul, Judaism, and the Gentiles*, 59–61; Watson has since backed away from this view: Watson, *Paul, Judaism, and the Gentiles*, 113). Paul does sharply distinguish between the Galatian Christians, whom he addresses with the second-person plural pronoun, and his opponents, to whom he refers in the third person. This may indicate that Paul's opponents were outsiders. Furthermore, Paul's focus on Jerusalem suggests that his opponents were either from Jerusalem or saw themselves as representatives of a Jerusalem-oriented theology (e.g., Martyn, "Law-Observant Mission," 307–24; Dunn, *Galatians*, 14–15; Schreiner, *Galatians*, 48–49). But these clues to the identity of the opponents may "be a consequence of the polemical language [Paul] is employing and may or may not reflect the actual circumstances" (Das, *Galatians*, 14). Ultimately, as John M. G. Barclay concludes, it is "probable" that Paul's opponents had "some links with the Jerusalem church" ("Mirror-Reading," 88). But the nature of these links cannot be known: Were they from Jerusalem? Or did they simply see themselves as representative

as having biblical support for this position. Did not circumcision apply to "any foreigner" who belonged to the house of Abraham (Gen 17:12)? And was it not the sign of an "everlasting covenant" (Gen 17:7-8, 13-14)?[114] In the minds of Paul's opponents, this simple concession to Jewish communities—which was supported by Scripture anyway—would pacify any hostility coming from local synagogues. To Paul, however, to preach circumcision and avoid persecution meant to abandon the scandal of the cross and submit again to slavery under the present evil age.

INSTANCE 4: THE PERSECUTION OF THE GALATIAN CHRISTIANS (3:4; 4:17-18, 29)

In 4:29, Paul says that "just as then the one born according to the flesh persecuted the one born according to the Spirit, so also it is now." Paul's immediately prior assertion that the Galatian Christians are "like Isaac... children of promise" makes clear that Paul speaks in 4:29 of the Galatian Christians suffering persecution. Is there any historical evidence for this? Hans Dieter Betz claims that Paul never says "that the Galatians have been persecuted."[115] F. F. Bruce writes, "There is no reference to their being positively persecuted for the faith."[116] Richard N. Longenecker claims, "For in the wider context of the letter there is no suggestion that the Galatian Christians had ever actually suffered any form of external persecution."[117] Similarly, Gordon D. Fee strongly asserts that "in contrast to most of Paul's other letters there is not the slightest hint in this one that the churches of Galatia were undergoing suffering."[118]

Galatians 3:4

Galatians 3:4 may serve to modify the assessment that the Galatian churches did not suffer persecution. Paul asks, "Did you suffer/experience (ἐπάθετε) so many things in vain?" The verb πάσχω may take either the

---

of Jerusalem's theology? Beyond this, the question of the origin of the opponents is left open. Either possibility—outsiders or insiders—can fit within this reconstruction.

114. Schreiner, *Galatians*, 50.
115. Betz, *Galatians*, 134.
116. Bruce, *Galatians*, 150.
117. Longenecker, *Galatians*, 104.
118. Fee, *God's Empowering Presence*, 387.

neutral sense "to experience" or the negative sense "to suffer" depending on context.[119] But the nineteen occurrences in the LXX (e.g., Esth 9:26; Amos 6:6; Zech 11:5), the six additional occurrences in the Pauline corpus (1 Cor 12:26; 2 Cor 1:6; Phil 1:29; 1 Thess 2:14; 2 Thess 1:5, 12), and thirty-five other occurrences in the NT (e.g., Matt 16:21; Acts 3:18; Heb 5:8; 1 Pet 2:19; Rev 2:10) all refer to suffering.[120] So "to suffer" is the normal sense of the word in the NT. Indeed, if πάσχω does not refer to suffering in 3:4 then, as Dunne writes, "Galatians 3.4 would then be a very odd exception."[121] Wilhelm Michaelis concludes that "the word is used *sensus bono* only when there is an addition to this effect or, very rarely, the context makes it sufficiently plain."[122] Some commentators believe that the context of 3:4 does indeed demand the neutral sense "to experience." Das writes, "The immediate context of Gal 3:1–5 decisively favors the positive 'experience.' The prior verse (3:3) reminds the Galatians of their beginning in the Spirit, and 3:5 returns to their continued enjoyment of the Spirit along with deeds of power."[123] Das and those scholars who take a similar position wrongly, in this instance, bifurcate the experience of the Spirit from suffering by isolating this passage from the wider context of Paul's theology. In his work on 2 Corinthians, Hafemann demonstrates that while the super-apostles pit the work of the Spirit and suffering against each other, Paul, on the other hand, embraces such weakness as normative.[124] In Galatians also, Paul connects the Spirit with suffering. It is "the one who is born of the Spirit" who is persecuted in 4:29. Additionally, Dunne demonstrates that "to suffer" was the unanimous

---

119. For examples of the neutral sense, see Plato, *Symp.* 174e; Josephus, *Ant.* 3.312. See BDAG, s.v. "πάσχω."

120. Dunne digs even deeper, writing, "In the post-NT era, all 52 occurrences of πάσχω in the Apostolic Fathers refer to suffering. Likewise, of the 19 occurrences in the LXX, each relates to suffering. The same can be said of the 28 occurrences in the Pseudepigrapha, with the possible exception of the use of πάσχω in the *Letter of Aristeas* 214 where it may have a more general sense" ("Suffering in Vain," 6–7).

121. Dunne, "Suffering in Vain," 6.

122. Michaelis, "πάσχω," 5:905.

123. Das wrongly claims that the default meaning should be "to experience" unless the negative sense is "specified by the context" (*Galatians*, 296). In fact, as demonstrated above, the opposite is true: The default meaning in the NT is "to suffer." Similarly, Fee makes the mistaken claim that "Pauline usage, significant as this is in most circumstances, is in this case the only thing in favor of translating the verb 'suffered'" (*God's Empowering Presence*, 387; italics original). So also Mußner, *Galaterbrief*, 208; Betz, *Galatians*, 134; Longenecker, *Galatians*, 104; deSilva, *Galatians*, 276.

124. Hafemann, *Suffering and the Spirit*, 220–21.

interpretation of patristic and medieval commentators.[125] Not until the seventeenth-century commentary of Justus Christoph Schomer did anyone suggest the interpretation "to experience."[126] These three lines of evidence converge to make a strong case for the negative sense "to suffer": (1) the lexical data, (2) the connection of the Spirit and suffering in Paul's theology, and (3) the consensus of earlier interpreters.

Is there then other historical evidence that the Galatian Christians suffered during the initial evangelization of the region? Certainly, as has been reviewed above, Paul and his missionary team suffered (Acts 13:50; 14:5, 19). But did the new believers in Galatia suffer alongside Paul and his team? In Thessalonica and Corinth, Luke narrates how persecution directed against Paul was extended to the new believers as well (Acts 17:5–9; 18:17). It is therefore possible that the Galatian Christians suffered alongside Paul and his missionary team at the time that they believed and received the Holy Spirit. Luke simply did not include their suffering in his narrative because it did not fit his purposes. Greater proof, however, comes from what Luke did include in the narrative: Paul warned the Galatian disciples that they must endure "many tribulations" in order to "enter the kingdom of God" (Acts 14:22).[127] Moo comments that the warning "suggests that this persecution may have extended to the new Christians as well."[128]

In light of this evidence, Paul's appeal in Gal 3:4 can be read in a manner similar to 1 Thess 1:4–6. In Thessalonica, the gospel came "not only in word, but also in power, in the Holy Spirit, and with full conviction" (1 Thess 1:5). The Thessalonian Christians "received the word in much affliction, with the joy of the Holy Spirit" (1 Thess 1:6). While in 1 Thessalonians this historical review serves to encourage the church to continue in faith (e.g., 1 Thess 4:1), in Galatians Paul reviews the early history of the church to express his astonishment that they are so quickly deserting the grace of Christ (Gal 1:6). In recent memory, they had received the Spirit by hearing the gospel with faith, and they suffered for this faith (Gal 3:2, 4). Will they now abandon the Spirit's miraculous work in order to find perfection through the law (3:3, 5)? In the context of Paul's larger argument, these rhetorical questions portray the Galatian Christians as hesitating between Paul's position—embracing the scandal

---

125. Dunne, "Suffering in Vain," 4.
126. Dunne, "Suffering in Vain," 4–5; Schomer, *Exegesis in Omnes Epistolas*, 11.
127. Bruce, *Acts*, 280; Parsons, *Acts*, 203; Moo, *Galatians*, 185.
128. Moo, *Galatians*, 185.

of the cross and enduring persecution (5:11)—and his opponent's position—boasting in the flesh in order to avoid persecution (6:12).

Galatians 4:17-18

While 3:4 indicates that the Galatian Christians had undergone persecution in the past, that does not necessarily mean that they are presently undergoing persecution. One possible reference to present persecution comes in 4:17–18. The repeated use of ζηλόω is suggestive, especially considering Paul's description of his former life as a persecutor in 1:13–14 and the background of Phinehan zeal discussed above. Dunne sees the first "ζηλόω in 4.17 as referring to [the opponents'] hostile behaviour."[129] The primary problem for such a view is that the Galatians themselves are identified as the object (ὑμᾶς) of the opponents' zeal. The object of ζηλόω identifies that thing or person to which the subject is devoted or over which the subject is jealous.[130] In 1 Cor 12:31, Paul commands the Corinthian church to make "the greater gifts" the object of their deep devotion (ζηλοῦτε δὲ τὰ χαρίσματα τὰ μείζονα; cf. 1 Cor 14:1, 39). In 2 Cor 11:2, the Corinthian church is the object of Paul's deep devotion because he has promised them in marriage to Christ (ζηλῶ γὰρ ὑμᾶς θεοῦ ζήλῳ). In Rom 10:2, Paul says that God is the object Jewish people's devotion (ζῆλον θεοῦ ἔχουσιν). In 2 Cor 7:7, Paul was the object of the Corinthian church's deep concern (τὸν ὑμῶν ζῆλον ὑπὲρ ἐμοῦ). So also, in Gal 1:14, Paul identifies his ancestral traditions as the object of his devotion (περισσοτέρως ζηλωτὴς ὑπάρχων τῶν πατρικῶν μου παραδόσεων). So too, in 4:17, the opponents display a devotion for the Galatians, not hostile behavior or aggression against them. Paul must correct his readers' perception of this devotion.[131] They have wrongly begun to treat Paul as their enemy (4:16) while succumbing to the flattery of the opponents (4:17).

Paul must, therefore, identify his opponents' true motives, which are not good (οὐ καλῶς): "They desire to exclude you in order that you might be zealous for them" (4:17). The primary difficulty with this verse

---

129. Dunne, *Persecution and Participation*, 172. Similarly Goddard and Cummins, "Ill or Ill-Treated?," 114–15.

130. BDAG, s.v. "ζηλόω."

131. Schreiner rightly claims that "Paul's words in the letter represent the divine perspective of the opponents and cannot be restricted merely to human judgment" (*Galatians*, 32).

is that Paul does not clearly identify what the opponents desire to exclude the Galatian Christians from: (1) Do the opponents wish to alienate the Galatian Christians from Paul?[132] (2) Is Paul identifying the social consequences of the focus on circumcision? Either one must adopt Jewish identity or be excluded from God's people, especially in terms of table fellowship.[133] (3) Or is Paul speaking about his understanding of the covenantal consequence of accepting circumcision? Those who accept circumcision will be "severed from Christ" (5:4).[134] Option one seems unlikely without the inclusion of an additional phrase in Greek such as "from us" or "from me," although their alienation from Paul would be a result of both option two and three.[135] In favor of option two, the situation at Antioch suggests that similar tactics of table exclusion were being employed or threatened by Paul's opponents in Galatia (2:12).[136] However, it is difficult to see how this obvious threat of exclusion could have been mistaken by the Galatian Christians as a positive zeal directed toward them. Rather Paul points out something that was not obvious to the Galatian Christians. As Schreiner comments, "These teachers surely claimed that they desired to *include* the Galatians in the true people of God, but in fact, they were excluding them from God's people if the Galatians followed them."[137] In Paul's polemic, this exclusion reveals that Paul's opponents do not really care about Christ or the Galatians. Their ultimate goal is self-exaltation—to have the Galatians exhibit zeal for them.[138] As Paul accuses them in 6:12–13, they desire to use the Gala-

---

132. NIV adds "from us"; CSB adds "from me." So Bruce, *Galatians*, 211.

133. Dunn, *Galatians*, 238; Das, *Galatians*, 468; Cobb, "ΕΚΚΛΕΙΩ en Galates 4,17," 567–85.

134. Schlier, *Brief an die Galater*, 150–51; Schreiner, *Galatians*, 288. Options two and three are not mutually exclusive but differ more in terms of emphasis. Clearly, social and covenantal issues are interrelated.

135. Hays, "Galatians," 295; Das, *Galatians*, 468; Cobb, "ΕΚΚΛΕΙΩ en Galates 4,17," 572–77. Christopher C. Smith wrongly sees the motif of an "excluded lover" ("Ἐκκλεῖσαι in Galatians 4:17," 480–99). See Longenecker, "Until Christ," 97; Cobb, "ΕΚΚΛΕΙΩ en Galates 4,17," 575–79. Betz wrongly discredits any theological meaning of the "exclusion," preferring to see Paul as appealing to the rhetorical theme of true friendship (*Galatians*, 230–31). See Schreiner, *Galatians*, 288.

136. Dunn, *Galatians*, 238; Martyn, *Galatians*, 423; Das, *Galatians*, 468; Dunne, *Persecution and Participation*, 173.

137. Schreiner, *Galatians*, 288. Italics original.

138. Cobb rightly writes, "Dissimulé derrière des apparences altruistes se cache le désir de faire des Galates un « trophée » (« ils vous jalousent ») et de créer un sentiment de gratitude mal placé" ("ΕΚΚΛΕΙΩ en Galates 4,17," 584).

tians as an object of boasting.[139] In 4:18, Paul clarifies himself: Zeal for the Galatians is not in itself problematic. Motives, however, determine whether zeal for someone is good or bad. In 4:19, Paul communicates the quality of his own zeal for the Galatians: While his opponents seek self-exaltation, Paul demonstrates the self-sacrificial love of a mother. While his opponents wish to exclude the Galatians from Christ, Paul desires to see Christ formed in them.

Even though Paul does not refer to any aggressive behavior on the part of his opponents in 4:17, he nevertheless may intend to associate his opponents with his previous way of life as a zealous persecutor. If this is the case, then Paul appeals here to the paradigmatic nature of his autobiography in 1:13–14 and the verbal association that ζηλόω creates between Paul as persecutor in 1:14 and the opponents in 4:17.[140] Such an association would be consistent with Paul's rhetorical purpose in 4:16–20. The Galatians wrongly regard Paul as an enemy while not perceiving the false motives behind the devotion that Paul's opponents have for them. Paul, therefore, corrects this perception, demonstrating himself as truly loving the Galatians while the opponents secretly plot their spiritual destruction.

Galatians 4:29

Considering Paul's polemical purposes, 4:29 deserves further examination. The word διώκω has consistently referred to hostile and violent persecution in Galatians (1:13, 23; 5:11; 6:12). So when Paul says that the present-day children of the Spirit (the Galatian Christians) are being persecuted by the present-day children of the flesh, the most natural reading is that the Galatian Christians are presently victims of hostile and violent persecution, akin to that previously enacted and experienced by Paul and avoided by the opponents.[141]

Assuming for the moment that this natural reading is correct, who are the children of the flesh that persecute the Galatian Christians? This identification relies on the target of the allegory as a whole (4:21—5:1). The two women correspond to the old and new covenants (4:24).[142] The chil-

---

139. Schreiner, *Galatians*, 288.

140. Dunn, *Galatians*, 237; Dunne, *Persecution and Participation*, 174.

141. The issues surrounding Paul's appeal to Ishmael persecuting Isaac will be examined in the next chapter.

142. The uncommon view of Davina C. Lopez does not fit within the larger purpose of Galatians. Lopez argues that Hagar and Sarah "represent two political choices:

dren of the new covenant are quite obviously the multi-ethnic churches of God. One part of Paul's goal in this identification is to admonish these new covenant, new Jerusalem children to stand firm in the freedom that is their birthright (4:26; 5:1).[143] By contrast, the Sinai covenant, which relates to the present Jerusalem, "is in slavery with her children" (4:24–25). To whom are the old covenant and her children enslaved? It is the present evil age (1:4) and τὰ στοιχεῖα τοῦ κόσμου (4:3, 8–9), which also formerly enslaved the Galatian Christians. In light of this, Paul's criticisms, obviously, apply to Judaism in general, which remained firmly devoted to the old covenant.[144] But Paul's more precise target are those whose "yoke of slavery" the Galatian Christians are tempted to submit to—his Jewish Christian opponents (5:1).[145] The other side of Paul's goal, then, is to identify his opponents as enslaved through an obsolete covenant to the present evil age and as seeking to enslave the Galatians again through their preaching of circumcision. To adequately warn the Galatians of the danger they face, Paul utilizes the rhetorical equivalent of "shock and awe" by linking the old covenant and its children with Hagar and Ishmael.[146] Paul's Jewish Christian opponents are enslaved offspring and family

---

continuation under Roman rule (Hagar, slavery, natural reproduction of domination) or service to the one God and collective self-determination (Sarah, freedom, unnatural motherhood breaking the cycle of domination)" (*Apostle to the Conquered*, 162). Citing 4:19, Lopez argues that Paul has adopted a non-dominant, non-masculine status and advocates for a "new creation" of international cooperation among defeated peoples, a group to which both Jews and Galatians belong (*Apostle to the Conquered*, 141, 150–51).

143. David Starling rightly argues that the deliberative rhetoric of the allegory "is aimed . . . at persuading the Galatians to act on the imperative with which the section closes" ("Justifying Allegory," 233–34). See also Scott, *Paul's Way*, 251.

144. Betz, *Galatians*, 246; Schreiner, *Galatians*, 302; Das, *Galatians*, 499. Contra Martyn, *Galatians*, 457–66. Admittedly, some interpreters have wrongly seen Paul as criticizing the Jews as an ethnic group. E.g., Lightfoot writes about "the present Jerusalem": "The metropolis of the Jews is taken to represent the whole race" (*Galatians*, 181).

145. Starling, "Justifying Allegory," 233–34.

146. F. S. Malan explains, "This identification of the law-abiding Jews, the progeny of Abraham, with the issue of the slave-woman of Abraham is intended to be a shock to the readers. It is calculated to shock them unto the realisation of what they are busy doing when they want to live under the law (Gl.4:21)" ("Strategy of Two Opposing Covenants," 433). Anne Davis labels this as the literary device of "apparent contradiction" ("Allegorically Speaking," 167–71). Matthew S. Harmon writes, "For a first-century Jew such a correlation would have been nothing short of scandalous" ("Allegory, Typology," 148). See also Betz, *Galatians*, 426; Hays, *Echoes of Scripture*, 112–14; Perriman, "Rhetorical Strategy," 36; Schreiner, *Galatians*, 293. Additionally, as Susan Elliott has written, part of the polemical shock may include language that links circumcision with the mutilation of temple slaves dedicated to the Anatolian mother of the gods ("Choose Your Mother," 661–83; Elliott, *Cutting Too Close*, 258–86). John, however, makes significant

relations of all who are bound to the old covenant and the present-age Jerusalem, including the Jewish nation generally.[147] So these opponents must also be those "born according to the flesh" who, like Ishmael, persecute those born according to the Spirit in 4:29.[148] If the children of the flesh had been identified simply as unbelieving Jews, then 4:29 would be unproblematic. As has been argued above, the internal evidence of 3:4 and the external evidence of Acts 13:13—14:23 suggest that in the past the Galatian Christians suffered persecution coming from local synagogues. Since Paul's opponents preach circumcision in order to avoid this same source of persecution, it seems probable that the Galatian Christians were in fact continuing to be persecuted by the local synagogues or were at the very least realistically threatened by the possibility of a new outbreak (6:12).[149] But since Paul seeks to identify his opponents as the children of the flesh, his accusation of persecution becomes problematic.

Is there evidence beyond 4:29 that Paul's opponents employed hostile persecution against the Galatian Christians? Dunne does not help here since he merely focuses on "the *imagery* of suffering and persecution in the letter, and the way that Paul *perceives* and *portrays* the crisis" rather than historical reconstruction.[150] So, Dunne attempts to limit himself to claiming that Paul *describes* his opponents as hostile and aggressive.[151]

But if 4:17, as has been argued above, refers to the flattering devotion that Paul's opponents displayed for the Galatians, then it seems unlikely

---

arguments against Elliott (*Galaterbrief im Kontext*, 183–86).

147. Das is particularly helpful here: "Although the apostle's primary purpose is to confront the Law-observant gentile mission, the claims he makes about the salvific inefficacy of the Law have profound implications for a Judaism apart from Christ (see also 2:21; 3:21). Certainly Paul's target is his Jewish-Christian rivals, but the modern attempt to rescue Paul from anti-Semitism must not ignore what he concretely says about the Mosaic Law as an ineffective instrument for a right standing before God" (*Galatians*, 488–89).

148. Burton, *Galatians*, 266; Mußner, *Galaterbrief*, 331; Martyn, *Galatians*, 445.

149. Persecution would not necessarily be constant but would vary in intensity based on circumstances. Also, such persecution could take various forms, not all of it involving violence, but also utilizing social and economic pressures.

150. Dunne, *Persecution and Participation*, 195. Italics original. Additionally, Dunne points to the use of ἀναγκάζω in 6:12 as indicating that Paul's opponents were "aggressive" in compelling the Galatians to be circumcised (*Persecution and Participation*, 56).

151. E.g., Dunne, "Cast Out the Aggressive Agitators," 247–48; Dunne, *Persecution and Participation*, 20–21. As should be expected, Dunne has difficulty avoiding historical reconstruction all together, and at times it can be unclear when he writes *merely* about Paul's images and when he makes judgments on the historical circumstances described by those images.

that the opponents were committing acts of persecution against the Galatians.[152] Furthermore, since Paul desires to utilize his polemic in order to reshape his readers' perception of the crisis, it seems unlikely that the opponents were doing anything that the Galatian Christians themselves would have perceived as persecution apart from Paul's letter. Barclay warns against the pitfall of "mishandling polemics."[153] Schreiner helpfully explains, "Barclay rightly perceives that Paul does not present the opponents as they would have presented themselves."[154] It should be added that neither does Paul present the opponents as the Galatian Christians would have presented them. While Paul's opponents present themselves as devoted to the Galatians, Paul claims, they are actually persecuting the Galatians by preaching a false gospel of circumcision.[155] Paul's polemical position, nonetheless, realistically communicates the severity of the threat. As Dunne correctly points out, this polemical use of διώκω would be consistent with other *images* employed by Paul.[156] They "trouble" and "agitate" the Galatians (1:7; 5:10, 12; cf. Acts 17:13; 1 Pet 3:14). They have "bewitched" the Galatians (3:1) and would enslave them (2:4; 4:9; 5:1).

Paul uses διώκω in 4:29 to create an "us versus them" narrative that should warn his readers concerning the perilous character of this other gospel. He associates his opponents with his former life as a Jewish persecutor who did not know Christ (1:13, 23). Not only are his opponents the family relations of all—including non-Christian Jews—who are enslaved to the old covenant, but their teaching is equivalent to the violent persecution that the Galatian Christians had endured in the past (and possibly in the present) from local synagogues (3:4). While his opponents are motivated to preach circumcision in order to escape persecution (6:12), in Paul's assessment their solution is in fact equivalent to the problem it seeks to solve. The preaching of circumcision is itself a form of spiritual persecution because the acceptance of this other gospel results in being

---

152. Mitternacht, "Foolish Galatians?" 427. Contra Dunne, *Persecution and Participation*, 172–73. Similarly Goddard and Cummins, "Ill or Ill-Treated?," 114–15.

153. Barclay, "Mirror-Reading," 80.

154. Schreiner, *Galatians*, 32.

155. Interestingly, Mitternacht seems convinced by the lines of evidence presented here, but since he does not factor in Paul's polemical purpose, he concludes that 4:29 can only refer to persecution inflicted upon the churches by Galatian Jews ("Foolish Galatians?," 427). See Burton, *Galatians*, 266.

156. Dunne, "Cast Out the Aggressive Agitators," 247–48; Dunne, *Persecution and Participation*, 20–21.

"severed from Christ" and "falling from grace" (5:4). Like Ishmael, they threatened the children of promise.

CONCLUSION

Having examined the four instances of persecution mentioned in Galatians and the various passages that possibly describe each, it will be helpful in conclusion to present a unified description of the historical reconstruction offered here. In his former life in Judaism, Paul persecuted the church of God and sought to destroy it (1:13, 23), but now that he preaches the faith that he once tried to destroy, he is the victim of persecution (5:11; 6:17). The Galatian Christians know this because, when Paul preached in Pisidian Antioch, Iconium, and Lystra, Jews from local synagogues incited persecution against him (Acts 13:13—14:23). Furthermore, the Galatian Christians themselves endured this same persecution, either alongside Paul or in the days that followed (3:4; Acts 14:22). It is this same threat of Jewish persecution that Paul's opponents seek to avoid by preaching circumcision as a strategy of *rapprochement* with local Jewish communities (6:12). These other preachers have winsomely preached circumcision to the Galatian Christians, showing both Scriptural proof for the necessity of circumcision (e.g., Gen 17:9–14) and displaying devotion for the Galatians (4:17). Because of this, the Galatian Christians are in the process of accepting this teaching.[157]

Paul writes Galatians in order to reshape the perception of the Galatian Christians. He is astonished that the Galatians would so quickly turn to a different gospel (1:6), and to demonstrate the gravity of the crisis, he pronounces a curse upon his opponents (1:8–9). His opponents wrongly interpret Scripture (3:6—4:11), and the devotion that they display for the Galatians comes from selfish motives (4:17–18; 6:12–13). In fact, they have bewitched the Galatians (3:1) and seek to enslave them (2:4; 4:9; 5:1). Instead of wanting what is best for the Galatians, circumcising the Galatians is for the opponents a basis of boasting, a means to escape persecution, and ultimately a way of removing the scandal of the cross (5:11; 6:12–13). The end result for the Galatians themselves will be separation from Christ (4:17; 5:4). In this fleshly attempt to keep the law, they are in fact being hindered from obeying the truth and from walking by the

---

157. Paul's warning in 5:2 suggests that they have not yet undergone circumcision. They are still in process of being swayed by the preaching of the opponents.

Spirit (5:7, 16). Unlike his selfish opponents, Paul like a selfless mother is filled with emotional anguish over their possible defection from Christ (4:19). They once showed him this same kind of love, not only enduring the trial of his physical illness but also seeking to do anything they could to help him (4:15),[158] but now they treat Paul like an enemy (4:16). Paul insists that his opponents do not really love the Galatians. Instead, they "persecute" them by preaching a dangerous false gospel (4:29). The Galatians should reject this false gospel and stand firm in the freedom that Christ has given them (4:30—5:1).

---

158. The expression "you would have gouged out your eyes and given them to me" in 4:15 simply communicates that the Galatians would have done anything they could to help Paul. So Fung, *Galatians*, 199; Longenecker, *Galatians*, 193.

6

Cosmic Conflict Manifested as Persecution in Galatians

EARLY CHRISTIANS IN THE second and third centuries, according to Paul Middleton, saw their persecution and martyrdom as contributing to the final outcome of a cosmic conflict in the spiritual realm.[1] Middleton further claims that this early Christian martyrology emerged, in part, from the influence of Paul's apocalyptic worldview.[2] This monograph has sought to build on Middleton's understanding of Paul's contribution to early Christian martyrology by examining the letter of Galatians in particular. Up to this point, this investigation has demonstrated, first, that in Galatians Paul fits the crisis in Galatia within the larger narrative framework of a cosmic conflict between God and the present evil age, a theme that significantly parallels both earlier OT Scripture and other early Jewish writings. Second, this investigation has sought to reconstruct the historical background to Galatians. While descriptions of Paul as persecutor and persecuted (1:13, 23; 5:11; 6:17), the opponents as avoiders of persecution (6:12), and the Galatians as persecuted in the past (3:4) refer to hostile harassment, the use of διώκω in 4:29 serves Paul's polemical purpose of reshaping his readers' perception of the opponents and their preaching.

This chapter merges these two components of the project in order to discover how cosmic conflict theologically informed Paul's understanding of persecution both as a historical phenomenon and as a polemical

---

1. Middleton, *Radical Martyrdom*, 6.
2. Middleton, *Radical Martyrdom*, 139–43.

charge against his opponents. Doing so demonstrates the thesis of this monograph: In Galatians, persecution manifests the cosmic conflict between God and the present evil age. Since multiple themes central to Galatians, including cosmic conflict and persecution, converge in Paul's use of Gen 21:9 in Gal 4:29, this significant verse is examined carefully and then used to inform the reading of other passages that contribute to the persecution theme in Galatians.

THE CHILDREN OF THE FLESH PERSECUTE THE CHILDREN OF THE SPIRIT (GALATIANS 4:29)

In their examinations of persecution in Galatians, both Ernst Baasland and John Anthony Dunne begin with 4:29.[3] In 4:29, the theme of persecution intersects with other central themes like sonship and the Spirit/flesh polarity.[4] The verse, however, features a problematic interpretation of Gen 21:9.[5] While Paul claims that Ishmael persecuted Isaac, Gen 21:9 does not explicitly say this. This section first examines the typology utilized by Paul in Gal 4:29 and then explains the basis of this instance of typology as well as the significance of Paul's exegesis.

Type and Antitype in 4:29

Galatians 4:29, following the allegory of which it is a part, identifies two groups: those born according to the flesh and those born according to the Spirit. These two groups correspond to Abraham's two sons, Ishmael and Isaac. In the allegory of 4:21—5:1, Paul discerns two aspects that distinguished Abraham's sons from one another: (1) the status of their mothers (slave/free; 4:21) and (2) the manner of their births (flesh/promise; 4:22).[6] Ishmael was born to a slave by human means, and Isaac was born to a free mother through the miraculous fulfillment of God's promise.

---

3. Baasland, "Persecution," 135; Dunne, *Persecution and Participation*, 47–48.

4. Dunne, *Persecution and Participation*, 48–49.

5. As becomes evident in 4:30 where Paul quotes Gen 21:10, Paul's statement in 4:29 contains his interpretation of Gen 21:9. See Dunn, *Galatians*, 256; Moo, *Galatians*, 310.

6. John M. G. Barclay rightly recognizes that these "twin axes . . . reflect motifs already present in the Genesis stories" (*Paul and the Gift*, 416). See Cousar, *Galatians*, 103–4.

The true seed and heir of Abraham was born through promise to the free woman.

Typology in the syntax. Longenecker, correctly, writes that "Paul sees [the experience of the Galatians] as an antitype of Ishmael's persecution of Isaac."[7] The syntax of 4:29 demonstrates this. In 4:29, Paul sets up a correlation by pairing the comparative conjunctions ὥσπερ and οὕτως. In this construction ὥσπερ marks the protasis with οὕτως marking the apodosis.[8] The addition of καί to the apodosis intensifies the logical connection.[9] In the Pauline corpus, this correlative construction occurs eight other times (Rom 5:12, 19, 21; 6:4, 19; 1 Cor 11:12; 15:22; 16:1).[10]

After contrasting Hagar with Sarah in the allegory, this construction allows 4:29 to shift the focus slightly by introducing the element of interaction between their offspring. The correlation of the two pronouns sets up a comparison between the past experience of Isaac with the present reality experienced by those who "like Isaac, are children of promise" (4:28). The use of οὕτως focuses the comparison specifically on the manner of the actions under consideration.[11] That is to say, the manner in which Ishmael treated Isaac is the same manner in which those born of the flesh treat the contemporary offspring of the Spirit. Furthermore, an analysis of how ὥσπερ . . . οὕτως functions in other instances demonstrates that the construction frequently compares the manner of a past event with the manner of an eschatological reality (Matt 12:40; 13:40;

---

7. Longenecker, *Galatians*, 216. Cf. Betz, *Galatians*, 249.

8. A. T. Robertson labels the pair "correlative accents" (*Grammar*, 429). So also Longenecker, *Galatians*, 216.

9. In the majority of instances, οὕτως occurs with καί, although καί is not necessary for the comparison. See Robertson, *Grammar*, 429.

10. Outside of Paul, James uses the construction once (Jas 2:26), and the Gospels utilize it seven times (Matt 12:40; 13:40; 24:27; 24:37; Luke 17:24; John 5:21, 26). Other variations on the ὡς (καθώς, καθάπερ) . . . οὕτως (οὕτως καί or simply καί) correlation occur more frequently. Blass categorizes these pairs as the correlative use of comparative conjunctions. Comparative conjunctions are then labeled as subordinating or hypotactic conjunctions (BDF, §453). The classification of BDF seems clearer than that of Wallace who lists correlative conjunctions without any reference to the pair currently under discussion as logical conjunctions and comparative conjunctions without any reference to their correlation as adverbial conjunctions (Wallace, *Greek Grammar*, 672, 675).

11. Although Wallace's classifications are imperfect, Wallace does helpfully add that these comparative conjunctions label manner or "how something is done" (*Greek Grammar*, 675).

24:27, 37; Luke 17:24; John 5:21, 26; Rom 5:21; 6:4, 19; 1 Cor 15:22). For example, Jesus makes the following comparison: "For as [ὥσπερ] the days of Noah were, so [οὕτως] the coming of the Son of Man will be" (Matt 24:37).

In addition, Paul uses two temporal adverbs to mark the typological comparison: τότε and νῦν. NT authors utilize these adverbs in eschatological contexts to signify a change in age, not merely to mark sequence. For example, Heb 12:26 compares the shaking of Sinai with the coming universal shaking of the final judgment: "At that time [τότε], his voice shook the earth, but now [νῦν] he has promised, 'Yet once more I will shake not only the earth but the heavens also.'" Similarly, in 2 Pet 3:6–7, the author compares the destruction of "the world that then [τότε] existed" in the days of Noah with the coming destruction of "the heavens and earth that now [νῦν] exist."

Paul intends to do more than make an analogy or give the Galatians an encouraging example of someone who has suffered in the past. Paul uses these comparative pronouns with the two temporal adverbs to demonstrate the typological relationship between the two instances of persecution. Longenecker helpfully summarizes the argument, "The particles ὥσπερ ("just as") and οὕτως ("so") serve to introduce the protasis and apodosis of the sentence, with their accompanying temporal adverbs τότε ("then") and νῦν ("now") being reflective of Paul's fundamental understanding of eschatological fulfillment."[12]

Type to antitype. Paul recognizes present-day slaves and present-day sons corresponding to Ishmael and Isaac. One group's identity emerges from human means while the other group's identity comes through the fulfillment of divine promise. Isaiah 54:1 explicates both the textual and historical correspondences between the patriarchal situation in Genesis and the future, as well as the escalation between type and antitype. The reference to the "barren one" in Isa 54:1 alludes to Sarah's barrenness (cf. Isa 51:2).[13] While at first glance "the one who has a husband" seems to contrast the marital status of two women, it more likely contrasts the differing origins of the two women's children.[14] One, like Hagar, has conceived

---

12. Longenecker, *Galatians*, 216.

13. Callaway, *Sing, O Barren One*, 63–65; Hays, *Echoes of Scripture*, 118–21; Jobes, "Jerusalem, Our Mother," 305–7. Contra Das, *Galatians*, 502.

14. Harmon, *She Must and Shall Go Free*, 180.

children through natural human means. By contrast, the barren woman, like Sarah, is commanded to rejoice on the basis of a promise: She will one day have children, and her future children will outnumber those of the woman who presently bears children by human means.

Isaiah reads the story of Sarah's barrenness as pregnant with the story of the nation of Israel.[15] Caneday explains, "It is fitting that, as mother of Israel, Sarah's desolation representatively foreshadows the nation's desolation out of which hope arises."[16] In Isaiah's prophecy, it is Jerusalem that will become desolate when God exiles Judah (Isa 64:10). The contrast of two women in Isa 54:1, therefore, is a contrast between the Jerusalem of the present and the Jerusalem of the future.[17] Isaiah's present Jerusalem was populated by those of human origin and thus stood condemned to desolation because of its sin. But God offers his people comfort, as he did Sarah before them, by means of a promise: The future Jerusalem that belongs to the new heavens and the new earth will bear children through God's merciful and miraculous deliverance (cf. Isa 65–66). While this expression of the promise directly addresses the needs of a desolate Jerusalem, it nevertheless remains in substance the same promise that was given to Abraham.[18]

When Paul writes in 4:24 that the story of Sarah and Hagar ἐστιν ἀλληγορούμενα, he does not mean, as some translations render it, that "this may be *interpreted* allegorically,"[19] but rather that Genesis itself "*speaks* allegorically" or that Genesis itself possesses "a deeper meaning."[20] Caneday explains, "The Genesis narrative itself, which is historical in character, was written so that the personages and events portrayed,

---

15. Callaway and Jobes call this a transformation, but that seems to imply that the story in Genesis is not about the destiny of a people (Callaway, *Sing, O Barren One*, 65; Jobes, "Jerusalem, Our Mother," 307). The corporate solidarity of Israel in Isaac makes Isaiah's interpretation understandable. See Robinson, *Corporate Personality*; Longenecker, *Biblical Exegesis*, 77. By contrast, Claus Westermann wrongly reads Isa 54:1 as alluding to "the age-old lament of the childless woman" generally without direct reference to Sarah (*Isaiah 40–66*, 272).

16. Caneday, "Covenant Lineage," 62.

17. Burton, *Galatians*, 442; Goldingay and Payne, *Isaiah 40–55*, 1:337; Willitts, "Isa 54,1 in Gal 4,24b–27," 195–97; Moo, *Galatians*, 306.

18. Caneday recognizes this, "Thus, Paul cites this passage [Isa 54:1], for it reflects the Lord's reaffirmation of his promise to Abraham" ("Covenant Lineage," 65).

19. So CSB, ESV, NIV.

20. Steven DiMattei shows that this was the predominant use of ἀλλεγορέω ("Paul's Allegory," 106–7). See also Harmon, "Allegory, Typology," 144–58.

symbolically represent things beyond themselves."[21] Isaiah, long before Paul, recognizes "that the narrative story in Genesis is laden with clusters of symbolic representations concerning salvation that is to come in latter days."[22] Paul then utilizes this Isaianic lens to ground his full understanding of correspondence between the two boys in Genesis and his readers in Galatia.[23] While Paul here describes Genesis as speaking allegorically, elsewhere he describes the same belief—that God providentially embedded earlier Scripture with a deeper meaning that could only be clearly understood in the light of Messiah—as typological (1 Cor 10:11) while the author of Hebrews describes it as parabolic (Heb 11:19).[24]

Paul challenges his readers to see themselves in the story of Abraham's two sons and by doing so to recover their liberty, writing "Do you not listen to the law" (4:21)? Not leaving anything to chance, he straightforwardly places the Galatians into the comparison: The Jerusalem above "is *our* mother" (4:26). "*You*, brothers, are children of promise like Isaac" (4:28). "Therefore, brothers, *we* are not children of the slave but of the free woman" (4:31). These statements simply rework what he has already said about them: "If you belong to Christ, then *you* are Abraham's seed, heirs according to promise" (3:29). "So *you* are no longer a slave but a son, and if a son, then an heir through God" (4:7). In 4:21—5:1, Paul raises the question "Which covenant is your mother?" in order to answer the question from 3:6—4:11, "Is Abraham and his God your father?"[25]

How can he make such confident assertions about their seed-identity? He does so on the basis of the same principles that identified Isaac

21. Caneday, "Covenant Lineage," 55.

22. Caneday, "Covenant Lineage," 60.

23. Caneday, "Covenant Lineage," 60; Harmon, "Allegory, Typology," 156; Dunne, *Persecution and Participation*, 186. Caneday helpfully compares what Paul does here through Isa 54:1 with how Hebrews uses Melchizedek through Ps 110:4 ("Covenant Lineage," 60). Harmon, through comparison with Philo, argues that this is actually what Paul means by allegory, "to read a text through the lens of another textual, philosophical, or theological framework to reveal a fuller meaning" ("Allegory, Typology," 153). This usage of the term "allegory" differs from later Christian practices that sought to find timeless, spiritual truths in OT narratives.

24. Caneday, "Covenant Lineage," 60; Harmon, "Allegory, Typology," 156; Carson, "Mystery and Fulfillment," 393–436.

25. Moo writes, "What is implicit in that earlier argument [3:7–29] becomes explicit here: it is not biological descent from Abraham that marks the true children of Abraham but descent through the line of promise" (*Galatians*, 293). For a fuller account of the relationship of 4:21–5:1 to 3:1–4:20, see Myers, "For It Has Been Written," 301–6. Cf. Elliott, "Choose Your Mother," 661–83.

rather than Ishmael as the heir in Genesis: They are children of promise (4:28). They are free (5:1).[26] By drawing on these principles that separated Isaac from Ishmael, Paul demonstrates the covenantal and eschatological distinction between the Galatian Christians and his opponents. The two groups belong to two different covenants, two different Jerusalems, and two different ages. One group is enslaved to the present evil age, and the other group has been liberated unto a new creation. The polarities that drive Paul's argument throughout the letter—human or divine, works of the law or faith of Christ, law or promise, slavery or freedom, the flesh or the Spirit—bear down upon these polar identities that emerge from a deeper reading of Genesis.[27]

Having identified their distinct lineages, how do these two covenant families relate to one another? According to Paul, the answer lies in the same narrative from which he has drawn the entire comparison. Just as Ishmael persecuted Isaac, so also the present-day flesh-born children persecute the Spirit-born children. What is at stake is not the mere injustice of such ill treatment but the threat that such treatment poses for the issue of inheritance. Sarah demanded that Hagar and Ishmael be cast out "for [γάρ] the son of the slave will never inherit along with the son of the free woman" (4:30; cf. Gen 21:10).[28] The relationship between type and antitype legitimates Paul's contemporizing of Sarah's demand as the actual speech of Scripture to the Galatian Christians (4:30).[29] Paul recognizes in the winsome teaching of his opponents an incredible danger. His

---

26. Martinus C. de Boer calls the reaffirmation of the identity of the Galatian believers Paul's "penultimate goal" (*Galatians*, 288).

27. Betz comments, "Because this dualism underlies the whole of Galatians it must be Paul's goal to arrive at this polarity here [4:29] too" (*Galatians*, 249).

28. According to Moo, the quotation allows Paul to make explicit that inheritance is "the defining issue" (*Galatians*, 311).

29. Hays, *Echoes of Scripture*, 116; Matera, *Galatians*, 178. Martyn wrongly argues that "the slave" refers specifically to the opponents, while "her son" refers to those Galatians who had embraced the opponents' teaching (*Galatians*, 446). Nor is it likely that Paul intends his readers to overhear the grounds of the command while not obeying the imperative itself. Susan G. Eastman correctly demonstrates that Paul does not *typically* use the second person singular imperative to address his readers ("Cast Out," 320–24; cf. Schreiner, *Galatians*, 306). But as Das rightly comments, "Paul is citing *a Scriptural text* as the basis for the Galatians' action. This is not just some isolated directive to Sarah or mere historical trivia.... Paul intends the Galatians to overhear the imperative and to note Abraham's obedient response. The Galatians are likewise to obey the command" (*Galatians*, 510; cf. Wright, *Paul and the Faithfulness of God*, 1136; Dunne, "Cast Out the Aggressive Agitators," 246–69). The Galatian churches are to exclude those who preach a false gospel.

spiritual children are in danger of abandoning their freedom and submitting again to a yoke of slavery (4:9; 5:1). By doing so, they would be abandoning their role as a son and heir through God (4:7). They would be severing themselves from Christ and the benefits of his cross (5:4).[30]

Summary. Before discussing the basis for or the exegetical legitimacy of the correspondence Paul sees between past and present, it should simply be observed that Paul presents this correspondence, not as mere analogy or example, but as typology. Many agree that typology consists of both historical correspondence and escalation.[31] The past corresponds to the present in terms of the identity of the heir of Abraham—free and born by promise—and in terms of the behavior of the non-elect against the elect—persecution.

Paul also presents escalation between the past and present in 4:29. First, quite obviously, there is an escalation in number. In the past, there was *one* born according to the flesh—Ishmael—and *one* born according to the Spirit—Isaac, but in the present, he speaks of groups—the opponents and the churches of Galatia. Second, escalation exists in terms of location. The global mission that Paul leads as apostle to the gentiles means that a conflict that was once localized in terms of one elect seed is now globalized since the gentiles also have become the sons of Abraham through faith. Thirdly, there is an escalation from promise to fulfillment that undergirds the previous two observations. Paul may be signifying this by the escalation of his language from 4:28–29. In 4:28, he identifies the Galatian churches as "children of promise," but in 4:29, he speaks of "those born according to the Spirit."[32] The promise that was given to Abraham and passed to his elect seed, Isaac, has been fulfilled in the singular Seed, Jesus Christ, and experienced through reception of the Spirit by the gentile sons of Abraham in Galatia. Whereas in the past, persecution of the elect by the non-elect was a localized event, in the fullness of

---

30. Betz explains, "Therefore, the citation of Gen 21:10 not only recommends what the Galatians should do about Paul's opponents, but also makes clear what they do to themselves if they do not carry out the divine order" (*Galatians*, 251).

31. E.g., Davidson, *Typology in Scripture*; Goppelt, *Typos*; Beale, *Handbook on the New Testament*, 13–25; Gentry and Wellum, *Kingdom through Covenant*, 102–8; Sequeira and Emadi, "Biblical-Theological Exegesis," 11–34; Hamilton, *Typology*, 26.

32. In 3:14, Paul refers to τὴν ἐπαγγελίαν τοῦ πνεύματος, in which τοῦ πνεύματος is an epexegetical genitive and can be translated "the promise that is the Spirit." So deSilva, *Galatians: Handbook*, 64. Paul's choice of "Spirit" in 4:29, as de Boer rightly explains, "is probably the result of his contemporizing intention" (*Galatians*, 306).

time such persecution has now been universalized because of the universalization of the people of God through the gospel and the actualization of the new creation and the heavenly Jerusalem in those believers.[33]

The Basis and Significance of Typology in 4:29

Paul sees the manner of Ishmael's treatment of Isaac as a type that corresponds to the manner of his opponents' treatment of the believers in Galatia. But how legitimate is Paul's exegesis of Gen 21:9? Is there exegetical warrant in Genesis itself for Paul's interpretation of Ishmael's laughter as persecution? Richard N. Longenecker provides the most comprehensive discussion of this dilemma.[34] Longenecker summarizes his conclusion, "Paul, of course, presumes a more developed account of the story of Ishmael and Isaac than the one presented in Scripture, for the Old Testament does not record anything about Ishmael's persecution of Isaac."[35] Longenecker suggests that Paul either appropriates rabbinic interpretation or methods.[36] In *Biblical Exegesis in the Apostolic Period*, Longenecker states that in Gal 4:29–30 Paul uses the rabbinic theme of persecution "turning it to his own purposes."[37] What purposes are those? He sees Paul as utilizing this tradition for an *ad hominem* defense of himself and his gospel.[38] He hypothesizes that Paul's opponents had used the story of Ishmael and Isaac to accuse Paul of preaching an "Ishmaelian" gospel. To counter this charge, Paul turns the interpretation against

---

33. Harmon, "Allegory, Typology," 156.

34. F. F. Bruce also gives space to the discussion. He cites much of the same evidence as Longenecker, but unlike Longenecker, he leaves the question of influence open, concluding about the rabbinic interpretations, "These observations are all later than Paul's day; whether there were earlier forms of any . . . which he knew we cannot say" (*Galatians*, 224). Similarly, Craig S. Keener also enumerates ancient traditions about Ishmael persecuting Isaac and their possible sources in Genesis, but Keener, like Bruce, does not in the end commit himself to an explanation of Paul's usage (*Galatians*, 432–33). Because Longenecker commits himself to the influence of rabbinic interpretations or methods upon Paul, the focus of this section will be upon Longenecker's comments rather than those of Bruce or Keener.

35. Longenecker, *Galatians*, 217.

36. Longenecker lists the following sources: Tg. Ps.-J. Gen 21:9–11; Tg. Onq. Gen 21:9; t. Soṭah 6.6; Pesiq. Rab. 48.2; Pirqe R. El. 30; Josephus, *Ant.* 1.215. See Longenecker, *Galatians*, 217.

37. Longenecker, *Biblical Exegesis*, 103–4.

38. Longenecker, *Biblical Exegesis*, 104; cf. Barrett, "Allegory of Abraham," 162–63.

his opponents.³⁹ Longenecker's hypothesis has enjoyed wide influence. Douglas J. Moo, for example, cites Longenecker's research and concludes that Paul's claim about persecution was "in light of its [Genesis 21:9] traditional interpretation."⁴⁰

Longenecker's hypothesis must be understood on the basis of his own hermeneutical presuppositions. He writes, "The Jewish roots of Christianity make it *a priori* likely that the exegetical procedures of the New Testament would resemble to some extent those of then contemporary Judaism."⁴¹ According to Longenecker, due to his Pharisaic training, Paul followed Jewish interpretive conventions like those recorded in the Mishnah.⁴² This presupposition means that when Paul's interpretation of a passage cannot be easily discerned from that passage's immediate context, Longenecker seeks an answer in a parallel interpretation from rabbinic literature. Such interpretations were at times non-contextual in nature and arbitrary. According to Longenecker, rabbinical literature demonstrates that Paul employed culturally appropriate argumentation when arbitrarily wielding Gen 21:9 as an *ad hominem* argument against his opponents.⁴³ Because of Paul's unique rabbinical context, Longenecker contends that today's readers cannot replicate Paul's procedure. Longenecker advocates defending apostolic faith and doctrine but not apostolic exegesis.⁴⁴ In cases like 4:29, Paul's exegesis is descriptive of his cultural context, not normative for all times and places.⁴⁵ What then can interpreters today learn from Paul and the other apostles? Longenecker answers, "We can learn from their exegetical methods how to contextualize that same gospel in our own day."⁴⁶

---

39. Longenecker writes, "In explicating their position, the Judaizers undoubtedly claimed that Paul's preaching represented an 'Ishmaelian' form of truth" (*Galatians*, 199–200). Why does Longenecker say that this is "undoubtedly" the case? Without direct evidence to the teachings of Paul's opponents, many doubts remain as to what they did or did not actually preach to the Galatians.

40. Moo, *Galatians*, 310. See also Dunn, *Galatians*, 256; George, *Galatians*, 346; de Boer, *Galatians*, 306; Das, *Galatians*, 507–8.

41. Longenecker, "Who Is the Prophet?" 383.

42. Longenecker, *Biblical Exegesis*, 189.

43. Longenecker, *Biblical Exegesis*, 103–4.

44. Longenecker, *Biblical Exegesis*, 198.

45. Longenecker, *Biblical Exegesis*, 193–98.

46. Longenecker, "'Who Is the Prophet?'" 385. On Longenecker's view of how such contextualization should proceed, see Longenecker, *New Testament Social Ethics*; *New Wine*.

Hays rightly criticizes Longenecker's position as "inherently unstable."[47] He explains that "it commits us to a peculiar intellectual schizophrenia in which we arbitrarily grant privileged status to past interpretations that we deem unjustifiable with regard to normal, sober hermeneutical canons."[48] If Paul's interpretation of earlier Scripture is arbitrary and *ad hominem*, then this undermines the doctrine that he teaches, and this, therefore, places Christian doctrine in a perilous position of affirming truth that is based on the apostle's arbitrary and illegitimate use of Scripture. In the end, this schizophrenic position, to echo Hays, actually proposes a schizophrenic Spirit who cannot inspire the apostle to rightly interpret the Spirit's own inspired Word.

For Longenecker, the only legitimate hermeneutical method is the historical-critical method (or, as he prefers, historico-grammatical).[49] But the rationalistic biases of the historical-critical method have been largely exposed in recent decades, requiring exegetes to recognize their own cultural biases and presuppositions. Discontent over the atomistic exegesis characteristic of strict adherence to the historical-critical method has revitalized concern for the topic of typology. Among those who desire to understand Paul's hermeneutic as explicable and exemplary, two competing understandings of typology have emerged. One understands typology primarily as the act of the reader who approaches a text figuratively rather than realistically.[50] Hays writes, "Typology is before all else a trope, an act of imaginative correlation."[51] From this perspective, typology is a *retrospective* figural reading of an earlier text in which *the reader* draws figural comparisons between past and present, imaginatively finding elements of correspondence and escalation.[52] While many scholars would

47. Hays, *Echoes of Scripture*, 181.
48. Hays, *Echoes of Scripture*, 181.
49. Longenecker, *Biblical Exegesis*, 198.
50. Frei, *Eclipse of Biblical Narrative*, 1–3; Treier, "Typology."
51. Hays, *Echoes of Scripture*, 100.
52. In his understanding of figural reading, Richard B. Hays has been influenced by the work of Erich Auerbach (Hays, *Reading Backwards*, 2; Auerbach, "Figura," 53–54; *Mimesis*, 73). On Auerbach, first, it should be noted that he worked from the laudable motivation of subverting Nazism. See Zakai and Weinstein, "Erich Auerbach," 320–38. Second, Auerbach differs from some who have adopted figural reading since he emphasizes that figural reading "differs from most of the allegorical forms known to us by the historicity both of the sign and what it signifies" ("Figura," 54). For other examples of those who describe typology as the retrospective act of the reader, see von Rad, *Old Testament Theology*, 363–66; France, *Jesus and the Old Testament*, 39–42; Seitz, *Figured Out*; Moberly, "Christ in All the Scriptures?" 79–100; Baker, *Two Testaments*, 181.

propose certain constraints upon the reader's imaginative activity (e.g., Hays's seven tests),[53] the fact remains that "the hermeneutical event occurs in my reading of the text."[54] By making typology an act of the reader rather than an act of the divine and/or human authors of Scripture, this reader-oriented understanding of typology offers no significant improvement upon Longenecker's approach since the reader employs earlier texts according to his own will or imagination for his own (at times, hypothetically, *ad hominem*) purposes.[55] The basis of the doctrine that emerges continues to be arbitrary since the texts that it is drawn from receive their figural meaning from the reader's imagination rather than the author's intention, even if certain hermeneutical constraints are placed upon that imagination. Whether legitimated by apostolic authority or Paul's imaginative hermeneutical skill, the positions represented by Longenecker and Hays both require a "leap of faith" by the Galatian believers to trust Paul, which actually undercuts Paul's own argument since he appeals to the voice of Scripture rather than his own authority or skill (4:21–22, 27, 30).[56]

Caneday offers this important correction: "To speak of *typological interpretation*, using the adjective to modify *interpretation*, creates confusion by focusing upon the *act of interpretation* rather than upon the *act of revelation*.... The reader discovers types and allegories that are already present in the text."[57] Paul believed that he was identifying typology that God had actually revealed in the text and that was now seen in the light of God's revelation in the Son. Types are "both *predictive* and *hidden*," explains Stephen J. Wellum.

---

53. Hays, *Echoes of Scripture*, 29–32.

54. Hays, *Echoes of Scripture*, 28. It should be noted that Hays identifies "a community of interpretation" as a constraint on "my reading" since a community's "hermeneutical conventions inform my reading" (Hays, *Echoes of Scripture*, 28). Thomas J. Millay argues that such post-critical hermeneutics cannot be identified with the exegesis of the early church fathers since each proceeds from fundamentally different worldviews ("Septuagint *Figura*," 93–104).

55. Robert Louis Wilken advocates for allegory on this basis, writing, "Context needs to be understood to embrace the Church, its liturgy, its way of life, its practices and institutions, its ideas and beliefs" ("In Defense of Allegory," 210). Thus, the reader extends the context of Scripture in order to accomplish the goals of the Church in his own day. This suggestion goes far beyond what has often been labeled "application" or "contextualization."

56. Caneday, "Covenant Lineage," 51.

57. Caneday, "Covenant Lineage," 68 n5.

They are *predictive* since God intends for them to anticipate Christ in a variety of ways. They are *hidden* not only due to their indirectness but also due to the fact that we come to know that they are types as God's redemptive plan unfolds and *later* texts pick up the recurring patterns.[58]

To identify types as predictive means to affirm that God designed history (persons, events, and institutions) to foreshadow his eschatological goal in Christ and that God testified to his design in the text of Scripture.[59] Since the predictive nature of a type is rooted in the providence of God, then that type is hidden, not due to God's intentional obscurity, but due to the progressive nature of God's revelation in history and text. This "fuller meaning" (*sensus plenior*) always resided in the divinely inspired text and is aligned with the authorial intent of the human author, but, as Douglas J. Moo and Andrew David Naselli explain, the meaning of the text "takes on deeper significance as God's plan unfolds (a *sensus praegnans*)."[60] If types are the product of God's act of revelation, then "interpreting types is not an 'imaginative' task but an exegetical one," as Aubrey Sequeira and Samuel C. Emadi argue, and types may be discovered through a grammatical-historical reading of the text in its canonical form and a biblical-theological reading of the text in its canonical context.[61]

In the case of Gal 4:29, Paul, unlike many historical-critical scholars, reads Genesis as a unified whole in its canonical form and discovers actual textual correspondence in God's progressive revelation between past and present events. Understanding typology as an act of revelation has two important consequences. First, this exegetical logic makes Paul's argument rational rather than merely emotional or authoritarian. Paul does not say, "Just trust me." He asks his readers to actually hear what Genesis says in its canonical form and canonical context. Second, covenantal continuity between the two sons of Abraham and the two groups identified with them in the allegory charges the event described

58. Gentry and Wellum, *Kingdom through Covenant*, 105.
59. Sequeira and Emadi, "Biblical-Theological Exegesis," 23.
60. Moo and Naselli, "Problem of the New Testament's Use," 736.
61. Sequeira and Emadi, "Biblical-Theological Exegesis," 23. Concerning the exegetical logic of Paul and other NT authors, Sequeira and Emadi, helpfully, write, "The exegetical logic of the NT authors demonstrates that types are historical, authorially intended, textually rooted, tied to Scripture's covenant structure, and undergo escalation from old covenant shadow to new covenant reality" (Sequeira and Emadi, "Biblical-Theological Exegesis," 12).

in Gen 21:9 with continuing significance for the churches of Galatia. The present-day children of the Spirit are not merely in a conflict *like* the one experienced by Isaac. They are in the *same* conflict as Isaac. Just as it was in the past, so it continues to be in the present. Thus, Paul does not *merely* employ the episode of Ishmael's laughter in 4:29 in order to attack his opponents (although he certainly does this) but because the episode belongs to the same cosmic conflict that the Galatian churches now experience.

Genesis 21:9 in the Context of Genesis

Sequeira and Emadi claim that "types are rooted in the *text* of the Old and New Testaments and can be exegetically demonstrated."[62] So, in the case of Paul's use of Gen 21:9 in Gal 4:29, is there exegetical warrant for Paul's interpretation of Ishmael's laughter as persecution?

Genesis 21:9 in the MT and LXX. The initial difficulty with understanding Paul's interpretation is that the text of Genesis itself does not explicitly say that Ishmael persecuted Isaac. In the MT of Gen 21:9, the Piel participle "laughing" (מצחק) is the second object of the verb "to see" (ראה) and functions as the complement to the primary object, "the son of Hagar" (את־בן־הגר). In this construction, מצחק is an accusative of state or situation. When Sarah saw Ishmael, he was in the state of "laughing." But what was the cause or nature of Ishmael's state of laughter? On this question, the MT is silent.

Neither does the meaning of צחק help the reader discern the nature of Ishmael's laughter. צחק occurs fifteen times in the MT both in verbal and nominal forms. These occurrences fall into five semantic categories.[63]

---

62. Sequeira and Emadi, "Biblical-Theological Exegesis," 22.
63. Compare findings with *HALOT*, s.v. "צחק".

TABLE 1: צחק IN THE MT

	Semantic Category	Instances
1	to laugh due to disbelief or shock; as a noun, laughter that is caused by disbelief or shock	Gen 17:17; 18:12, 13, 15 (2x)
2	to laugh due to joy; as a noun, laughter that is caused by joy	Gen 21:6 (2x)
3	to mock, deride; as a noun, entertainment that is an object of mocking	Judg 16:25; Ezek 23:32; possibly Gen 39:14
4	to laugh as a euphemism for sexual activity or riotous debauchery	Gen 26:8; 39:17; Exod 32:6; possibly Gen 39:14
5	as a participle, someone who jokes	Gen 19:14

The alternate spelling שׂחק occurs more frequently with thirty-seven verbal instances and fifteen nominal instances.[64] Instances of שׂחק may also be divided into five categories.[65]

TABLE 2: שׂחק IN THE MT

	Semantic Category	Instances
1	to mock, deride; as a noun, entertainment that is an object of mocking	Judg 16:25, 27; 2 Chr 30:10; Job 5:22; 12:4 (2x); 29:24; 30:1; 39:7, 18, 22; 41:21; Pss 2:4; 37:14; 52:8; 59:9; Prov 1:26; 31:25; Jer 15:17; 20:7; 48:26–27, 39; Lam 1:7; 3:14; Hab 1:10 (2x)
2	to laugh due to joy, celebrate; as a noun, laughter that is caused by joy	1 Sam 18:7; 2 Sam 6:5, 21; 1 Chr 13:8; 15:29; Job 8:21; Ps 126:2; Prov 8:30, 31; 14:3; Eccl 2:2; 3:4; 7:3; 10:19; Jer 30:19; 31:4
3	as a noun, a joke or laughter that is characteristic of a fool	Prov 10:23; 29:9; Eccl 7:6
4	to play in a childlike manner, playfully joke	Job 40:20, 29; Ps 104:26; Prov 26:19; Zech 8:5
5	to play competitively, fight	2 Sam 2:14

These findings give a range of possibilities, but they do not solve the dilemma. Was Ishmael laughing for joy, in play, in mockery, or as a

---

64. The nominal form occurs with either a *holem* or *holem-vav*: שְׂחֹק or שְׂחוֹק. The two forms, צחק and שׂחק, occur as synonyms in Judges 16:25.

65. Compare findings with *HALOT*, s.v. "שׂחק".

euphemism for sexual activity? Ultimately, the nature of Ishmael's laughter cannot be determined by the lexical data or the syntax of Gen 21:9 in Hebrew.

Since Paul's quotation of Gen 21:10 in 4:30 resembles the LXX, it may be legitimately assumed that Paul's interpretation had its origin in the Greek version of Genesis. But the LXX also fails to solve the issue. First, it has similar syntax to the MT. In the LXX, Sarah beheld the son of Hagar "playing" (παίζοντα). The sentence contains a double accusative with "the son" (τὸν υἱόν) as the object and the participle "playing" (παίζοντα) as the complement. Second, παίζω has significant semantic overlap with the Hebrew verbs צחק and שׂחק. It occurs nineteen times in the LXX in five semantic groupings.⁶⁶

Table 3: Παίζω in the LXX

	Semantic Category	Instances
1	to laugh due to joy, celebrate (possibly dance)	2 Sam 6:5, 21; 1 Chr 13:8; 15:29; Jer 37:19; 38:4; 1 Esd 5:3
2	to play in a childlike manner, playfully joke	Job 40:29; Prov 26:19; Isa 3:16; Zech 8:5; Sir 32:12; 47:3
3	to mock, deride	Judg 16:25; Jer 15:17
4	to laugh as a euphemism for sexual activity or riotous debauchery	Gen 26:8; Exod 32:6
5	to play competitively, fight	2 Sam 2:14

In these aspects, the LXX does not differ significantly from the MT. The LXX however adds the prepositional phrase μετὰ Ισαακ τοῦ υἱοῦ αὐτῆς as a modifier of παίζοντα. The only other place in the LXX where παίζω appears with μετά is Gen 26:8 when Isaac is seen playing sexually with Rebecca. But in other extant ancient Greek literature μετά follows παίζω only three times. In all three instances, μετά marks those that someone is playing with in a childlike or joyful way.⁶⁷

---

66. The only occurrence in the NT is 1 Cor 10:7 where Paul is quoting Exod 32:4. Compare findings to LEH, s.v. "παίζω".

67. LSJ only lists the instance from Herodotus (LSJ, s.v. "παίζω").

Table 4: Παίζω + μετά in Greek literature

Source	Greek Text	English Translation
Aristophanes, *Av.* 660	... κατάλειφ' ἡμῖν δεῦρ' ἐκβιβάσας, ἵνα παίσωμεν μετ' ἐκείνης.	... leave her [the nightingale] with us here, in order that we might play with her.
Herodotus, *Hist.* 1.114	... ἔπαιζε δὲ μετ' ἄλλων ἡλίκων ἐν ὁδῷ.	[Describing the childhood of Cyrus the Great] ... and he played with others of the same age in the road.
HH 3.204–6	... οἳ δ' ἐπιτέρπονται θυμὸν μέγαν εἰσορόωντες Λητώ τε χρυσοπλόκαμος καὶ μητίετα Ζεὺς υἷα φίλον παίζοντα μετ' ἀθανάτοισι θεοῖσι.	[After describing Apollo playing the lyre and dancing] ... and those rejoicing with great thyme, golden-haired Leto and wise Zeus, look upon their beloved son [Apollo], playing among the immortal gods.

In a further similarity to Gen 21:9 LXX, *Homeric Hymn 3* uses the present active participle accusative masculine singular of παίζω. Despite this similarity, the fact remains that no example in ancient Greek literature exists of μετά marking the object of someone's mocking, much less physical persecution. With only the above instances for comparison, it seems that the LXX either intends to portray Ishmael as playing with Isaac in an innocent childlike manner or that like the MT it leaves the matter open.[68]

Genesis 21:9 in rabbinic literature. Paul's interpretation of Gen 21:9 in Gal 4:29 cannot be drawn conclusively from the vocabulary or syntax of the MT or LXX. For this reason, Longenecker turns to rabbinical literature as the basis of Paul's reading. Such an interpretation, however, was certainly not monolithic among the rabbis. The midrash on the verse in the Genesis Rabbah lists four competing interpretations of Ishmael's laughter.[69] First, Rabbi Akiba, noting the use of צחק in Gen 34:17, claimed that Sarah saw

---

68. Jerome's Vulgate similarly leaves the interpretation of Genesis 21:9 open: *cumque vidisset Sarra filium Agar Aegyptiae ludentem dixit ad Abraham*. *Ludo* has a similar semantic range to צחק and παίζω (LS, s.v. "ludo").

69. Gen. Rab. 53.11. The Tosefta contains the same four interpretations but attributes them differently (t. Soṭah 6.6). See Meeks, "'And Rose up to Play,'" 69–70. Bruce cautiously reminds readers that these interpretations are later than Paul and that therefore their influence in Paul's day is uncertain (*Galatians*, 224).

Ishmael committing sexual immorality.[70] Rabbi Ishmael, however, with reference to צחק in Exod 32:6 claimed that Ishmael committed idolatry.[71] Third, Rabbi Simeon ben Yohai, the author of the midrash, claimed that Ishmael mocked those who rejoiced over Isaac's birth since as the firstborn he would receive the inheritance.[72] He grounded his interpretation in Sarah's response in Gen 21:10. Of the interpretive options given in the midrash, only Rabbi Azariah in the name of Rabbi Levi posited any sort of physical persecution, claiming that Ishmael shot arrows at Isaac. He based his interpretation on Prov 26:18–19: "Like a madman shooting flaming arrows of death is one who deceives his neighbor and says, 'I was only joking [הלא־משחק אני]!'"[73] Still other Jewish interpreters saw nothing at all sinister in Ishmael's laughter. Notably, Jub 17:4 says, "And Sarah saw Ishmael playing and dancing" along with Abraham at the feast.[74] Josephus does not even mention Ishmael's laughter but explains his expulsion on the basis of Sarah's jealousy.[75]

Rabbinic literature demonstrates a variety of interpretations of Ishmael's laughter. Some rabbis did indeed believe that Ishmael either mocked or physically persecuted Isaac, but others did not follow these interpretations, either interpreting Ishmael's actions as idolatry, sexual immorality, or completely innocent. This variety does not disprove Longenecker's hypothesis, but it should at least caution interpreters from positing the influence of rabbinical interpretations and methods upon Paul.[76]

In a response essay to Longenecker, G. K. Beale offers two further objections to Longenecker's hermeneutical approach. First, since most examples of Jewish interpretation were written after AD 70, to speak of "a non-contextual *rabbinic* method" in the apostolic age may be

---

70. Gen. Rab. 53.11. Similarly David J. Zucker proposes pederasty as one possible explanation of the situation ("What Sarah Saw," 57–58).

71. Gen. Rab. 53.11. So also Exod. Rab. 1.1; similarly Tg. Ps.-J. Gen 21:9 and Tg. J. Gen 21:9 have Ishmael giving strange worship, possibly to the Lord; even so Tg. Ps.-J. does however demonstrate the expectation of future persecution. In Tg. Ps.-J. Gen 21:10, Sarah appeals to Abraham to cast out Ishmael lest he "make war with Isaac."

72. Gen. Rab. 53.11. So also Tg. Onq. Gen 21:9.

73. Gen. Rab. 53.11. So also Pesiq. Rab. 48.2. See Schwartz, "Ishmael at Play," 209–12.

74. Quoted from Charlesworth, *Old Testament Pseudepigrapha*. See Schwartz, "Ishmael at Play," 207–9.

75. Josephus, *Ant.* 1.215. For a broader overview that includes interpretations in medieval art, see England, "Ishmael Playing?," 16–35.

76. Dunne, *Persecution and Participation*, 179–81.

anachronistic.[77] Second, Longenecker's assertion that the apostles closely followed Jewish procedures may not adequately account for the uniqueness of Christian experience and theology.[78] So, in view of the inconclusive lexical data and the variety of rabbinical interpretations, might a contextual reading of Genesis produce a better explanation of Paul's interpretation?[79]

Genesis 21:9 within the cosmic conflict theme of Genesis. Since Galatians parallels Genesis in terms of a theme of cosmic conflict, might reading Gen 21:9 within the context of that theme reveal how Paul understood the verse? Chapter 3 reviewed the cosmic conflict theme found in Genesis. To summarize here, Gen 1:1 defines the setting of the narrative as the entire universe. Even the election of Abraham occurs for global purposes (Gen 12:3; cf. 41:57). The conflict emerges in the cosmic-oriented narrative of Genesis because of human sin, which results in cosmic disorder. Genesis 3:15 defines the expectation for the metanarrative that follows. Two offspring—the seed of the woman and the seed of the serpent—will clash, but ultimately the seed of the woman will fatally strike the serpent. Yahweh further defines this eschatological hope through his promise of a kingdom to Abraham—a promise that can only be fulfilled through Yahweh's invasive action (Gen 12:1–2; 15).

The clash of the two seeds receives its initial interpretation in the narrative of Cain and Abel.[80] These biological brothers reveal through their actions that they belong to different spiritual lineages.[81] The struggle predicted in Gen 3:15 clearly does not refer to a human fear of snakes nor

---

77. Beale, "Did Jesus and His Followers Preach?," 388. Italics original.

78. Beale, "Did Jesus and His Followers Preach?," 388.

79. Dunne also concludes that the rabbinical hypothesis does not make the best sense of the evidence (*Persecution and Participation*, 181–82). Dunne, however, claims that Paul interprets Ishmael's laughter through the lens of Isa 52:13—53:12. He seeks to make his case through correspondence between παῖς and its cognates in both passages. The argument is not strong, and it only shifts the problem to the legitimacy of Paul's reading Gen 21:9 *through* the lens of Isa 52:13—53:12 (*Persecution and Participation*, 186–91). Below, this dissertation makes the argument that Paul reads Gen 21:9 within the context of Genesis as whole.

80. Westermann, *Genesis 1–11*, 285–86; Waltke, *Genesis*, 93–94; Arnold, *Genesis*, 79–80.

81. Waltke, rightly, points to the significant word בכר that distinguishes the offering of Abel from Cain: "Abel brings the best, fat from 'the firstborn.' Cain's sin is tokenism" (*Genesis*, 97). For an overview of interpretations of God's rejection of Cain's sacrifice, see Wenham, *Genesis 1–15*, 104.

does it predict a division of humanity on the basis of ethnic distinctions. Instead, the division is between those who receive Yahweh's favor and those who are dominated by sin. Additionally, the narrative clarifies the nature of the struggle between these two seeds: The struggle is "to the death." This initial fratricide becomes paradigmatic for the narratives that follow.[82] Not only does Genesis feature a repeated pattern of fraternal strife but it also features a repetition of Cain's motive in committing fratricide. Cain kills Abel because of his envy over God's favor.[83] His actions can be understood as an attempt to counteract the favor of God given to Abel. Emadi rightly comments, "Many of Genesis' major motifs originate in this episode—particularly sibling rivalry, jealousy, and the favoring of the younger son."[84]

Fraternal spiritual divisions continue in the narratives of Isaac and Ishmael, Jacob and Esau, as well as Joseph and his brothers.[85] In every case the seed of the woman can be identified by the favor of God, especially through the promise of blessing. By contrast the seed of the serpent demonstrates the distinguishing characteristic of subjugation to sin. As the most unexpected case, Joseph's brothers serve as a salient example. Their pervasive sinfulness stains the pages of the text: the slaughter at Shechem (Gen 34:25–29), their possession of idols (Gen 35:2–4), their callous elimination of Joseph (Gen 37:12–36), and their sexual immorality (Gen 35:22; 38). In one sense, the stories of Genesis are origins stories because they explain the condemnation of Israel's enemies: the Canaanites, Moabites, Ammonites, Ishmaelites, and Edomites (e.g., Gen 9:18–28; 19:30–38). The marking out of Joseph's brothers as likewise subjugated by the serpent may also explicate the sinfulness of Israel herself. But, at the very least, it creates a sharp contrast between the wicked brothers and the righteous Joseph.

This perpetual polarity between the righteous and the wicked turns the characters of Genesis into stock characters.[86] While certainly doing

---

82. Dan W. Forsyth labels the narrative as the "mythical, primary form of sibling rivalry" in Genesis ("Sibling Rivalry," 470). See Wénin, "Fraternité," 24–35; Sigmon, "Between Eden and Egypt," 18–35; Emadi, "Covenant, Typology," 98–102.

83. Although the primary concern of Genesis is the favor of God upon the elect son, this does not negate an emphasis on paternal favor that also pervades the book. See Steinmetz, *From Father to Son*, 31.

84. Emadi, "Covenant, Typology," 98.

85. Other familial variations also occur: Abraham and Lot (or at least their servants); Jacob and Laban; Rachel and Leah.

86. The term "stock character," borrowed from literature and drama, emphasizes that

so with great variation, they repeat the roles of the seed of the serpent and the seed of the woman—the roles of Cain and Abel. These stock characters interact in what Robert Alter terms a "biblical type-scene."[87] A biblical type-scene replicates a common scene, duplicating important motifs while also identifying significant points of variation (e.g., encountering one's future mate at a well).[88] The type-scene created in the murder of Abel is recapitulated in the episodes that follow. For example, although Esau does not kill Jacob, he certainly desires to do so, saying, "The days of mourning for my father are approaching; then I will kill my brother Jacob" (Gen 27:41). Like Cain, Esau was motivated to fratricide by not receiving the blessing of God. So, also, Joseph's brothers intend to kill the favorite son. Only Reuben's intervention prevents them from doing so (Gen 37:20–22). Instead, they eliminate Joseph by selling him into slavery and lying about his death to their father, an act practically equivalent to murder. Again, competition for God's blessing, which in Joseph's case had been foretold by his dreams, motivated this practical fratricide (Gen 37:5–11; 19–20). So, Genesis repeatedly features scenes of fraternal conflict in which the blessed brother finds himself in mortal danger because of the jealousy of the rejected brother(s). While great variation exists between each episode of the type-scene, a significant level of continuity creates an expectation within the hearer as to how the story *should* naturally proceed. Alter explains,

> What I am suggesting is that the contemporary audiences of these tales, being perfectly familiar with the convention, took particular pleasure in seeing how in each instance the convention could be, through the narrator's art, both faithfully followed and renewed for the specific needs of the hero under consideration. In some cases, moreover, the biblical authors, counting on their audience's familiarity with the features and function of the type-scene, could merely allude to the type-scene or present a transfigured version of it.[89]

---

certain character types can be easily identified by readers/audiences without requiring much development from the author (e.g., "Mr. Right" in romantic comedies). In its usage here, the term does not imply that these characters are parodies of themselves as is sometimes meant by the term. See "Stock character," Baldick, *Dictionary of Literary Terms*, 243.

87. Alter, *Art of Biblical Narrative*, 51.
88. Alter, *Art of Biblical Narrative*, 51.
89. Alter, *Art of Biblical Narrative*, 58.

Considering the divine inspiration of Scripture, however, these type-scene episodes are not *merely* literary conventions but are types of the predicted conflict in Gen 3:15. Emadi writes, "Each of these sibling rivalries or 'seed conflicts' develops the paradigmatic conflict first announced in Genesis 3:15 and then portrayed in Cain's murder of Abel. While only the Genesis 4 conflict ends in murder, the threat of fratricide against the covenant seeds looms throughout each of these conflicts."[90]

The relationship of Isaac and Ishmael must be read as a type-scene of fraternal strife within the context of cosmic conflict. Initially, the circumstances surrounding Ishmael's birth only hint at his identification as the seed of the serpent. The slavery of Hagar possibly ties Ishmael to the subjugation of Cain (Gen 16:1; cf. Gen 4:7), but a clearer echo of Eden sounds in Gen 16:2: Just as Adam listened to the voice of his wife (כִּי־שָׁמַעְתָּ לְקוֹל אִשְׁתֶּךָ; Gen 3:17), Abram listened to the voice of Sarai (וַיִּשְׁמַע אַבְרָם לְקוֹל שָׂרָי; Gen 16:2). These initial hints that something is amiss in the conception and birth of Ishmael become explicit when the angel of Yahweh predicts Ishmael's ungodly character. Hagar is told that he will be "a wild donkey of a man" (Gen 16:12).[91] Yahweh refuses Abraham's prayer that Ishmael would live before God (Gen 17:18–19). Instead, God will establish his covenant with Isaac (Gen 17:19–21). So, even before the birth of Isaac, God identifies Isaac as the legitimate seed and object of his favor while Ishmael is characterized as wild and ungodly.[92] Additionally, the angel of Yahweh says that Ishmael will have "his hand against everyone and everyone's hand against him, and he shall dwell over against all his kinsmen" (Gen 16:12). The NIV takes this final line as idiomatic: "and he will live in hostility toward all his brothers."[93]

---

90. Emadi, "Covenant, Typology," 99. Similarly, Steinmetz identifies "a clear pattern of potential threat to the son's life in the process of the transfer of the blessing from his father" and sees this violence as the primary threat in Genesis for the transmission of the Abrahamic blessing (*From Father to Son*, 31).

91. Cf. Jer 2:24; Hos 8:9. See Hamilton, *Genesis 1–17*, 454; Wenham, *Genesis 16–50*, 11; Waltke, *Genesis*, 255.

92. Von Rad, *Genesis*, 194.

93. So also Sarna, *Genesis*, 121; Waltke, *Genesis*, 255. André Wénin identifies three narrative features—Isaac's settling at Lahai-roi (Gen 16:14; 24:62; 25:11), his preferring the Ishmael-like Esau over Jacob, and Esau's marrying of Ishmael's daughter to please Isaac (28:6–9)—that signify Isaac's nostalgic yearning for a sibling relationship that prematurely ended ("Ismaël et Isaac," 490). Perhaps, though, these allusions to the earlier cycle serve to present Isaac as preferring his firstborn in the same way that Abraham preferred Ishmael in contrast with God's plan to bless the younger brother (cf. Gen 17:18).

This characterization of Ishmael follows the pattern of hostility predicted in Gen 3:15 and demonstrated by Cain. It, therefore, creates an expectation of fraternal strife in the relationship of Isaac and Ishmael. Having not received God's favor, it seems only a matter of time before Ishmael will strike with fratricidal intent.

Furthermore, when Ishmael laughs in Gen 21:9, he does so in a literary context that charges צחק with particular significance through repetition.[94] Both Abraham and Sarah laughed at the thought of having a child in their old age (Gen 17:17; 18:12, 15). Appropriately, they name the child יצחק (Gen 21:3), and Sarah announces, "Laughter [צחק], God has made for me! Everyone who hears will laugh [יצחק] with me!" (Gen 21:6). Considering Sarah's announcement, Ishmael's laughter should be welcomed, but coming as it does from her son's rival, she reacts decisively to protect the source of her laughter.[95] The aural similarity between מצחק in Gen 21:9 and the name יצחק may even suggest that Sarah saw Ishmael as taking on the role of Isaac.[96] Perhaps, though, a simpler explanation captures the repetition of laughter better. Laughter highlights the election of Isaac, who is both the unlikely fulfillment of Yahweh's promise to Abraham and Sarah as well as the heir to the covenant. Ishmael's act of laughter contrasts him with the person named laughter, Isaac. At any rate, Sarah's reaction reveals that Ishmael's laughter sparked fear in her that Isaac would be forced to share his inheritance with the son of an Egyptian slave.[97]

God endorses Sarah's demand, further confirming the legitimacy of Sarah's fears (Gen 21:12).[98] Both Yahweh and Sarah give the same reason

---

94. Bruce, *Galatians*, 223; Zucker, "Isaac," 105–10.

95. Similarly Nikaido, "Hagar and Ishmael," 236–37.

96. Similarly Coats, *Genesis*, 153; Murphy, "Sista-Hoods," 88; Robinson, "Characterization," 208.

97. Sarah may feel threated by the foreign (and, thus, pagan) influence of Hagar and Ishmael upon her son (Zucker, "What Sarah Saw," 57–58). Ironically, Sarah fears that her son will be equal to the son of slaves from Egypt, when her descendants will actually be slaves in Egypt.

98. Wénin insightfully reminds readers, concerning Sarah at the festival of weaning, that "le moment est délicat pour elle sur le plan affectif" ("Ismaël et Isaac," 492). Sarah almost certainly acted from a complex of emotional motivations ranging from jealousy toward Hagar and her child to a maternal desire to protect her own offspring. Despite whatever may have motivated Sarah, the author of Genesis gives clues in the surrounding context to what one might call the theological purpose of Sarah's demand that Ishmael be exiled. Note, especially, the use of זרע in Gen 21:12–13, linking the episode of Ishmael's expulsion with the seed motif going back to Gen 3:15.

for Ishmael's exile: Isaac is and must, therefore, remain the sole heir (Gen 21:10). Abraham's seed will be named through Isaac alone (Gen 21:12). Although the vocabulary and syntax of Gen 21:9 itself does not indicate the nature or cause of Ishmael's laughter, the context—both the wider context of fraternal strife as cosmic conflict and the more immediate context of Isaac's election—identifies the laughing Ishmael as a danger to the elect Isaac. The semantic range of צחק allows for a level of ambiguity that the author may exploit to both resonate with the laughter motif and to insinuate that Ishmael in some way mocked Isaac. In this context, it seems reasonable that the author of Genesis intended readers to hear this laughter as mocking or at the very least to join Sarah in her perception of the laughter as indicating danger.

Can this really be called persecution though? Certainly, the potential for physical violence is never realized in this case. The same motive, however, that fueled the fratricidal impulses of Cain, Esau, and Joseph's brothers moved Ishmael as well. Ishmael plays a stock role in the narrative, and in Genesis, the stock character of the serpent's seed always desires to harm the one who has received the blessing of God. Thus, when Sarah sees Ishmael laughing at the feast, she recognizes the danger that Ishmael poses against her own son and responds in order to preempt this threat. Sarah's intervention serves as the significant variation in this biblical type-scene of fraternal strife. Sarah sagaciously perceives persecution in Ishmael's laughter so that the potential for physical persecution never becomes realized. Sarah's preemptive actions save Isaac from loss of inheritance or even death. Instead, Ishmael and his mother exit the scene in a final correspondence between Ishmael and Cain. Both, having been driven away, settle (ישב) in another land (Gen 4:16; 21:21; cf. Gen 3:24).[99]

Genesis 21:9 within the Cosmic Conflict Theme of Galatians

If Paul reads Genesis as a unified whole and sees the fraternal strife between Ishmael and Isaac as one episode of the cosmic conflict predicted in Genesis 3:15, then this further validates his assertion in Galatians 4:29 that the persecution of the children of the Spirit is to be expected. "Just as then . . . so also now" (4:29).[100] Paul does not claim that the Galatian

---

99. Contra Nikaido who reads the separation motif as contributing to the heroic portrayal of Ishmael ("Hagar and Ishmael," 233–34).

100. The entire allegory depends on a unified interpretation of Genesis. Caneday rightly criticizes scholars for tending "to locate the origin of *the allegory* within Paul's

COSMIC CONFLICT MANIFESTED AS PERSECUTION IN GALATIANS 167

Christians are *similar* to Isaac. They are the *same* as Isaac. They are legitimate sons and heirs of Abraham, and therefore they suffer the *same* persecution that the heir has always suffered.[101] In 5:17, he will claim that "the desires of the flesh are against the Spirit." So, also, the children of the flesh are always against the children of the Spirit. The Galatian Christians have been freed from this present evil age through the invasive actions of God, and they now belong to the new creation and the Jerusalem above.

But their personal eschatological transformation has placed them in a new position within the cosmic conflict between God and the present evil age. These liberated sons of God are now the targets of those whose identity continues to be bound to the present evil age and the present Jerusalem. Just as Ishmael was a threat to Isaac's inheritance, so also the false gospel of Paul's opponents threatens the inheritance of the Galatian Christians. Just as fraternal strife in Genesis manifested the cosmic conflict of Gen 3:15, so also the false-teaching "persecution" of Paul's opponents manifests the cosmic conflict that continues (yet escalates) in the fullness of time. His opponents must be "cast out" like Hagar so that their leaven does not infect the entire lump (4:30; 5:9).

READING OTHER TEXTS IN LIGHT OF GALATIANS 4:29

How might reading 4:29 in this way affect the way other passages about persecution should be read? This section proposes possible exegetical results of interpreting persecution as cosmic conflict.

Galatians 1:13–14, 23

Krister Stendahl has argued that Paul's Damascus road experience was a call rather than a conversion. He objects that the change experienced by Paul was not a change in religion as the word "conversion" communicates to modern ears. Stendahl writes, "Serving the one and the same God,

---

interpretative skillfulness rather than within the Genesis narrative itself" ("Covenant Lineage," 50).

101. Baasland rightly states, "If the persecution theme in itself was the only point of interest, he might very well have chosen Esau's persecution of Jacob, and been treading on much safer ground exegetically. But the point that Paul wishes to drive home lies exactly in the very characters of Ishmael and Isaac" ("Persecution," 137). It should be noted that if the persecution theme was the only point then the best example would have been Abel (cf. Matt 23:35; Luke 11:51; Heb 11:4; 12:24).

Paul receives a new and special calling in God's service.... The emphasis in the accounts is always on this assignment, not on the conversion."[102] Stendahl rightly recognizes that Paul utilizes the language of prophetic calling in 1:15, echoing Isa 49:1.[103] Stendahl also rightly recognizes that the modern concept of religious conversion as a sociological phenomenon wrongly colors the modern reader's perception of Paul's experience.

Nevertheless, Stendahl fails to pay careful attention to 1:13 when he claims that Paul saw himself as "serving the one and the same God" before and after his encounter with Jesus on the road to Damascus.[104] Paul writes that he persecuted and sought to destroy τὴν ἐκκλησίαν τοῦ θεοῦ. This phrase corresponds to the Hebrew קהל יהוה.[105] That Paul views his former way of life in Judaism as consisting of persecuting and ravaging *the assembly of Yahweh* has two important implications for his retrospective judgment on that former way of life. First, by making this statement, he counts himself as having been outside the assembly of Yahweh in the past. Certainly, in his previous way of life, he did not regard himself as excluded from the assembly of Yahweh. Rather, he thought of himself as that assembly's zealous defender. Only now that God was pleased to reveal his Son to Paul does he retrospectively make this judgment.[106] Second, he was not merely outside the assembly of Yahweh, but he was

---

102. Stendahl, *Paul among Jews*, 7. Followed by Dunn, *Galatians*, 65; Hays, "Galatians," 215. Similarly Betz, *Galatians*, 69.

103. Stendahl, *Paul among Jews*, 8. See also Munck, *Paul and Salvation*, 24–35; Sandnes, *Paul, One of the Prophets?*; Ciampa, *Presence and Function*, 111–23; Wilk, *Bedeutung des Jesajabuches*, 292–93; Harmon, *She Must and Shall Go Free*, 75–79.

104. Stendahl, *Paul among Jews*, 7.

105. Thomas R. Schreiner argues that Paul may use the phrase ἐκκλησία θεοῦ rather than the LXX phrase ἐκκλησία κυρίου "to avoid the confusion between the Father and Christ that would be precipitated by the word *Lord*" (*Paul, Apostle*, 331–32). Thus, Paul does not refer specifically to the Judean churches. Contra de Boer, *Galatians*, 87. Peter Oakes rightly concludes, "Paul could, unusually, describe the whole Jesus movement as a single assembly, in order to evoke its continuity with the Israelite assembly" (*Galatians*, 54–55). See also Schlier, *Brief an die Galater*, 22; Mußner, *Galaterbrief*, 79; Burton, *Galatians*, 45; Matera, *Galatians*, 58; Dunn, *Galatians*, 59; George, *Galatians*, 114; de Boer, *Galatians*, 88; Moo, *Galatians*, 100–101; Beale, "Background of Ἐκκλησία Revisited," 151–68.

106. Such a judgment was no small thing to a former Pharisee. By doing so, he grouped himself with the excluded parties of Deut 23—eunuchs, those of mixed Israelite ethnicity, and the pagan nations of the Ammonites and Moabites (Deut 23:2–9). This combination of language bites with irony. In his "former life in Judaism," Paul condemns himself as being non-Israelite—outside "the assembly of God" and thus equivalent to the Ammonites and Moabites.

actively opposed to that assembly and, therefore, opposed to God himself.[107] Under the weight of these implications, Stendahl's thesis cannot stand.[108] While formerly Paul conceived of himself as defending the God of Israel, the new Paul sees his past efforts as the exact opposite—fighting against the God of Israel.[109] While Paul did not experience a religious conversion in the modern sociological sense, he clearly sees himself as experiencing a conversion of identity from child of the flesh to child of the Spirit, from fighting against God to serving God. The reaction of the Judean churches in 1:23–24 confirms the significance of Paul's transformed identity from persecutor to preacher.[110] Paul has changed sides in the cosmic conflict between God and the present evil age, and his own autobiography creates a paradigm for understanding the present crisis in Galatia.[111]

Galatians 3:4

The previous chapter argued that πάσχω in 3:4 should be translated "to suffer." Fee objects to this translation because he believes "that in contrast to most of Paul's other letters there is not the slightest hint in this one that the churches of Galatia were undergoing suffering, not to mention suffering τοσαῦτα (so many things)."[112] Therefore, Fee believes that the

---

107. De Boer comments, "The genitive 'of God' in any event clearly shows whose side God was on in Paul's retrospective look at his 'way of life earlier in Judaism.' He now knows that he persecuted the church that has been gathered by God" (*Galatians*, 88). Cf. Martyn, *Galatians*, 154; Barclay, *Paul and the Gift*, 357.

108. Additionally, Moo writes that "it is a logical error to think that because Paul speaks of his calling as a purpose of the experience that it is the *only* purpose of that experience" (*Galatians*, 105). See also Gaventa, *From Darkness to Light*; Donaldson, "Zealot and Convert," 655–82; Segal, *Paul the Convert*; Das, *Galatians*, 147–52.

109. Ben Witherington III comments, "His symbolic universe was not merely altered, in some respects it was turned upside down" (*Grace in Galatia*, 111).

110. Oakes, *Galatians*, 60. The sharp contrast in 1:23 between the past (ποτε) and the present (νῦν) may also reflect Paul's eschatological understanding of his personal transformation. Similarly Baasland, "Persecution," 137.

111. Lyons, *Pauline Autobiography*; Gaventa, "Galatians 1 and 2," 309–26; Hansen, "Paradigm of the Apocalypse," 194–209.

112. Fee, *God's Empowering Presence*, 387.

translation "to suffer" disconnects the question from the "appeal to their experience of the Spirit" and gives it "no specific reference to the immediate context."[113] But in light of the rest of the letter, the proclamation of the Son, the reception of the Spirit, the working of miracles, and even the suffering of persecution in 3:1–5 are all family traits of the seed of Abraham.[114] Like Isaac, the Galatian Christians have been born "according to the Spirit" (4:29), and the children of the Spirit have always suffered at the hands of the children of the flesh.[115] Paul, therefore, can appeal to the past suffering of the Galatian Christians for a positive purpose: Their suffering in the past serves to affirm the change of identity they experienced when they heard the gospel vividly preached and received the Spirit.[116] How can they know that they are true heirs of Abraham? They suffer persecution just like Isaac before them.[117] Furthermore, the specific form of Paul's question highlights this meaning behind their suffering. He asks, "Did you suffer so many things *in vain*—if indeed it was in vain?" Either their suffering was purposeful and meaningful or it was not.[118] If they abandon Paul's gospel, then their suffering was "needless" or "without good cause."[119] Thus, they would affirm the position of Paul's opponents that persecution was something to be avoided (6:12).[120] If so, what was the use of enduring it in the past? But if they persevere in the preaching of the cross, then they suffered as children "born according to the power of the Spirit" (4:29) who also have the hope of salvation in the eschatological judgment.[121]

---

113. Fee, *God's Empowering Presence*, 387. So also Mußner, *Galaterbrief*, 208; Betz, *Galatians*, 134; Longenecker, *Galatians*, 104; Das, *Galatians*, 296.

114. Dunne, *Persecution and Participation*, 73–78.

115. Dunne, "Suffering in Vain," 10. Contra Charles H. Cosgrove, who writes that "the theme of suffering and the Spirit never becomes an object of reflection in Galatians" (*Cross and the Spirit*, 187).

116. Contra Baasland who claims it also means suffering from "individual struggle against the desires of the flesh" ("Persecution," 140). While that may be true, it does not seem to be referred to here.

117. This does not contradict the observation that the suffering of Galatians conforms them to their crucified Messiah. See Dunne, "Suffering in Vain," 9; Oakes, *Galatians*, 104. Nevertheless, the identification of their suffering with the suffering of Isaac is stated more explicitly in Galatians than with the suffering of Christ who "gave himself *for our sins*" (1:4; cf. 2:20).

118. Similarly, Paul worries that his own labors over them will be "in vain" (4:11).

119. Burton, *Galatians*, 150.

120. Lightfoot, *Galatians*, 135; George, *Galatians*, 213; McKnight, *Galatians*, 141.

121. Schreiner cites 1 Cor 15:2 and Gal 4:11 to demonstrate that εἰκῇ in soteriological

Galatians 5:11 and 6:12

Galatians 5:11 and 6:12 complement one another. Paul is persecuted because he no longer preaches circumcision while his opponents use circumcision to avoid persecution for the cross of Christ.[122] Paul, however, refuses to abandon the scandal of the cross.[123] The general principle is clear: The preaching of the cross in the present evil age brings persecution. Circumcision of the flesh does not bring persecution. As Mußner explains, "Die Verfolgung des Apostels hängt ursächlich zusammen mit seiner Predigt."[124] Why is this principle true? It is the logic of cosmic conflict. Wright claims that "*eschatology defines election*" and explains that "the 'new creation' determines the identity of the single family, the 'seed' promised to Abraham, and in doing so utterly relativizes the marks of circumcision."[125] The children born according to the power of the flesh—the preachers of circumcision—belong to the present evil age and therefore pose that age no threat. All their concerns belong to this realm of the flesh. They are motivated to circumcise the Galatians "to make a good showing *in the flesh*" and "to boast *in your flesh*" (6.12–13).[126] They

---

contexts indicates the futility of a faith that does not persevere to the end (*Galatians*, 185). Cf. Dunne, *Persecution and Participation*, 76.

122. The reference to Paul's preaching of circumcision refers to his "former life in Judaism" (1:13). See Fung, *Galatians*, 238–39. Contra Howard, *Paul*. The phrase τῷ σταυρῷ in 6:12 is a dative of cause. They avoid being persecuted *because of* the cross. See Burton, *Galatians*, 350; Mußner, *Galaterbrief*, 412; Bruce, *Galatians*, 269; Wallace, *Greek Grammar*, 167–68; Schreiner, *Galatians*, 377; deSilva, *Galatians: Handbook*, 141.

123. It may be, as Schreiner proposes, that the opponents charged Paul with avoiding conflict over circumcision because the rite was offensive to the gentiles (*Galatians*, 326–27). If this is the case, Paul is turning their argument against them. He is not afraid of a scandal and the persecution that results.

124. Mußner, *Galaterbrief*, 362. Cf. Baasland, "Persecution," 138.

125. Wright, *Paul and the Faithfulness of God*, 1143. Italics original. See also Plummer, *Paul's Understanding*, 121–38; Plummer, "Role of Suffering," 6–19.

126. The references to σάρξ brackets Paul's final attack against his opponents (6:12–13). See Schlier, *Brief an die Galater*, 206–7; Fung, *Galatians*, 304; Weima, "Gal 6.11–18," 95–96; Martyn, *Galatians*, 561; Moo, *Galatians*, 392; Barclay, *Paul and the Gift*, 394. De Boer explains, "Those 'wanting to make a good showing in the Flesh' do not know that there has been a change of regimes (3:25); they still orient their lives to the Flesh instead of to the Spirit (cf. 6:8), with all the dangers for communal life that involves (cf. 5:13–24)" (*Galatians*, 398). Similarly, deSilva writes, "In a context dealing with circumcision, the resonances of 'flesh' as physical matter return. As a realm of what is weak, slavish, opposed to promise (see, e.g., 4:21–31), this would have negative connotations of its own, but these connotations are amplified by the repetitive use of σάρξ in 5:16–24 (and perhaps 6:7–10) to denote the self-centered cravings and inclinations that are hostile to the leading of the Spirit" (*Galatians*, 140).

do this because circumcision and uncircumcision belong to the value structures of this present evil age, but the cross puts to death that old world and inaugurates a new creation.[127] Those who preach the cross, therefore, proclaim the defeat of the present evil age and the abolition of its value structures. God has liberated his children from its dominion (1:4; 4:3–7). In light of this eschatological transition, Paul sees only two parties: those born according to the flesh and those born according to the Spirit. While Paul's opponents advocate circumcision in order to avoid Jewish persecution (6:12), in so doing they "persecute"—in Paul's polemical rhetoric—the Galatian Christians (4:29). Those who avoid persecution persecute others because only two possibilities exist: Either one is persecuted, or one is a persecutor. Ishmael persecuted Isaac, threatening Isaac's inheritance (4:29–30), and so now those who belong to the realm of the flesh—the present evil age—persecute those who belong to the new creation.[128]

Galatians 6:17

Galatians 6:17 gives the most explicit connection between the suffering of Christ and the suffering of Paul and other believers. Paul's scars of persecution mark him as belonging to Jesus since his suffering imitates the suffering of his master, Jesus.[129] Underlying this assertion is Paul's understanding of union with Christ. God promised Abraham a singular Seed, who is Christ (3:16), and one can claim to be "Abraham's seed, heirs according to promise" only "if you belong to Christ" (3:29). Additionally, Paul's freedom motif stands alongside his concept of slavery to Christ (e.g., 1:4, 10; 4:3; 5:1). According to Jeremy W. Barrier, this makes sense in Paul's cultural context: "Manumission typically transferred the

127. Mußner, *Brief an die Galater*, 411; Martyn, "Apocalyptic Antinomies," 412–15; Weima, "Gal 6.11–18," 100–102; Wright, *Paul and the Faithfulness of God*, 1143; Barclay, *Paul and the Gift*, 395. It is unlikely that the opponents had completely abandoned the message of a crucified Christ. Rather, Paul criticizes them because by preaching circumcision *alongside* the cross they actually empty the cross of its power and significance. He states this in 2:21: "I do not nullify the grace of God, for if righteousness were through the law, *then Christ died for nothing.*" See Dunn, *Galatians*, 337; Schreiner, *Galatians*, 377.

128. Das writes, "For Paul, the supposed entry rite was in reality an exit rite! . . . The cross and circumcision represent two very different approaches to acceptance by God" (*Galatians*, 637). Cf. Barrett, *Freedom and Obligation*, 69.

129. Betz, "στίγμα," 7:657–64; BDAG, s.v. "στίγμα"; L&N, 8.55, 33.481, 90.84; Longenecker, *Galatians*, 299; Dunne, *Persecution and Participation*, 100.

relationship of slave/master over to client/patron, which in all honesty was not liberation, but rather a small adjustment within the power hierarchy."[130] Therefore, "Paul did not see liberation as the annulment of slavery, but rather saw liberation only in terms of the transference of allegiance from one master to another."[131] To be liberated from the present evil age means a transfer of allegiance to "the Lord Jesus Christ" (1:3), to be "a slave of Christ" (1:10), and to "belong to Christ" (3:29).[132] Yet, at the same time, allegiance to Christ brings a "freedom that we have in Christ Jesus" (2:4) and a freedom for which "Christ has set us free" (5:1). It is the freedom of having also become sons and heirs in addition to slaves to Christ (3:29; 4:4–7). While τοῦ Ἰησοῦ in 6:17 is syntactically a descriptive genitive and thus only signifies a general relationship between Paul's στίγματα and Jesus,[133] this theological discourse on slavery, freedom, and sonship gives the phrase greater significance.[134] Paul's marks relate to Jesus not in terms of a mere moral example of one who also suffered but in terms of eschatological family relation.[135] Isaac, the type of Abraham's seed, experienced persecution. So also, Christ, the antitype of Abraham's seed, suffered on the cross. Paul, united with Christ by faith, bears the same family resemblance. Just as Isaac was marked by persecution, so also Paul bears the marks of Jesus, and in the realm of the Spirit

---

130. Barrier, "Marks of Oppression," 360. Cf. Harrill, "Paul and Slavery," 575–607.

131. Barrier, "Marks of Oppression," 361. Against the textual evidence, however, Barrier claims that Paul understood his allegiance as transferring from Caesar to Christ ("Marks of Oppression," 362). Rather, Paul has been liberated from the law and its condemning function within the present evil age (2:19–21). Barrier also oddly suggests that the metaphor of slavery to Christ is "less than desirable" and that Christians today should "seek other alternatives and better metaphors in which to interpret the Christians' identity with Christ" ("Marks of Oppression," 362).

132. This emphasis on allegiance is similar to the recent argument of Bates, *Salvation by Allegiance Alone*. Undoubtedly, faith involves allegiance to the Lord Jesus Christ. Nevertheless, Galatians clearly emphasizes Abraham's trust in God's promise as the model of justifying faith.

133. DeSilva, *Galatians: Handbook*, 146. By using the name "Jesus" without any title such as Christ or Lord, Paul may allude to the death of Jesus. So Borse, "Wundmale und der Todesbescheid," 93; Dunn, *Galatians*, 347; Das, *Galatians*, 654.

134. While certainly possessing great emotional power, this theological context means that Paul does not merely appeal to these marks simply as a rhetorical ploy to manipulate his reader's emotions. See Witherington, *Grace in Galatia*, 454.

135. There remains, as Schreiner notes, a difference in the nature of Paul's suffering from Christ's since Christ's suffering redeemed sinners (*Galatians*, 384; cf. Borse, "Wundmale und der Todesbescheid," 91).

these family marks possess value rather than circumcision of the flesh.¹³⁶ If understood in terms of family resemblance, Martyn is correct when he writes that "his scars are nothing other than the present epiphany of the crucifixion of Jesus."¹³⁷

CONCLUSION

Paul's use of Gen 21:9 in Gal 4:29 presents persecution as a manifestation of the cosmic conflict between God and the present evil age. In Genesis, the relationship of Ishmael and Isaac recapitulates the theme of fraternal strife that originates with Cain and Abel and expresses the cosmic conflict between the seed of the serpent and the seed of the woman in Gen 3:15. In this context of fraternal strife as cosmic conflict, when Sarah hears Ishmael's laughter, she recognizes the threat that Ishmael poses to Isaac's inheritance of the divine promise. Sarah preempts this threat by demanding that Abraham cast out Hagar and Ishmael, and by doing so, she saves Isaac's inheritance and possibly also his life. In Galatians, Paul identifies this as a type. There is historical correspondence: Just as then Ishmael persecuted Isaac—just as then the seed of the serpent persecuted the seed of the woman—so also now Paul's opponents—those born according to the power of the flesh—persecute the Galatian believers—those born according to the power of the Spirit.

Yet, there is also escalation as the persecution of God's people expands across the world to God's multinational Abrahamic seed. At times persecution takes the form of the historical phenomena of hostile harassment (1:13–14, 23; 3:4; 5:11; 6:12), but Paul may also polemically charge false teachers with persecution because every attempt to endanger the inheritance of God's Spirit-born children can legitimately be called persecution (4:29). Why? Because the children of this age utilize both the strategies of hostile harassment and false teaching to endanger God's heirs. Isaac is no mere example. Every believer is a child of promise like

---

136. Weima rightly recognizes that the primary contrast is between the persecution avoidance of Paul's opponents and the persecution endurance of Paul, but this does not negate the contrast between circumcision and persecution ("Gal 6.11–18," 98–99). Paul presents two options of valuation. One belonging to the world—circumcision and uncircumcision—and one belonging to the new creation—persecuted and persecutor. See Wright, *Paul and the Faithfulness of God*, 1145.

137. Martyn, *Galatians*, 569; Mußner, *Brief an die Galater*, 420. The idea that these στίγματα served as a talisman remains possible also. See Dunn, *Galatians*, 346; Witherington, *Grace in Galatia*, 454.

Isaac (4:28), and therefore everyone who belongs to Christ through faith is "Abraham's seed, heirs according to promise" just as Isaac was (3:29). But unlike Isaac, believers in the fullness of time have received the fulfillment of God's promise as the gentiles receive the Spirit by faith (3:14). Nevertheless, these Spirit-born children are persecuted in the *same* conflict because they dwell in the present age while belonging to the new creation and the Jerusalem above. The flesh-born children of this present world attack the heirs of the new creation as they have always done since the beginning of time. Paul pleads with the churches at Galatia to hear what the Scripture says (4:21, 30), to cast out the false teachers (4:30), and by so doing to stand fast in their freedom (5:1). He implores them to perceive the crisis in Galatia rightly. This is no religious dispute. This is the war of the ages, and their spiritual family is on the side of the persecuted, the side of the cross, and the side of victory.

7

Conclusion

SINCE THE PUBLICATION OF Ernst Baasland's article in 1984, an increasing number of scholars have attempted to address persecution, the "neglected feature" of Galatians.[1] While other perspectives on the theme have been helpful, this monograph offers a simple explanation of Paul's theology of persecution in Galatians based on a close reading of Galatians itself. Influenced by Paul Middleton's work on Christian martyrology in the second and third centuries, this monograph has argued that in Galatians Paul views persecution as a manifestation of the cosmic conflict between God and the present evil age.[2] Furthermore, Paul's understanding of persecution as cosmic conflict does not emerge from his own mind but, rather, emerges as his understanding of the world based on earlier Scripture, especially Genesis and Isaiah.

SUMMARY

After chapter 1 introduced the thesis of this monograph and the history of research, chapters 2–4 focused on a theme of cosmic conflict in Galatians and other Jewish texts. Chapter 2 demonstrated that an apocalyptic cosmic conflict is indeed a significant theme in Galatians and defined the nature of that conflict. In Galatians, Paul uses the theme to place the crisis in Galatia within a broader context of a conflict between God and the present evil age. This exegetical investigation called for a modification

---

1. Baasland, "Persecution," 135–50.
2. Middleton, *Radical Martyrdom*.

in Middleton's definition of cosmic conflict. Whereas Middleton defined cosmic conflict as a war between God and a personal being named Satan, in Galatians the cosmic conflict is between God and an impersonal yet personified entity labeled "this present evil age" (1:4).[3] In the letter, Paul identifies three primary ways that this cosmic conflict manifests itself in the crisis at Galatia: (1) within the believer and the community, (2) between Jew and gentile, and (3) between persecutor and persecuted.

Chapters 3–4 examined Paul's theological context by identifying cosmic conflict as a thematic parallel between Galatians and a sample of earlier Jewish documents. These chapters then compared Paul's depiction of cosmic conflict with these other texts. Chapter 3 investigated the theme of cosmic conflict in Genesis, Psalms, Isaiah, and Habakkuk and identified three loci of that theme: (1) the polarity of the righteous/wicked, (2) the problem of sin and suffering, and (3) the solution of God's invasive action. While significant differences were highlighted among these four biblical books, these differences represent the organic growth of OT eschatology through the progress of revelation. Chapter 4 examined the theme in other early Jewish texts (Daniel; 1 Enoch; 4 Ezra; 2 Baruch; Jubilees; 1 Maccabees; 2 Maccabees; 4 Maccabees; 1QS; CD; 1QM). These texts, like Galatians, demonstrated a dependence upon earlier Israelite Scripture, sharing both a theme of cosmic conflict and the three loci that give shape to that theme. But beyond this general unity around a theme, these early Jewish texts exhibited immense diversity, especially concerning the nature of God's future invasive actions. In this theological context, Paul transformed the theme of cosmic conflict from earlier Scripture in three primary ways: (1) He read Scripture in light of the coming of the Son and the Spirit. (2) Because of the work of the Son and the Spirit, he believed that the new creation had already been inaugurated, although not yet fully realized, in the church. (3) Paul believed that the gentiles were to be included in the people of God through faith in the gospel of Christ apart from the law.

Chapter 5 shifted to the topic of persecution in Galatia and answered the historical questions about the persecution referred to in the letter. The letter refers to four instances of persecution or likely persecution: (1) Paul, in his former life in Judaism, persecuted the church of God (1:13, 23). (2) But now as a preacher of Christ, Paul endures persecution (5:11; 6:17). (3) By preaching circumcision, Paul's opponents avoid possible persecution from local synagogues (6:12). (4) The Galatian Christians

---

3. Middleton, *Radical Martyrdom*, 6.

had suffered persecution from local synagogues in the past (3:4), but now they are being "persecuted" in a different way—through the preaching of a false gospel that will sever them from Christ (4:29). In Galatians, Paul uses the theme of persecution to polemically reshape the perception of his readers. His opponents pose as friends, but they have no love for the Galatian believers (e.g., 4:16–19). Their preaching is persecution because it threatens to separate the Galatian believers from Christ and thus from their inheritance as sons (5:4). Therefore, the Galatian believers must reject the false gospel of Paul's opponents and stand firm in their freedom (5:1).

By bringing together the earlier studies on cosmic conflict (chapters 2–4) and persecution in Galatia (chapter 5), chapter 6 examined the theological significance of Paul's use of διώκω in 4:29. In a typological relationship, the Spirit-born children in Galatia are persecuted in the same conflict as Isaac. Paul's opponents are the children of the flesh, and their false teaching is meant to deprive the Galatian Christians of their inheritance. Just as Sarah recognized the threat posed by Ishmael and saved Isaac, so too the Galatians must hear Sarah's voice—the voice of Scripture—that commands them to cast out the false teachers (4:30). They must open their eyes and choose a side in this cosmic conflict. They must choose between the freedom that is the gift of God or slavery to this present evil age.

RESULTS OF PERSECUTION AS COSMIC CONFLICT

There are three further results of understanding persecution as a manifestation of cosmic conflict. First, if persecution manifests the cosmic conflict between God and this age, then persecution may also validate the gospel's authenticity. Paul's primary goal in writing Galatians is to demonstrate the authenticity of his gospel (1:6–9), and persecution contributes to that goal. Paul is persecuted because he preaches the true gospel (5:11), and his opponents are not persecuted because they preach a false gospel (6:12). Persecution, therefore, validates the true message just as the avoidance of persecution invalidates the false teaching of Paul's opponents. Paul makes this argument more carefully than it might initially appear. Paul does not employ the logical fallacy that a claim must be true if people are willing to suffer for it.[4] It is not persecution alone that

---

4. This fallacious argument can often be found in popular Christian apologetics. The substance of it often appears like this: If the apostles and early Christians were willing

validates the gospel but persecution *as a manifestation of cosmic conflict*. Paul identifies their experience as consistent with the worldview that he taught them. The hostility of the domain of the flesh confirms that they have believed in the authentic message of the Spirit and have changed sides in the cosmic conflict. This consistency between the message believed and the suffering experienced confirms and validates Paul's gospel.

Second, if persecution manifests the cosmic conflict between God and this age, then persecution distinguishes God's true people.[5] In Paul's polemic, only two options exist: persecuted or persecutor. Paul himself transitioned from persecutor to persecuted (1:13, 23). Paul's opponents avoid being persecuted and, therefore, despite their apparent zeal for the Galatians, they are persecuting the Galatians with their false gospel (4:29; 6:12). But for Paul, this division is not *merely* polemical. It is fundamental to his worldview. Either one is born according to the power of the Spirit or one is born according to the power of the flesh, and the flesh-born children always persecute the Spirit-born children (4:29). Persecution is not merely a possible circumstance that the local church may encounter. It is the expectation (cf. 2 Tim 3:12). Persecution is a repeated and escalating pattern in salvation history. The church of God lives within a cosmic conflict that repeatedly manifests itself through persecution. Therefore, the inevitability of persecution for God's Spirit-born children serves as an important aspect of both Paul's ecclesiology and eschatology (or perhaps one should say "of his eschatological ecclesiology"). Paul, like Martin Luther after him, therefore, identifies persecution as a visible mark of the true church.[6]

Third, if Paul identifies the false teaching of his opponents as persecution in 4:29, then both hostile harassment and false teaching are equivalent in essence because they belong to the same cosmic conflict.

---

to die for the gospel, then the gospel must be true. But does the same logic apply to Socrates? Are his claims true simply because he was willing to be killed for them?

5. The claim that persecution distinguishes the true people of God is not novel but basing the claim upon this cosmic conflict interpretation is unique. See Hubing, *Crucifixion and New Creation*, 186; Dunne, *Persecution and Participation*, 43–87.

6. Martin Luther argues for seven holy possessions of the church, which are visible marks of the genuine assembly of God's holy people. According to Luther, the seventh visible mark of God's holy people is "the holy possession of the sacred cross" ("On the Councils of the Church," 41:164). While Luther's Roman Catholic opponents claimed to possess splintered relics from the true cross of Christ, Luther argued that the true church possessed the holy cross by enduring suffering for Christ. Consistent with Luther's broader theology of the cross, the true church is to be seen in suffering rather than in the power manifest by the papacy. Despite Luther's influence, persecution has largely been ignored as a topic in ecclesiology.

This, of course, assumes that Paul accurately testifies to the way things truly are and does not simply use his polemics as a rhetorical ploy for power. While it may be helpful in some respects, especially in church history, to distinguish between the outward threat of persecution and the inward threat of false teaching, Paul does not make such a distinction in Galatians. Both of these phenomena come from the same source and therefore are part of the same threat. To Paul, hostile harassment is persecution, *and* false teaching is persecution. Both are methods of attack against God's children that seek to separate them from their inheritance and enslave them anew to this present evil age. Furthermore, the response to both methods of attack is the same: stand firm in the true gospel of Jesus Christ (e.g., Gal 5:1; 1 Thess 3:1–5).

SIGNIFICANCE FOR GLOBAL CHRISTIANITY TODAY

God called Paul to preach his Son among the gentiles (1:16). Paul believed that no ethnic, cultural, or geographical limitation could be placed on the universal message of liberation from this present evil age that is revealed in Christ. Never before in the history of Christianity has this been more evident than today. As the center of Christianity shifts to the Global South, the gospel of Jesus Christ resounds as a message for all people. "There is neither Jew nor Greek, there is neither slave nor free, there is no male and female" (3:28a). There is no Global North or Global South. "For you are all one in Christ Jesus" (3:28b). Yet, as the universal gospel crosses more ethnic, cultural, and geographical boundaries than ever before, the conflict that has come down through the ages from Isaac to the churches of Galatia to global Christianity today will continue to escalate until Christ returns.

In light of this, it can be claimed that persecution is a regular, visible mark of the local church. Every church will participate in persecution in some way. Many churches will suffer hostile harassment, and some believers will die. We know "that we are destined for this" (1 Thess 3:3). Other churches suffer through the conflict they endure with false teachers. Believers around the world will continue to be "tossed by the waves and blown by every wind of teaching, by human cunning in the schemes of deceit" (Eph 4:14). Churches with an overrealized eschatology, which denies the necessity of persecution (e.g., churches that preach the prosperity gospel), are unfaithful to the biblical pattern set forth by Paul. Like the churches of Galatia before us, the Holy Spirit calls believers around the world today to perceive the crises that threaten them rightly. A cosmic conflict rages between the flesh and the Spirit, and believers must stand firm in the freedom that comes to us as a gift through the death of God's Son.

Bibliography

Abegg, Martin G., Jr. "The Covenant of the Qumran Sectarians." In *The Concept of the Covenant in the Second Temple Period*, edited by Stanley E. Porter and Jacqueline C. R. de Roo, 81-97. JSJSup 71. Leiden: Brill, 2003.
Abel, Felix Marie. *Les livres des Maccabees*. EBib. Paris: Éditions du Cerf, 1961.
Abir, Peter Antonysamy. *The Cosmic Conflict of the Church: An Exegetico-Theological Study of Revelation 12, 7-12*. European University Studies: Series 23, Theology 547. Frankfurt am Main, Germ.: Lang, 1995.
Abma, Richtsje. *Bonds of Love: Methodic Studies of Prophetic Texts with Marriage Imagery (Isaiah 50:1-3 and 54:1-10, Hosea 1-3, Jeremiah 2-3)*. SSN 40. Assen: Van Gorcum, 1999.
———. "Travelling from Babylon to Zion: Location and Its Function in Isaiah 49-55." *JSOT* 22, no. 74 (1997) 3-28.
Adams, Edward. *Constructing the World: A Study in Paul's Cosmological Language*. Edinburgh: T. & T. Clark, 2000.
Alexander, T. Desmond. "Genealogies, Seed and the Compositional Unity of Genesis." *TynBul* 44, no. 2 (1993) 255-70.
Alfrink, B. J. "L'idée de résurrection d'après Dan 12:1-2." *Biblica* 4, no. 2 (1959) 355-71.
Allen, Leslie C. *Psalms 101-150*. WBC. Nashville: Nelson, 2002.
———. "Some Prophetic Antecedents of Apocalyptic Eschatology and Their Hermeneutical Value." *ExAud* 6 (1990) 15-28.
Alter, Robert. *The Art of Biblical Narrative*. New York: Basic Books, 1981.
Altick, Richard D., and John J. Fenstermaker. *The Art of Literary Research*. New York: Norton, 1993.
Andersen, Francis I. *Habakkuk*. AB 25. New York: Doubleday, 2001.
Anderson, John E. "Awaiting an Answered Prayer: The Development and Reinterpretation of Habakkuk 3 in Its Contexts." *ZAW* 123, no. 1 (2011) 57-71.
Arnold, Bill T. *Genesis*. NCBC. Cambridge: Cambridge University Press, 2009.
Arnold, Clinton E. "Returning to the Domain of the Powers: Stoicheia as Evil Spirits in Galatians 4:3, 9." *NovT* 38, no. 1 (1996) 55-76.
Auerbach, Erich. "Figura." In *Scenes from the Drama of European Literature*, 11-76. Theory and History of Literature 9. Minneapolis: University of Minnesota Press, 1984.
———. *Mimesis: The Representation of Reality in Western Literature*. New York: Doubleday, 2003.

Auffret, Pierre. "Complements sur la structure littèraire du Ps 2 et son rapport au Ps 1." *BN* 35 (1986) 7–13.
———. "Essai sur la structure littèraire du psaume 1." *BZ* 22 (1978) 26–45.
———. *The Literary Structure of Psalm 2*. Translated by D. J. A. Clines. JSOTSup 3. Sheffield: JSOT, 1977.
Baasland, Ernst. "Persecution: A Neglected Feature in the Letter to the Galatians." *ST* 38, no. 2 (1984) 135–50.
Bachmann, Michael. "4QMMT und Galaterbrief, מעשי התורה und ΕΡΓΑ ΝΟΜΟΥ." *ZNW* 89 (1998) 91–113.
Baker, David W. *Nahum, Habakkuk and Zephaniah*. TOTC. Downers Grove, IL: IVP Academic, 2009.
Baker, D. L. *Two Testaments, One Bible: The Theological Relationship between the Old and New Testaments*. Downers Grove, IL: IVP Academic, 2010.
Baldick, Chris. *The Concise Oxford Dictionary of Literary Terms*. Oxford: Oxford University Press, 2001.
Balch, David L. "The Suffering of Isis/Io and Paul's Portrait of Christ Crucified (Gal 3:1) Frescoes in Pompeian and Roman Houses and in the Temple of Isis in Pompei." *JR* 83, no. 1 (2003) 24–55.
Baltzer, Klaus. *Deutero-Isaiah*. Translated by Margaret Kohl. Hermeneia. Minneapolis: Fortress, 2001.
Barclay, John M. G. *Jews in the Mediterranean Diaspora: From Alexander to Trajan (323 BCE–117 CE)*. Edinburgh: T. & T. Clark, 1996.
———. "Mirror-Reading a Polemical Letter: Galatians as a Test Case." *JSNT* 31 (1987) 73–93.
———. *Obeying the Truth: A Study of Paul's Ethics in Galatians*. Studies of the New Testament and Its World. Edinburgh: T. & T. Clark, 1988.
———. *Paul and the Gift*. Grand Rapids: Eerdmans, 2015.
Barnes, T. D. "Legislation against the Christians." *JRS* 58, nos. 1–2 (1968) 32–50.
———. "Pre-Decian Acta Martyrum." *JTS* 19, no. 2 (1968) 509–31.
Barnett, Paul. *The Second Epistle to the Corinthians*. NICNT. Grand Rapids: Eerdmans, 1997.
Barrett, C. K. "The Allegory of Abraham, Sarah, and Hagar in the Argument of Galatians." In *Essays on Paul*, 154–70. Philadelphia: Westminster, 1982.
———. *Freedom and Obligation: A Study of the Epistle to the Galatians*. Philadelphia: Westminster, 1985.
Barrier, Jeremy W. "Marks of Oppression: A Postcolonial Reading of Paul's *Stigmata* in Galatians 6:17." *BibInt* 16, no. 4 (2008) 336–62.
Barr, James. "The Question of Religious Influence: The Case of Zoroastrianism, Judaism, and Christianity." *JAAR* 53, no. 2 (1985) 201–35.
———. *The Semantics of Biblical Language*. Oxford: Oxford University Press, 1961.
Barth, Karl. *Church Dogmatics I/2*. Edited by G. W. Bromiley and T. F. Torrance. Translated by G. T. Thomson and Harold Knight. London: T. & T. Clark, 2004.
Bartlett, John R. *The First and Second Books of the Maccabees*. CBC. Cambridge: Cambridge University Press, 1973.
———. *1 Maccabees*. Guides to Apocrypha and Pseudepigrapha. Sheffield: Sheffield Academic Press, 1998.
Bates, Matthew W. *Salvation by Allegiance Alone: Rethinking Faith, Works, and the Gospel of Jesus the King*. Grand Rapids: Baker Academic, 2017.

Bauckham, Richard. *Gospel of Glory: Major Themes in Johannine Theology.* Grand Rapids: Baker Academic, 2015.

Bauer, Walter, et al. *A Greek-English Lexicon of the New Testament and Other Early Christian Literature.* 3rd ed. Chicago: University of Chicago, 2000.

Baumgarten, Albert I. "The Perception of the Past in the Damascus Document." In *The Damascus Document: A Centennial of Discovery,* edited by Joseph M. Baumgarten et al., 1–16. STDJ 34. Leiden: Brill, 2000.

Beale, G. K. "The Background of Ἐκκλησία Revisited." *JSNT* 38, no. 2 (2015) 151–68.

———. "Did Jesus and His Followers Preach the Right Doctrine from the Wrong Texts? An Examination of the Presuppositions of Jesus' and the Apostles' Exegetical Method." In *The Right Doctrine from the Wrong Texts? Essays on the Use of the Old Testament in the New,* edited by G. K. Beale, 387–404. Grand Rapids: Baker, 1994.

———. *Handbook on the New Testament Use of the Old Testament: Exegesis and Interpretation.* Grand Rapids: Baker, 2012.

———. *A New Testament Biblical Theology: The Unfolding of the Old Testament in the New.* Grand Rapids: Baker Academic, 2011.

———. "The Old Testament Background of Paul's Reference to 'the Fruit of the Spirit' in Galatians 5:22." *BBR* 15, no. 1 (2005) 1–38.

Beale, G. K., and Benjamin L. Gladd. *Hidden but Now Revealed: A Biblical Theology of Mystery.* Downers Grove, IL: InterVarsity, 2014.

Beker, J. Christiaan. *Paul's Apocalyptic Gospel: The Coming Triumph of God.* Philadelphia: Fortress, 1982.

———. *Paul the Apostle: The Triumph of God in Life and Thought.* Philadelphia: Fortress, 1980.

———. *Suffering and Hope: The Biblical Vision and the Human Predicament.* Grand Rapids: Eerdmans, 1994.

———. *The Triumph of God: The Essence of Paul's Thought.* Translated by Loren T. Stuckenbruck. Minneapolis: Fortress, 1990.

Bentzen, Aage. "On the Ideas of 'the Old' and 'the New' in Deutero-Isaiah." *ST* 1 (1947) 183–87.

Berges, Ulrich. *The Book of Isaiah: Its Composition and Final Form.* Translated by Millard C. Lind. HBM 46. Sheffield: Sheffield Phoenix, 2012

———. *Das Buch Jesaja: Komposition und Endgestalt.* HBS 16. Freiburg: Herder, 1998.

———. "Personifications and Prophetic Voices of Zion in Isaiah and Beyond." In *The Elusive Prophet: The Prophet as a Historical Person, Literary Character and Anonymous Artist,* edited by Johannes C. de Moor, 54–82. Leiden: Brill, 2001.

Best, Ernest. *Second Corinthians.* Interpretation. Louisville: John Knox, 1987.

Betz, Hans Dieter. *Galatians.* Hermeneia. Philadelphia: Fortress, 1979.

Betz, Otto. "στίγμα." In *TDNT,* translated by Geoffrey W. Bromiley, 7:657–64. Grand Rapids: Eerdmans, 1964–76.

Bird, Michael F. *An Anomalous Jew: Paul among Jews, Greeks, and Romans.* Grand Rapids: Eerdmans, 2016.

Bird, Michael F., and Preston M. Sprinkle, eds. *The Faith of Jesus Christ: Exegetical, Biblical, and Theological Studies.* Peabody, MA: Hendrickson, 2009.

Bisbee, Gary A. *Pre-Decian Acts of Martyrs and Commentarii.* Philadelphia: Fortress, 1988.

Black, David Alan. "Weakness Language in Galatians." *GTJ* 4, no. 1 (1983) 15–36.

Black, Matthew. *The Book of Enoch or 1 Enoch: A New English Edition*. SVTP 7. Leiden: Brill, 1985.
Blackwell, Ben C., et al. "An Introduction." In *Paul and the Apocalyptic Imagination*, edited by Ben C. Blackwell et al., 3–21. Minneapolis: Fortress, 2016.
Blass, Friedrich, et al. *A Greek Grammar of the New Testament and Other Early Christian Literature*. Chicago: University of Chicago, 1961.
Blenkinsopp, Joseph. *Isaiah 40–55*. AB 19A. New York: Doubleday, 2002.
Blinzer, Josef. "Lexikalisches zu dem Terminus τὰ Στοιχεῖα τοῦ Κόσμου bei Paulus." In *Studiorum Paulinorum Congressus Internationalis Catholicus*, 2:429–43. Rome: Pontifical Biblical Institute, 1961.
Boccaccini, Gabriele. "The Evilness of Human Nature in *1 Enoch*, *Jubilees*, Paul, and *4 Ezra*: A Second Temple Jewish Debate." In *Fourth Ezra and Second Baruch: Reconstruction after the Fall*, edited by Matthias Henze and Gabriele Boccaccini, 63–79. JSJSup 164. Leiden: Brill, 2013.
Boda, Mark J. *A Severe Mercy: Sin and Its Remedy in the Old Testament*. Siphrut 1. Winona Lake, IN: Eisenbrauns, 2009.
Borse, Udo. "Die Wundmale und der Todesbescheid." *BZ* 14, no. 1 (1970) 88–111.
Bourdieu, Pierre. "Ökonomisches Kapital, Kulturelles Kapital, Soziales Kapital." In *Soziale Ungleichheiten*, 183–98. Soziale Welt 2. Göttingen: Schwartz, 1983.
Brandenburger, Egon. *Die Verborgenheit Gottes im Weltgeschehen: das literarische und theologische Problem des 4. Esrabuches*. ATANT 68. Zürich: Theologischer Verlag, 1981.
Breytenbach, Cilliers. *Paulus und Barnabas in der Provinz Galatien: Studien zu Apostelgeschichte 13f: 16,6: 18,23 und den Adressaten des Galaterbriefes*. AGJU 38. Leiden: Brill, 1996.
Brock, Sebastian P. "Abraham and the Ravens: A Syriac Counterpart to Jubilees 11–12 and Its Implications." *JSJ* 9, no. 2 (1978) 135–52.
Brooke, George J. "The Kittim in the Qumran Pesharim." In *Images of Empire*, edited by Loveday Alexander, 135–59. JSOTSup 122. Sheffield: Sheffield Academic Press, 1991.
———. "Text, Timing, and Terror: Thematic Thoughts on the *War Scroll* in Conversation with the Writings of Martin G. Abegg, Jr." In *The War Scroll, Violence, War and Peace in the Dead Sea Scrolls and Related Literature: Essays in Honour of Martin G. Abegg on the Occasion of His 65th Birthday*, edited by Kipp Davis et al., 49–66. STDJ 115. Leiden: Brill, 2016.
Bruce, F. F. *The Book of the Acts*. NICNT. Grand Rapids: Eerdmans, 1988.
———. *The Epistle to the Galatians*. NIGTC. Grand Rapids: Eerdmans, 1982.
Brueggemann, Walter. "Bounded by Obedience and Praise: The Psalms as Canon." *JSOT* 16, no. 50 (1991) 63–92.
———. *Isaiah 40–66*. Westminster Bible Companion. Louisville: Westminster John Knox, 1998.
Brueggemann, Walter, and William H. Bellinger Jr. *Psalms*. NCBC. Cambridge: Cambridge University Press, 2014.
Buber, Martin. *Kampf um Israel: Reden und Schriften*. Berlin: Schocken Verlag, 1933.
Bullock, C. Hassell. "Double-Tracking in the Psalms, Book 5, as a Hermeneutical Method." *JETS* 60, no. 3 (2017) 479–88.
Bultmann, Rudolf. *Theology of the New Testament*. Translated by Kendrick Grobel. Waco, TX: Baylor, 2007.

Bundrick, David R. "Ta Stoicheia Tou Kosmou (Gal 4:3)." *JETS* 34, no. 3 (1991) 353–64.
Burk, Denny. "Is Paul's Gospel Counterimperial? Evaluating the Prospects of the 'Fresh Perspective' for Evangelical Theology." *JETS* 51, no. 2 (2008) 309–37.
Burkes, Shannon. "'Life' Redefined: Wisdom and Law in Fourth Ezra and *Second Baruch*." *CBQ* 63, no. 1 (2001) 55–71.
Burton, Ernest DeWitt. *The Epistle to the Galatians*. ICC. Edinburgh: T. & T. Clark, 1980.
Butticaz, Simon. "Vers une Anthropologie Universelle? La Crise Galate: Fragile Gestion de l'ethnicité Juive." *NTS* 61, no. 4 (2015) 505–24.
Callaway, Mary. *Sing, O Barren One: A Study in Comparative Midrash*. SBLDS 91. Atlanta: Scholars, 1986.
Calvin, John. *Commentaries on the Epistles of Paul to the Galatians and Ephesians*. Translated by William Pringle. Calvin's Commentaries. Edinburgh: Calvin Translation Society, 1854.
Campbell, Douglas A. *The Deliverance of God: An Apocalyptic Rereading of Justification in Paul*. Grand Rapids: Eerdmans, 2009.
———. "Galatians 5.11: Evidence of an Early Law-Observant Mission by Paul?" *NTS* 57, no. 3 (2011) 325–47.
Campbell, Jonathan G. "Essene-Qumran Origins in the Exile: A Scriptural Basis?" *JJS* 46, no. 1–2 (1995) 143–56.
———. *The Use of Scripture in the Damascus Document 1–8, 19–20*. BZAW 228. Berlin: De Gruyter, 1995.
Caneday, Ardel B. "Covenant Lineage Allegorically Prefigured: 'Which Things Are Written Allegorically' (Galatians 4:21–31)." *SBJT* 14, no. 3 (2010) 50–77.
Carmignac, Jean. *La Règle de la Guerre des Fils de Lumière contre les Fils de Ténèbres*. Autour de la Bible. Paris: Letouzey et Ané, 1958.
Carr, David M. *Writing on the Tablet of the Heart: Origins of Scripture and Literature*. Oxford: Oxford University Press, 2005.
Carson, D. A. "Mystery and Fulfillment: Toward a More Comprehensive Paradigm of Paul's Understanding of the Old and the New." In *Justification and Variegated Nomism*, edited by D. A. Carson et al., 2:393–436. Grand Rapids: Baker, 2001.
Charlesworth, James H. "4 Ezra and 2 Baruch: Archaeology and Elusive Answers to Our Perennial Questions." In *Interpreting 4 Ezra and 2 Baruch: International Studies*, edited by Gabriele Boccaccini and Jason M. Zurawski, 155–72. LSTS 87. London: T. & T. Clark, 2014.
Charlesworth, James H., ed. *The Old Testament Pseudepigrapha*. 2 vols. Garden City, NY: Doubleday, 1983.
Chase, Mitchell Loyd. "Resurrection Hope in Daniel 12:2: An Exercise in Biblical Theology." PhD diss., The Southern Baptist Theological Seminary, 2013.
Childs, Brevard S. *Introduction to the Old Testament as Scripture*. Philadelphia: Fortress, 1979.
———. *Isaiah*. OTL. Louisville: Westminster John Knox, 2001.
Ciampa, Roy E. *The Presence and Function of Scripture in Galatians 1 and 2*. WUNT 2.102. Tübingen: Mohr Siebeck, 1998.
———. Review of *She Must and Shall Go Free: Paul's Isaianic Gospel in Galatians* by Matthew S. Harmon. *JETS* 55, no. 1 (2012) 199–202.
Coats, George W. *Genesis with an Introduction to Narrative Literature*. FOTL 1. Grand Rapids: Eerdmans, 1983.

Cobb, Donald. "EKKΛEIΩ en Galates 4,17: Exclure de L'alliance?" *RB* 123, no. 4 (2016) 567–85.
Cody, Aelred. "When Is the Chosen People Called a *Gôy*?" *VT* 14, no. 1 (1964) 1–6.
Coggins, R. J., and Michael A. Knibb. *The First and Second Books of Esdras*. CBC. Cambridge: Cambridge University Press, 1979.
Cohen, Norman J. "Two That Are One: Sibling Rivalry in Genesis." *Judaism* 32, no. 3 (1983) 331–42.
Collins, Adela Yarbro. "Introduction: Early Christian Apocalypticism." *Semeia* 36 (1986) 1–11.
Collins, John J. *The Apocalyptic Imagination: An Introduction to the Jewish Matrix of Christianity*. The Biblical Resource Series. Grand Rapids: Eerdmans, 1998.
———. *Apocalypticism in the Dead Sea Scrolls*. Literature of the Dead Sea Scrolls. London: Routledge, 2002.
———. *The Apocalyptic Vision of the Book of Daniel*. HSM 16. Missoula, MT: Scholars, 1977.
———. *Daniel with an Introduction to Apocalyptic Literature*. FOTL 20. Grand Rapids: Eerdmans, 1984.
———. *The Dead Sea Scrolls: A Biography*. Princeton: Princeton University Press, 2013.
———. "Introduction: Towards the Morphology of a Genre." *Semeia* 14 (1979) 1–20.
———, ed. *The Oxford Handbook of Apocalyptic Literature*. Oxford: Oxford University Press, 2014.
———. *Seers, Sibyls, and Sages in Hellenistic-Roman Judaism*. Leiden: Brill, 2001.
Cook, Stephen L. *Prophecy and Apocalypticism: The Postexilic Social Setting*. Minneapolis: Fortress, 1995.
Cosgrove, Charles H. *The Cross and the Spirit: A Study in the Argument and Theology of Galatians*. Macon, GA: Mercer University Press, 1988.
Cousar, Charles B. *Galatians*. Interpretation. Atlanta: John Knox, 1982.
Craigie, Peter C. *Psalms 1–50*. WBC. Waco, TX: Word, 1983.
Crawford, Cory D. "On the Exegetical Function of the Abraham/Ravens Tradition in *Jubilees* 11." *HTR* 97, no. 1 (2004) 91–97.
Cross, Frank Moore. *The Ancient Library of Qumran*. Garden City, NY: Doubleday, 1961.
———. *Canaanite Myth and Hebrew Epic: Essays in the History of the Religion of Israel*. Cambridge, MA: Harvard University Press, 1973.
———. "The Divine Warrior in Israel's Early Cult." In *Biblical Motifs: Origins and Transformations*, edited by Alexander Altmann, 11–30. Cambridge, MA: Harvard University Press, 1966.
———. "New Directions in the Study of Apocalyptic." *JTC* 6 (1969) 157–65.
Dahood, Mitchell J. *Psalms 1–50*. AB 16. Garden City, NY: Doubleday, 1966.
Das, A. Andrew. *Galatians*. Concordia Commentary. St. Louis: Concordia, 2014.
———. *Paul and the Stories of Israel: Grand Thematic Narratives in Galatians*. Minneapolis: Fortress, 2016.
———. *Solving the Romans Debate*. Minneapolis: Fortress, 2007.
Davenport, Gene L. *The Eschatology of the Book of Jubilees*. Studia Post-Biblica 20. Leiden: Brill, 1971.
Davidson, Richard M. *Typology in Scripture: A Study of Hermeneutical ΤΥΠΟΣ Structures*. Berrien Springs, MI: Andrews University Press, 1981.

Davies, J. P. *Paul among the Apocalypses? An Evaluation of the "Apocalyptic Paul" in the Context of Jewish and Christian Apocalyptic Literature*. LNTS 562. London: T. & T. Clark, 2016.
Davies, Philip R. "And Enoch Was Not, For Genesis Took Him." In *Biblical Traditions in Transmission: Essays in Honour of Michael A. Knibb*, edited by Charlotte Hempel and Judith M. Lieu, 97–107. JSJSup 111. Leiden: Brill, 2006.
———. *The Damascus Covenant: An Interpretation of the "Damascus Document."* JSOTSup 25. Sheffield: JSOT 1983.
Davis, Anne. "Allegorically Speaking in Galatians 4:21–5:1." *BBR* 14, no. 2 (2004) 161–74.
Davis, Basil S. *Christ as Devotio: The Argument of Galatians 3:1–14*. Lanham, MD: University Press of America, 2002.
———. "The Meaning of ΠΡΟΕΓΡΑΦΗ in the Context of Galatians 3.1." *NTS* 45, no. 2 (1999) 194–212.
De Boer, Martinus C. "Apocalyptic as God's Eschatological Activity in Paul's Theology." In *Paul and the Apocalyptic Imagination*, edited by Ben C. Blackwell et al., 45–63. Minneapolis: Fortress, 2016.
———. *The Defeat of Death: Apocalyptic Eschatology in 1 Corinthians 15 and Romans 5*. JSNTSup 22. Sheffield: JSOT 1988.
———. *Galatians*. NTL. Louisville: Westminster John Knox, 2011.
———. "The Meaning of the Phrase Τὰ Στοιχεῖα Τοῦ Κόσμου in Galatians." *NTS* 53, no. 2 (2007) 204–24.
———. "Paul and Jewish Apocalyptic Eschatology." In *Apocalyptic and the New Testament: Essays in Honor of J. Louis Martyn*, edited by Joel Marcus and Marion L. Soards, 169–90. JSNTSup 24. Sheffield: Sheffield Academic Press, 1989.
DeClaissé-Walford, Nancy L. "The Meta-Narrative of the Psalter." In *The Oxford Handbook of the Psalms*, edited by William P. Brown, 363–76. Oxford: Oxford University Press, 2014.
Delitzsch, Franz. *Psalms*. Translated by Francis Bolton. Peabody, MA: Hendrickson, 1996.
Dempster, Stephen G. *Dominion and Dynasty: A Theology of the Hebrew Bible*. NSBT. Downers Grove IL: InterVarsity, 2003.
———. "The Servant of the Lord." In *Central Themes in Biblical Theology: Mapping Unity in Diversity*, edited by Scott J. Hafemann and Paul R. House, 128–78. Grand Rapids: Baker Academic, 2007.
DeRouchie, Jason S. "The Blessing-Commission, the Promised Offspring, and the *Toledot* Structure of Genesis." *JETS* 56, no. 2 (2013) 219–47.
deSilva, David A. "The Author of 4 Maccabees and Greco-Roman Paideia: Facets of the Formation of a Hellenistic Jewish Rhetor." *BBR* 26, no. 4 (2016) 501–31.
———. *4 Maccabees: Introduction and Commentary on the Greek Text in Codex Sinaiticus*. Septuagint Commentary. Leiden: Brill, 2006.
———. *Galatians: A Handbook on the Greek Text*. BHGNT. Waco, TX: Baylor University Press, 2014.
———. "The Human Ideal, the Problem of Evil, and Moral Responsibility in 4 Maccabees." *BBR* 23, no. 1 (2013) 57–77.
———. *Introducing the Apocrypha: Message, Context, and Significance*. Grand Rapids: Baker Academic, 2002.
———. *The Letter to the Galatians*. NICNT. Grand Rapids: Eerdmans, 2018.

———. "Using the Master's Tools to Shore Up Another's House: A Postcolonial Analysis of 4 Maccabees." *JBL* 126, no. 1 (2007) 99–127.

De Vos, J. Cornelis. "Jerusalem: Why on Earth Is It in Heaven? A Comparison of Galatians 4:21–31 and 2 Baruch 4:1–7." In *Exploring the Narrative: Jerusalem and Jordan in the Bronze and Iron Ages*, edited by E. J. van der Steen et al., 326–37. New York: Continuum, 2014.

Dexinger, Ferdinand. *Henochs Zehnwochenapokalypse und offene Probleme der Apokalyptikforschung*. Studia Post-Biblica 29. Leiden: Brill, 1977.

DiMattei, Steven. "Paul's Allegory of the Two Covenants (Gal 4.21–31) in Light of First-Century Hellenistic Rhetoric and Jewish Hermeneutics." *NTS* 52, no. 1 (2006) 102–22.

Dinkler, Erich. "Jesu Wort Vom Kreuztragen." In *Neutestamentliche Studien für Rudolf Bultmann zu Seinem 70*, edited by Walther Eltester, 110–29. BZNW 21. Berlin: Töpelmann, 1957.

Docherty, Susan. *The Jewish Pseudepigrapha: An Introduction to the Literature of the Second Temple Period*. Minneapolis: Fortress, 2015.

Dommershausen, Werner. *1 Makkabäer; 2 Makkabäer*. NEchtB. Würzburg: Echter-Verlag, 1995.

Donaldson, Terence L. "The 'Curse of the Law' and the Inclusion of the Gentiles: Galatians 3:13–14." *NTS* 32 (1986) 94–112.

———. *Judaism and the Gentiles: Jewish Patterns of Universalism (to 135 CE)*. Waco, TX: Baylor University Press, 2007.

———. "Zealot and Convert: The Origin of Paul's Christ-Torah Antithesis." *CBQ* 51, no. 4 (1989) 655–82.

Doran, Robert. *2 Maccabees*. Hermeneia. Minneapolis: Fortress, 2012.

Dow, Lois K. Fuller. *Images of Zion: Biblical Antecedents for the New Jerusalem*. New Testament Monographs 26. Sheffield: Sheffield Phoenix, 2010.

Drawnel, Henryk. "The Mesopotamian Background of the Enochic Giants and Evil Spirits." *DSD* 21 (2014) 14–38.

Duchesne-Guillemin, Jacques. "Le Zervanisme et Les Manuscrits De La Mer Morte." *Indo-Iranian Journal* 1, no. 1 (1957) 96–99.

Duhaime, Jean. "La Règle de La Guerre de Qumrân et l'apocalyptique." *ScEs* 36, no. 1 (1984) 67–88.

———. "The War Scroll from Qumran and the Greco-Roman Tactical Treatises." *RevQ* 13 (1988) 133–51.

———. *The War Texts: 1QM and Related Manuscripts*. New York; London: T. & T. Clark, 2004.

Dumbrell, William J. *The Faith of Israel: A Theological Survey of the Old Testament*. Grand Rapids: Baker Academic, 2002.

———. "The Role of the Servant in Isaiah 40–55." *RTR* 48, no. 3 (1989) 105–13.

Duncan, George Simpson. *The Epistle of Paul to the Galatians*. MNTC. New York: Harper, 1934.

Dunne, John Anthony. "Cast Out the Aggressive Agitators (Gl 4:29–30) Suffering, Identity, and the Ethics of Expulsion in Paul's Mission to the Galatians." In *Sensitivity to Outsiders: Exploring the Dynamic Relationship between Mission and Ethics in the New Testament and Early Christianity*, edited by Jacobus Kok et al., 246–69. WUNT 2.364. Tübingen: Mohr Siebeck, 2013.

———. *Persecution and Participation in Galatians*. WUNT 2.454. Tübingen: Mohr Siebeck, 2017.
———. "Suffering and Covenantal Hope in Galatians: A Critique of the 'Apocalyptic Reading' and Its Proponents." *SJT* 68, no. 1 (2015) 1–15.
———. "Suffering in Vain: A Study of the Interpretation of ΠΑΣΧΩ in Galatians 3.4." *JSNT* 36, no. 1 (2013) 3–16.
Dunn, James D. G. *Beginning from Jerusalem. Christianity in the Making 2*. Grand Rapids: Eerdmans, 2009.
———. *The Epistle to the Galatians*. Black's New Testament Commentary. Peabody, MA: Hendrickson, 1993.
———. "The Incident at Antioch (Gal 2:11–18)." *JSNT* 18 (1983) 3–57.
———. *The New Perspective on Paul*. Grand Rapids: Eerdmans, 2008.
Dupont-Sommer, André. *Les écrits esséniens découverts près de la mer Morte*. Paris: Payot, 1980.
———. "Le problème des influences étrangères sur la secte juive de Qoumrân." *RHPR* 35, no. 1 (1955) 75–92.
———. *Le Quatrième livre des Machabées*. BEHEH 274. Paris: Champion, 1939.
Eastman, Susan G. "'Cast Out the Slave Woman and Her Son': The Dynamics of Exclusion and Inclusion in Galatians 4.30." *JSNT* 28, no. 3 (2006) 309–36.
———. "The Evil Eye and the Curse of the Law: Galatians 3.1 Revisited." *JSNT* 83 (2001) 69–87.
———. "Israel and the Mercy of God: A Re-Reading of Galatians 6.16 and Romans 9–11." *NTS* 56, no. 3 (2010) 367–95.
———. *Recovering Paul's Mother Tongue: Language and Theology in Galatians*. Grand Rapids: Eerdmans, 2007.
Eaton, John H. *Psalms of the Way and the Kingdom: A Conference with the Commentators*. JSOTSup 199. Sheffield: Sheffield Academic Press, 1995.
Eidevall, Göran. *Prophecy and Propaganda: Images of Enemies in the Book of Isaiah*. ConBOT 56. Winona Lake, IN: Eisenbrauns, 2009.
Elliott, Susan. "Choose Your Mother, Choose Your Master: Galatians 4:21–5:1 in the Shadow of the Anatolian Mother of the Gods." *JBL* 118, no. 4 (1999) 661–83.
———. *Cutting Too Close for Comfort: Paul's Letter to the Galatians in Its Anatolian Cultic Context*. JSNTSup 248. London: T. & T. Clark, 2003.
Elman, Yaakov. "Zoroastrianism and Qumran." In *Dead Sea Scrolls at 60: Scholarly Contributions of New York University Faculty and Alumni*, edited by Lawrence H. Schiffman and Shani Tzoref, 91–98. STDJ 89. Leiden: Brill, 2010.
Emadi, Samuel Cyrus. "Covenant, Typology, and the Story of Joseph: A Literary-Canonical Examination of Genesis 37–50." PhD diss., The Southern Baptist Theological Seminary, 2016.
Endres, John C. "Eschatological Impulses in Jubilees." In *Enoch and the Mosaic Torah: The Evidence of Jubilees*, edited by Gabriele Boccaccini and Giovanni Ibba, 323–37. Grand Rapids: Eerdmans, 2009.
Englard, Yaffa. "Ishmael Playing? Exegetical Understandings and Artistic Representations of the Verb Meṣaḥēq in Genesis 21.9." *Biblical Reception* 2 (2013) 16–35.
Epp, Eldon Jay. "Paul's Diverse Imageries of the Human Situation and His Unifying Theme of Freedom." In *Unity and Diversity in New Testament Theology: Essays in*

Honor of George E Ladd, edited by Robert A. Guelich, 100–116. Grand Rapids: Eerdmans, 1978.

Eshel, Hanan. "The Kittim in the *War Scroll* and in the Pesharim." In *Historical Perspectives: From the Hasmoneans to Bar Kokhba in Light of the Dead Sea Scrolls*, edited by David M. Goodblatt et al., 29–44. STDJ 37. Leiden: Brill, 2001.

Esler, Philip Francis. *Galatians*. New Testament Readings. London: Routledge, 1998.

Everson, A. Joseph. "The Canonical Location of Habakkuk." In *Thematic Threads in the Book of the Twelve*, edited by Paul L. Redditt and Aaron Schart, 165–74. BZAW 325. Berlin: De Gruyter, 2003.

Fairchild, Mark R. "Paul's Pre-Christian Zealot Associations: A Re-Examination of Gal 1.14 and Acts 22.3." *NTS* 45, no. 4 (1999) 514–32.

Farmer, William R. *Maccabees, Zealots, and Josephus: An Inquiry into Jewish Nationalism in the Greco-Roman Period*. New York: Columbia University Press, 1956.

Fast, Henry. "The Pauline Concept of Cosmic Conflict." MA thesis, Wheaton College, 1961.

Fee, Gordon D. *God's Empowering Presence: The Holy Spirit in the Letters of Paul*. Peabody, MA: Hendrickson, 1994.

Fishbane, Michael A. "Composition and Structure in the Jacob Cycle (Gen 25:19–35:22)." *JJS* 26 (1975) 15–38.

Fishwick, Duncan. *The Imperial Cult in the Latin West: Studies in the Ruler Cult of the Western Provinces of the Roman Empire*. Vol. 2.1. Études Préliminaires aux Religions Orientales dans L'Empire Romain 108. Leiden: Brill, 1991.

Flusser, David. *Qumran and Apocalypticism*. Translated by Azzan Yadin. Vol. 1. Judaism of the Second Temple Period. Grand Rapids: Eerdmans, 2007.

Forsyth, Dan W. "Sibling Rivalry, Aesthetic Sensibility, and Social Structures in Genesis." *Ethos* 19, no. 4 (1991) 453–510.

Foulkes, Francis. "The Acts of God: A Study of the Basis of Typology in the Old Testament." In *The Right Doctrine from the Wrong Texts? Essays on the Use of the Old Testament in the New*, edited by G. K. Beale, 342–71. Grand Rapids: Baker, 1994.

Fowler, John M. *Kampf im Kosmos*. Hamburg: Gemeinschaft der Siebenten-Tags-Adventisten, 2002.

France, R. T. *Jesus and the Old Testament: His Application of Old Testament Passages to Himself and His Mission*. Downers Grove, IL: InterVarsity, 1971.

Freedman, David Noel. *Psalm 119: The Exaltation of Torah*. Biblical and Judaic Studies 6. Winona Lake, IN: Eisenbrauns, 1999.

Freedman, David Noel, and Jeffrey C. Geoghegan. "Another Stab at the Wicked Priest." In *The Bible and the Dead Sea Scrolls: The Second Princeton Symposium on Judaism and Christian Origins*, edited by James H. Charlesworth, 2:17–24. Waco, TX: Baylor University Press, 2006.

Frei, Hans W. *The Eclipse of Biblical Narrative: A Study in Eighteenth and Nineteenth Century Hermeneutics*. New Haven: Yale, 1974.

Frend, W. H. C. *Martyrdom and Persecution in the Early Church: A Study of Conflict from the Maccabees to Donatus*. Oxford: Blackwell, 1965.

Frye, Richard N. "Qumran and Iran: The State of Studies." In *Christianity, Judaism and Other Greco-Roman Cults: Studies for Morton Smith at Sixty*, edited by Jacob Neusner, 167–73. SJLA 12. Leiden: Brill, 1975.

Fung, Ronald Y. K. *The Epistle to the Galatians*. NICNT. Grand Rapids: Eerdmans, 1988.

Furnish, Victor Paul. *II Corinthians*. AB 32A. Garden City, NY: Doubleday, 1984.
Gammie, John G. "Spatial and Ethical Dualism in Jewish Wisdom and Apocalyptic Literature." *JBL* 93, no. 3 (1974) 356–85.
García Martínez, Florentino. "Qumran Origins and Early History: A Groningen Hypothesis." *FO* 25 (1988) 113–36.
García Martínez, Florentino, and Adam S. van der Woude. "A 'Groningen' Hypothesis of Qumran Origins and Early History." *RevQ* 14, no. 4 (1990) 521–41.
Garlington, Don B. "Paul's 'Partisan'Ἐκ' and the Question of Justification in Galatians." *JBL* 127, no. 3 (2008) 567–89.
Garrett, Duane A. *Rethinking Genesis: The Sources and Authorship of the First Book of the Pentateuch*. Grand Rapids: Baker, 1991.
Gaventa, Beverly Roberts. *From Darkness to Light: Aspects of Conversion in the New Testament*. OBT 20. Philadelphia: Fortress, 1986.
———. "Galatians 1 and 2: Autobiography as Paradigm." *NovT* 28, no. 4 (1986) 309–26.
———. "The Maternity of Paul: An Exegetical Study of Galatians 4:19." In *The Conversation Continues: Studies in Paul & John in Honor of J. Louis Martyn*, edited by Robert T. Fortna and Beverly Roberts Gaventa, 189–201. Nashville: Abingdon, 1990.
———. *Our Mother Saint Paul*. Louisville: Westminster John Knox, 2007.
———. "The Singularity of the Gospel Revisited." In *Galatians and Christian Theology: Justification, the Gospel, and Ethics in Paul's Letter*, edited by Mark W. Elliott et al., 187–99. Grand Rapids: Baker Academic, 2014.
Gentry, Peter J. "The Literary Macrostructures of the Book of Isaiah and Authorial Intent." In *Bind Up the Testimony: Explorations in the Genesis of the Book of Isaiah*, edited by Daniel I. Block and Richard L. Schultz, 227–54. Peabody, MA: Hendrickson, 2015.
Gentry, Peter J., and Stephen J. Wellum. *Kingdom through Covenant: A Biblical-Theological Understanding of the Covenants*. Wheaton, IL: Crossway, 2012.
George, Timothy. *Galatians*. NAC. Nashville: Broadman & Holman, 1994.
Gillingham, Susan. *A Journey of Two Psalms: The Reception of Psalms 1 and 2 in Jewish and Christian Tradition*. Oxford: Oxford University Press, 2013.
Goddard, A. J., and Stephen Anthony Cummins. "Ill or Ill-Treated? Conflict and Persecution as the Context of Paul's Original Ministry in Galatia (Galatians 4.12–20)." *JSNT* 52 (1993) 93–126.
Goff, Matthew. "Looking for Sapiential Dualism at Qumran." In *Dualism in Qumran*, edited by Géza G. Xeravits, 20–38. LSTS 76. London: T. & T. Clark, 2010.
———. "Warriors, Cannibals and Teachers of Evil: The Sons of the Angels in Genesis, the Book of the Watchers and the Book of Jubilees." *SEÅ* 80 (2015) 79–97.
Goldingay, John. *Daniel*. WBC. Dallas: Word, 1989.
———. *Isaiah 56–66*. ICC. London: Bloomsbury, 2014.
Goldingay, John, and David F. Payne. *Isaiah 40–55*. Vol. 1. ICC. London: T. & T. Clark, 2006.
Goldstein, Jonathan A. *I Maccabees*. AB 41. Garden City, NY: Doubleday, 1976.
———. *II Maccabees*. AB 41A. Garden City, NY: Doubleday, 1983.
Goppelt, Leonhard. *Typos: The Typological Interpretation of the Old Testament in the New*. Translated by D. H. Madvig. Grand Rapids: Eerdmans, 1982.

Gorman, Michael J. "The Apocalyptic New Covenant and the Shape of Life in the Shape according to Galatians." In *Paul and the Apocalyptic Imagination*, edited by Ben C. Blackwell et al., 317–37. Minneapolis: Fortress, 2016.

———. *Becoming the Gospel: Paul, Participation, and Mission*. Grand Rapids: Eerdmans, 2015.

———. *Cruciformity: Paul's Narrative Spirituality of the Cross*. Grand Rapids: Eerdmans, 2001.

———. *Inhabiting the Cruciform God: Kenosis, Justification, and Theosis in Paul's Narrative Soteriology*. Grand Rapids: Eerdmans, 2009.

Grabiner, Steven. *Revelation's Hymns: Commentary on the Cosmic Conflict*. LNTS 511. London: T. & T. Clark, 2015.

Grant, Jamie A. *The King as Exemplar: The Function of Deuteronomy's Kingship Law in the Shaping of the Book of Psalms*. AcBib 17. Atlanta: SBL, 2004.

Gunkel, Hermann. *Genesis*. Translated by Mark E. Biddle. Mercer Library of Biblical Studies. Macon, GA: Mercer University Press, 1997.

———. *Schöpfung und Chaos in Urzeit und Endzeit: eine religionsgeschichtliche Untersuchung über Gen 1 und Ap Joh 12*. Göttingen: Vandenhoeck & Ruprecht, 1895.

Gurtner, Daniel M. "Eschatological Rewards for the Righteous in 2 Baruch." In *Interpreting 4 Ezra and 2 Baruch: International Studies*, edited by Gabriele Boccaccini and Jason M. Zurawski, 107–15. LSTS 87. London: T. & T. Clark, 2014.

Hafemann, Scott J. "'Because of Weakness' (Galatians 4:13): The Role of Suffering in the Mission of Paul." In *The Gospel to the Nations: Perspectives on Paul's Mission*, edited by Peter Bolt and Mark Thompson, 131–46. Downers Grove, IL: InterVarsity, 2000.

———. *Suffering and the Spirit: An Exegetical Study of II Cor. 2:14—3:3 within the Context of the Corinthian Correspondence*. WUNT 2.19. Tübingen: Mohr Siebeck, 1986.

Ha, Hong Pyo. "The Emergence of Proto-Apocalyptic Worldviews in the Neo-Babylonian Period: An Analysis of Selected Passages from Ezekiel and Isaiah 40–55." PhD diss., Drew University, 2009.

Hamilton, James M., Jr. *God's Glory in Salvation through Judgment: A Biblical Theology*. Wheaton, IL: Crossway, 2010.

———. "The Seed of the Woman and the Blessing of Abraham." *TynBul* 58, no. 2 (2007) 253–73.

———. "The Skull Crushing Seed of the Woman: Inner-Biblical Interpretation of Genesis 3:15." *SBJT* 10, no. 2 (2006) 30–54.

———. *Typology—Understanding the Bible's Promise-Shaped Patterns: How Old Testament Expectations Are Fulfilled in Christ*. Grand Rapids: Zondervan Academic, 2022.

———. "Was Joseph a Type of the Messiah? Tracing the Typological Identification between Joseph, David, and Jesus." *SBJT* 12, no. 4 (2008) 52–77.

Hamilton, Victor P. *The Book of Genesis: Chapters 1–17*. NICOT. Grand Rapids: Eerdmans, 1990.

———. *The Book of Genesis: Chapters 18–50*. NICOT. Grand Rapids: Eerdmans, 1995.

Hanneken, Todd Russell. *The Subversion of the Apocalypses in the Book of Jubilees*. EJL 34. Atlanta: Society of Biblical Literature, 2012.

Hansen, G. Walter. "A Paradigm of the Apocalypse: The Gospel in the Light of Epistolary Analysis." In *Gospel in Paul: Studies on Corinthians, Galatians and Romans for*

Richard N Longenecker, edited by L. Ann Jervis and Peter Richardson, 194–209. Sheffield: Sheffield Academic Press, 1994.

Hanson, Paul D. "Apocalypticism." In *The Interpreter's Dictionary of the Bible: Supplementary Volume*, edited by Keith Crim, 29–30. Nashville: Abingdon, 1976.

———. *The Dawn of Apocalyptic: The Historical and Sociological Roots of Jewish Apocalyptic Eschatology*. Philadelphia: Fortress, 1979.

Hardin, Justin K. *Galatians and the Imperial Cult: A Critical Analysis of the First-Century Social Context of Paul's Letter*. WUNT 2.237. Tübingen: Mohr Siebeck, 2008.

Harland, Philip A. *Associations, Synagogues, and Congregations: Claiming a Place in Ancient Mediterranean Society*. Minneapolis: Fortress, 2003.

Harmon, Matthew S. "Allegory, Typology, or Something Else? Revisiting Galatians 4:21—5:1." In *Studies in the Pauline Epistles: Essays in Honor of Douglas J. Moo*, edited by Matthew S. Harmon and Jay E. Smith, 144–58. Grand Rapids: Zondervan, 2014.

———. *She Must and Shall Go Free: Paul's Isaianic Gospel in Galatians*. BZNW 168. Berlin: De Gruyter, 2010.

Harnisch, Wolfgang. *Verhängnis und Verheissung der Geschichte: Untersuchungen zum Zeit- und Geschichtsverständnis im 4. Buch Esra und in der syr. Baruchapokalypse*. Göttingen: Vandenhoeck & Ruprecht, 1969.

Harrill, J. Albert. "Paul and Slavery." In *Paul in the Greco-Roman World: A Handbook*, edited by J. Paul Sampley, 575–607. Harrisburg, PA: Trinity Press International, 2003.

Harrington, Daniel J. *The Maccabean Revolt: Anatomy of a Biblical Revolution*. Wilmington, DE: Michael Glazier, 1988.

Harris, Murray J. *The Second Epistle to the Corinthians*. NIGTC. Grand Rapids: Eerdmans, 2005.

Hartman, Louis Francis, and Alexander A. Di Lella. *The Book of Daniel*. AB 23. Garden City, NY: Doubleday, 1978.

Hays, Richard B. "Apocalyptic *Poiēsis* in Galatians: Paternity, Passion, and Participation." In *Galatians and Christian Theology: Justification, the Gospel, and Ethics in Paul's Letter*, edited by Mark W. Elliott et al., 200–219. Grand Rapids: Baker Academic, 2014.

———. *The Conversion of the Imagination: Paul as Interpreter of Israel's Scripture*. Grand Rapids: Eerdmans, 2005.

———. *Echoes of Scripture in the Letters of Paul*. New Haven: Yale University Press, 1989.

———. *The Faith of Jesus Christ: The Narrative Substructure of Galatians 3:1—4:11*. Grand Rapids: Eerdmans, 2002.

———. "The Letter to the Galatians." In *The New Interpreter's Bible*, edited by Leander E. Keck, 11:181–348. Nashville: Abingdon, 2000.

———. *Reading Backwards: Figural Christology and the Fourfold Gospel Witness*. Waco, TX: Baylor University Press, 2014.

Heger, Paul. "Another Look at Dualism in Qumran Writings." In *Dualism in Qumran*, edited by Géza G. Xeravits, 39–101. LSTS 76. London: T. & T. Clark, 2010.

Hengel, Martin. *The Zealots: Investigations into the Jewish Freedom Movement in the Period from Herod I until 70 AD*. Translated by David Smith. Edinburgh: T. & T. Clark, 1989.

Henten, Jan Willem van. *The Maccabean Martyrs as Saviours of the Jewish People: A Study of 2 and 4 Maccabees*. JSJSup 57. Leiden: Brill, 1997.

Henze, Matthias. "'4 Ezra' and '2 Baruch': Literary Composition and Oral Performance in First-Century Apocalyptic Literature." *JBL* 131, no. 1 (2012) 181–200.

———. *Jewish Apocalypticism in Late First Century Israel: Reading* Second Baruch *in Context*. Texts and Studies in Ancient Judaism 142. Tübingen: Mohr Siebeck, 2011.

Hirsch, Emanuel. "Zwei Fragen zu Galater 6." *ZNW* 29 (1930) 192–97.

Hodges, Frederick M. "The Ideal Prepuce in Ancient Greece and Rome: Male Genital Aesthetics and Their Relation to *Lipodermos*, Circumcision, Foreskin Restoration, and the *Kynodesmē*." *Bulletin of the History of Medicine* 75, no. 3 (2001) 375–405.

Hooker, Morna D. "Interchange and Atonement." *BJRL* 60 (1978) 462–81.

———. "Interchange and Suffering." In *Suffering and Martyrdom in the New Testament: Studies Presented to G. M. Styler by the Cambridge New Testament Seminar*, edited by William Horbury and Brian McNeil, 70–83. Cambridge: Cambridge University Press, 1981.

———. "Interchange in Christ." *JTS* 22, no. 2 (1971) 349–61.

Hopkins, Keith. "Christian Number and Its Implications." *JECS* 6, no. 2 (1998) 185–226.

Hossfeld, Frank-Lothar, and Erich Zenger. *Die Psalmen I: Psalm 1–50*. NEchtB. Würzburg: Echter Verlag, 1993.

———. *Psalms 3: A Commentary on Psalms 101–150*. Translated by Linda M. Maloney. Hermeneia. Minneapolis: Fortress, 2011.

House, Paul R. "The Day of the Lord." In *Central Themes in Biblical Theology: Mapping Unity in Diversity*, edited by Scott J. Hafemann and Paul R. House, 177–224. Grand Rapids: Baker Academic, 2007.

———. "Endings as New Beginnings: Returning to the Lord, the Day of the Lord, and Renewal in the Book of the Twelve." In *Thematic Threads in the Book of the Twelve*, edited by Paul L. Redditt and Aaron Schart, 313–38. BZAW 325. Berlin: De Gruyter, 2003.

———. *The Unity of the Twelve*. JSOTSup 97. Sheffield: Almond, 1990.

Howard, George. *Paul: Crisis in Galatia: A Study in Early Christian Theology*. SNTSMS 35. Cambridge: Cambridge University Press, 1990.

Hubbard, Moyer V. *New Creation in Paul's Letters and Thought*. SNTSMS 119. Cambridge: Cambridge University Press, 2004.

Hubing, Jeff. *Crucifixion and New Creation: The Strategic Purpose of Galatians 6.11–17*. LNTS 508. London: T. & T. Clark, 2015.

Huddleston, Jonathan. *Eschatology in Genesis*. FAT 2.57. Tübingen: Mohr Siebeck, 2012.

Hugenberger, G. P. "The Servant of the Lord in the 'Servant Songs' of Isaiah: A Second Moses Figure." In *The Lord's Anointed: Interpretation of Old Testament Messianic Texts*, edited by P. E. Satterthwaite et al., 105–40. Grand Rapids: Baker, 1995.

Hunn, Debbie. "Pleasing God or Pleasing People? Defending the Gospel in Galatians 1–2." *Biblica* 91, no. 1 (2010) 24–49.

Ibba, Giovanni. *Il "Rotolo Della Guerra" Edizione Critica*. Turin, Italy: Silvio Samorani, 1998.

Iyer, Meena. *Faith and Philosophy of Zoroastrianism*. Indian Religions Series 7. Delhi: Kalpaz, 2009.

Jackson, T. Ryan. *New Creation in Paul's Letters: A Study of the Historical and Social Setting of a Pauline Concept*. WUNT 2.272. Tübingen: Mohr Siebeck, 2010.

Jassen, Alex P. "The Dead Sea Scrolls and Violence: Sectarian Formation and Eschatological Imagination." *BibInt* 17, no. 1–2 (2009) 12–44.

———. "Violent Imaginaries and Practical Violence in the *War Scroll*." In *The War Scroll, Violence, War and Peace in the Dead Sea Scrolls and Related Literature: Essays in Honour of Martin G. Abegg on the Occasion of His 65th Birthday*, edited by Kipp Davis et al., 175–203. STDJ 115. Leiden: Brill, 2016.

Jensen, Joseph. "Yahweh's Plan in Isaiah and in the Rest of the Old Testament." *CBQ* 48, no. 3 (1986) 443–55.

Jeremias, Gert. *Der Lehrer der Gerechtigkeit*. Studien zum Umwelt des Neuen Testaments 2. Göttingen: Vandenhoeck & Ruprecht, 1963.

Jervis, L. Ann. *At the Heart of the Gospel: Suffering in the Earliest Christian Message*. Grand Rapids: Eerdmans, 2007.

———. *Galatians*. NIBC. Peabody, MA: Hendrickson, 1999.

Jewett, Robert. "Agitators and the Galatian Congregation." In *The Galatians Debate: Contemporary Issues in Rhetorical and Historical Interpretation*, edited by Mark D. Nanos, 334–47. Peabody, MA: Hendrickson, 2002.

Jobes, Karen H. "Jerusalem, Our Mother: Metalepsis and Intertextuality in Galatians 4:21–31." *WTJ* 55, no. 2 (1993) 299–320.

John, Felix. *Der Galaterbrief im Kontext historischer Lebenswelten im antiken Kleinasien*. FRLANT 264. Göttingen: Vandenhoeck & Ruprecht, 2016.

Johnson, Marshall D. "The Paralysis of Torah in Habakkuk 1:4." *VT* 35, no. 3 (1985) 257–66.

Jongeling, Bastiaan. *Le rouleau de la guerre des manuscrits de Qumrân*. SSN 4. Assen: Van Gorcum, 1962.

Kahl, Brigitte. *Galatians Reimagined: Reading with the Eyes of the Vanquished*. Minneapolis: Fortress, 2014.

———. "Reading Galatians and Empire at the Great Altar of Pergamon." *USQR* 59 (2005) 21–43.

Kaminski, Carol M. *From Noah to Israel: Realization of the Primaeval Blessing after the Flood*. JSOTSup 413. London: T. & T. Clark, 2004.

Kampen, John. "Wisdom, Poverty, and Non-Violence in *Instruction*." In *The War Scroll, Violence, War and Peace in the Dead Sea Scrolls and Related Literature: Essays in Honour of Martin G. Abegg on the Occasion of His 65th Birthday*, edited by Kipp Davis et al., 215–36. STDJ 115. Leiden: Brill, 2016.

Käsemann, Ernst. "On the Subject of Primitive Christian Apocalyptic." In *New Testament Questions of Today*, 108–37. Philadelphia: Fortress, 1969.

Keener, Craig S. *Acts: An Exegetical Commentary*. Grand Rapids: Baker Academic, 2012.

———. *1–2 Corinthians*. NCBC. Cambridge: Cambridge University Press, 2005.

———. *Galatians: A Commentary*. Grand Rapids: Baker Academic, 2019.

———. *The Mind of the Spirit: Paul's Approach to Transformed Thinking*. Grand Rapids: Baker Academic, 2016.

Keesmaat, Sylvia C. *Paul and His Story: (Re)Interpreting the Exodus Tradition*. JSNTSup 181. Sheffield: Sheffield Academic Press, 1999.

Kelhoffer, James A. *Persecution, Persuasion, and Power: Readiness to Withstand Hardship as a Corroboration of Legitimacy in the New Testament*. WUNT 2.270. Tübingen: Mohr Siebeck, 2010.

Kidner, Derek. *Psalms 1–72*. TOTC. Downers Grove, IL: InterVarsity, 1973.

Kikawada, Isaac M., and Arthur Quinn. *Before Abraham Was: The Unity of Genesis 1–11*. Nashville: Abingdon, 1985.

Kilgallen, John J. "Hostility to Paul in Pisidian Antioch (Acts 13,45)—Why?" *Biblica* 84, no. 1 (2003) 1–15.

Kim, Seyoon. *Christ and Caesar: The Gospel and the Roman Empire in the Writings of Paul and Luke*. Grand Rapids: Eerdmans, 2008.

———. *Paul and the New Perspective: Second Thoughts on The Origin of Paul's Gospel*. Grand Rapids: Eerdmans, 2002.

Kleer, Martin. *Der liebliche Sänger der Psalmen Israels: Untersuchungen zu David als Dichter und Beter der Psalmen*. Bodenheim: Philo, 1996.

Kleinknecht, Karl Theodor. *Der leidende Gerechtfertigte: die alttestamentlich-jüdische Tradition vom ‚leidenden Gerechten' und ihre Rezeption bei Paulus*. WUNT 2.13. Tübingen: Mohr Siebeck, 1984.

Klink, Edward W., and Darian R. Lockett. *Understanding Biblical Theology: A Comparison of Theory and Practice*. Grand Rapids: Zondervan, 2012.

Knibb, Michael A. *Essays on the Book of Enoch and Other Early Jewish Texts and Traditions*. SVTP 22. Leiden: Brill, 2009.

Koch, Klaus. "Esras erste Vision: Weltzeiten und Weg des Höchsten." *BZ* 22, no. 1 (1978) 46–75.

Kohler, Ludwig, et al. *The Hebrew and Aramaic Lexicon of the Old Testament*. Translated and edited under the supervision of Mervyn E. J. Richardson. 4 vols. Leiden: Brill, 1994–99.

Koptak, Paul E. "Rhetorical Identification in Paul's Autobiographical Narrative: Galatians 1:13–2:14." *JSNT* 40 (1990) 97–113.

Kratz, Reinhard Gregor. "Die Tora Davids: Psalm 1 und Die Doxologische Fünfteilung des Psalters." *ZTK* 93, no. 1 (1996) 1–34.

Kugel, James L. *A Walk through Jubilees: Studies in the Book of Jubilees and the World of Its Creation*. JSJSup 156. Leiden: Brill, 2012.

Kuhn, Karl G. "Die Sektenschrift und die iranische Religion." *ZTK* 49, no. 3 (1952) 296–316.

Kwon, Yon-Gyong. *Eschatology in Galatians: Rethinking Paul's Response to the Crisis in Galatia*. WUNT 2.183. Tübingen: Mohr Siebeck, 2004.

La Piana, George. "Foreign Groups in Rome during the First Centuries of the Empire." *HTR* 20, no. 4 (1927) 183–403.

Laato, Antti. "The Chronology in the Damascus Document of Qumran." *RevQ* 15, no. 4 (1992) 605–7.

———. *Who Is the Servant of the Lord? Jewish and Christian Interpretations on Isaiah 53 from Antiquity to the Middle Ages*. Studies in Rewritten Bible 4. Winona Lake, IN: Eisenbrauns, 2012.

LaCocque, André. *Daniel in His Time*. Studies on Personalities in the Old Testament. Columbia, SC: University of South Carolina Press, 1988.

Lambrecht, Jan. "Critical Reflections on Paul's 'Partisan Ἐκ' as Recently Presented by Don Garlington." *ETL* 85, no. 1 (2009) 135–41.

Lampe, G. W. H. "New Testament Doctrine of *Ktisis*." *SJT* 17, no. 4 (1964) 449–62.

Lenglet, Adrien. "La structure littéraire de Daniel 2–7." *Biblica* 53 (1972) 169–90.

Leuenberger, Martin. "Ort und Funktion der Wolkenvision und ihrer Deutung in der syrischen Baruchapokalypse: eine These zu deren thematischer Entfaltung." *JSJ* 36, no. 2 (2005) 206–46.

Levison, John R. "The Two Spirits in Qumran Theology." In *The Bible and the Dead Sea Scrolls: The Second Princeton Symposium on Judaism and Christian Origins*, edited by James H. Charlesworth, 2:169–94. Waco, TX: Baylor University Press, 2006.
Lewis, Charleton T., and Charles Short, eds. *A Latin Dictionary*. Oxford: Clarendon, 1879.
Lichtenberger, Hermann. "Gottes Nähe in einer Zeit ohne Gebet: Zum Geschichtsbild des 2. Makkabäerbuches." In *Gottes Nähe im Alten Testament*, edited by Gönke Eberhardt and Kathrin Liess, 135–49. Stuttgarter Bibel-studien. Stuttgart: Katholisches Bibelwerk, 2004.
Liddell, Henry George, et al. *A Greek-English Lexicon*. 9th ed. Oxford: Clarendon, 1996.
Lied, Liv Ingeborg. "Current Scholarship on Baruch: 2000–2009." *CBR* 9, no. 2 (2011) 238–76.
———. *The Other Lands of Israel: Imaginations of the Land in 2 Baruch*. JSJSup 129. Leiden: Brill, 2008.
Lightfoot, J. B. *The Epistle of St. Paul to the Galatians*. Grand Rapids: Zondervan, 1971.
Lim, Timothy H. "The Wicked Priests of the Groningen Hypothesis." *JBL* 112, no. 3 (1993) 415–25.
Longenecker, Bruce W. "'Until Christ Is Formed in You': Suprahuman Forces and Moral Character in Galatians." *CBQ* 61, no. 1 (1999) 92–108.
Longenecker, Richard N. *Biblical Exegesis in the Apostolic Period*. Grand Rapids: Eerdmans, 1999.
———. *Galatians*. WBC. Dallas: Word, 1990.
———. *New Testament Social Ethics for Today*. Grand Rapids: Eerdmans, 1984.
———. *New Wine into Fresh Wineskins: Contextualizing the Early Christian Confessions*. Peabody, MA: Hendrickson, 1999.
———. *Paul, Apostle of Liberty*. Grand Rapids: Eerdmans, 2015.
———. "'Who Is the Prophet Talking About?' Some Reflections on the New Testament Use of the Old." In *The Right Doctrine from the Wrong Texts? Essays on the Use of the Old Testament in the New*, edited by G. K. Beale, 375–86. Grand Rapids: Baker, 1994.
Lopez, Davina C. *Apostle to the Conquered: Reimagining Paul's Mission*. Paul in Critical Contexts. Minneapolis: Fortress, 2008.
Louw, Johannes P., and Eugene A. Nida, eds. *Greek-English Lexicon of the New Testament: Based on Semantic Domains*. 2nd ed. New York: United Bible Societies, 1989.
Lucas, Ernest C. *Daniel*. ApOTC. Downers Grove, IL: InterVarsity, 2002.
Lust, Johan, et al., eds. *Greek-English Lexicon of the Septuagint*. Rev. ed. Stuttgart: Deutsche Bibelgesellschaft, 2003
Luther, Martin. "The Freedom of a Christian." In *Luther's Works*, vol. 31, translated by Jaroslav Pelikan, 327–77. Philadelphia: Fortress, 1957.
———. *Luther's Works*. Vol. 26, *Lectures on Galatians (1535) Chapters 1–4*. Translated by Jaroslav Pelikan. Philadelphia: Fortress, 1963.
———. "On the Councils of the Church." In *Luther's Works*, vol. 41, translated by Jaroslav Pelikan, 149–64. Philadelphia: Fortress, 1966.
Lyons, George. *Pauline Autobiography: Toward a New Understanding*. SBLDS 73. Chico, CA: Scholars, 1986.
Mackey, Jason Alan. "The Light Overcomes the Darkness: Cosmic Conflict in the Fourth Gospel." PhD diss., The Southern Baptist Theological Seminary, 2014.

Magyarosi, Barna. *Holy War and Cosmic Conflict in the Old Testament: From the Exodus to the Exile*. Adventist Theological Society Dissertation Series 9. Berrien Springs, MI: Adventist Theological Society, 2010.

Malan, F. S. "The Strategy of Two Opposing Covenants: Galatians 4:21—5:1." *Neot* 26, no. 2 (1992) 425–40.

Marshall, I. Howard. *Acts*. TNTC. Downers Grove, IL: IVP Academic, 2008.

Martin, Troy W. "Apostasy to Paganism: The Rhetorical Stasis of the Galatian Controversy." *JBL* 114, no. 3 (1995) 437–61.

———. "Pagan and Judeo-Christian Time-Keeping Schemes in Gal 4.10 and Col 2.16." *NTS* 42, no. 1 (1996) 105–19.

———. "Whose Flesh? What Temptation? (Galatians 4.13–14)." *JSNT* 74 (1999) 65–91.

Martyn, J. Louis. "Apocalyptic Antinomies in Paul's Letter to the Galatians." *NTS* 31, no. 3 (1985) 410–24.

———. "The Apocalyptic Gospel in Galatians." *Int* 54, no. 3 (2000) 246–66.

———. "Christ, the Elements of the Cosmos, and the Law in Galatians." In *The Social World of the First Christians: Essays in Honor of Wayne A. Meeks*, edited by L. Michael White and O. Larry Yarbrough, 16–39. Minneapolis: Fortress, 1995.

———. "The Daily Life of the Church in the War between the Spirit and the Flesh." In *Theological Issues in the Letters of Paul*, 251–66. Nashville: Abingdon, 1997.

———. "Epistemology at the Turn of the Ages." In *Theological Issues in the Letters of Paul*, 89–110. Nashville: Abingdon, 1997.

———. *Galatians*. AB 33A. New York: Doubleday, 1997.

———. "God's Way of Making Right What Is Wrong." In *Theological Issues in the Letters of Paul*, 141–56. Nashville: Abingdon, 1997.

———. "A Law-Observant Mission to Gentiles." In *The Galatians Debate: Contemporary Issues in Rhetorical and Historical Interpretation*, edited by Mark D. Nanos, 348–61. Peabody, MA: Hendrickson, 2002.

———. "A Law-Observant Mission to Gentiles: The Background of Galatians." *SJT* 38, no. 3 (1985) 307–24.

Mason, Steve. "Jews, Judaeans, Judaizing, Judaism: Problems of Categorization in Ancient History." *JSJ* 38 (2007) 457–512.

Matera, Frank J. *Galatians*. Sacra Pagina. Collegeville, MN: Liturgical, 1992.

———. *2 Corinthians*. NTL. Louisville: Westminster John Knox, 2003.

McCann, J. Clinton. "The Shape and Shaping of the Psalter: Psalms in Their Literary Context." In *The Oxford Handbook of the Psalms*, edited by William P. Brown, 350–62. Oxford: Oxford University Press, 2014.

McKenzie, John L. *Second Isaiah*. AB 20. Garden City, NY: Doubleday, 1968.

McKnight, Scot. *Galatians*. NIVAC. Grand Rapids: Zondervan, 1995.

———. "I Am Church: Ecclesial Identity and the Apostle Paul." *The Covenant Quarterly* 72, no. 3–4 (2014) 217–32.

Meeks, Wayne A. "'And Rose up to Play': Midrash and Paraenesis in 1 Corinthians 10:1–22." *JSNT* 16 (1982) 64–78.

Michaelis, Wilhelm. "πάσχω." In *TDNT*, translated by Geoffrey W. Bromiley, 5:904–38. Grand Rapids: Eerdmans, 1964–76.

Michaud, Henri. "Un mythe Zervanite dans un des manuscrits de Qumrân." *VT* 5, no. 2 (1955) 137–47.

Middleton, Paul. "'Dying We Live' (2 Cor. 6.9): Discipleship and Martyrdom in Paul." In *Paul, Grace and Freedom: Essays in Honour of John K. Riches*, edited by Paul Middleton et al., 82–93. T. & T. Clark Biblical Studies. London: T. & T. Clark, 2009.

———. *Radical Martyrdom and Cosmic Conflict in Early Christianity*. LNTS 307. London: T. & T. Clark, 2006.

Milik, Jozef T. *Ten Years of Discovery in the Wilderness of Judaea*. Translated by John Strugnell. SBT 26. London: SCM, 1959.

Millay, Thomas J. "Septuagint *Figura*: Assessing the Contribution of Richard B. Hays." *SJT* 70, no. 1 (2017) 93–104.

Miller, Patrick D. "The Beginning of the Psalter." In *The Shape and Shaping of the Psalter*, edited by J. Clinton McCann, 84–92. JSOTSup 159. Sheffield: JSOT 1993.

———. "Deuteronomy and Psalms: Evoking a Biblical Conversation." *JBL* 118, no. 1 (1999) 3–18.

———. *The Divine Warrior in Early Israel*. HSM 5. Cambridge, MA: Harvard University Press, 1973.

———. "The End of the Psalter: A Response to Erich Zenger." *JSOT* 80 (1998) 103–10.

———. "Kingship, Torah Obedience and Prayer." In *Neue Wege der Psalmenforschung*, edited by Klaus Seybold and Erich Zenger, 127–42. Freiburg: Herder, 1995.

Mitchell, David C. *The Message of the Psalter: An Eschatological Programme in the Books of Psalms*. JSOTSup 252. Sheffield: Sheffield Academic Press, 1997.

Mitchell, Stephen. *Anatolia: Land, Men, and Gods in Asia Minor*. Vol. 1, *The Celts in Anatolia and the Impact of Roman Rule*. Oxford: Clarendon, 1993.

———. *Anatolia: Land, Men, and Gods in Asia Minor*. Vol. 2, *The Rise of the Church*. Oxford: Clarendon, 1995.

Mitternacht, Dieter. "Foolish Galatians?—A Recipient-Oriented Assessment of Paul's Letter." In *The Galatians Debate: Contemporary Issues in Rhetorical and Historical Interpretation*, edited by Mark D. Nanos, 408–33. Peabody, MA: Hendrickson, 2002.

Moberly, R. W. L. "Christ in All the Scriptures? The Challenge of Reading the Old Testament as Christian Scripture." *JTI* 1 (2007) 79–100.

Moltmann, Jürgen. *Theology of Hope: On the Ground and the Implications of a Christian Eschatology*. Translated by James W. Leitch. New York: Harper & Row, 1967.

Moo, Douglas J. "Creation and New Creation." *BBR* 20, no. 1 (2010) 39–60.

———. *Galatians*. BECNT. Grand Rapids: Baker Academic, 2013.

Moo, Douglas J., and Andrew David Naselli. "The Problem of the New Testament's Use of the Old Testament." In *The Enduring Authority of the Christian Scriptures*, edited by D. A. Carson, 702–46. Grand Rapids: Eerdmans, 2016.

Morland, Kjell Arne. *The Rhetoric of Curse in Galatians: Paul Confronts Another Gospel*. Atlanta: Scholars, 1995.

Moss, Candida R. *Ancient Christian Martyrdom: Diverse Practices, Theologies, and Traditions*. ABRL. New Haven: Yale University Press, 2012.

———. *The Myth of Persecution: How Early Christians Invented a Story of Martyrdom*. New York: HarperOne, 2013.

———. *The Other Christs: Imitating Jesus in Ancient Christian Ideologies of Martyrdom*. Oxford: Oxford University Press, 2010.

Motyer, J. A. *The Prophecy of Isaiah: An Introduction and Commentary*. Downers Grove, IL: InterVarsity, 1993.

Muddiman, John. "An Anatomy of Galatians." In *Crossing the Boundaries: Essays in Biblical Interpretation in Honour of Michael D. Goulder*, edited by Stanley E. Porter et al., 257–70. BibInt 8. Leiden: Brill, 1994.

Munck, Johannes. *Paul and the Salvation of Mankind*. Translated by Frank Clarke. Atlanta: John Knox, 1977.

Murdock, William R. "History and Revelation in Jewish Apocalypticism." *Int* 21, no. 2 (1967) 167–87.

Murphy, Frederick James. "2 Baruch and the Romans." *JBL* 104, no. 4 (1985) 663–69.

———. *The Structure and Meaning of Second Baruch*. SBLDS 78. Atlanta: Scholars, 1985.

———. "The Temple in the Syriac *Apocalypse of Baruch*." *JBL* 106, no. 4 (1987) 671–83.

Murphy-O'Connor, Jerome. "The Essenes and Their History." *RB* 81, no. 2 (1974) 215–44.

Murphy, Rosalyn F. T. "Sista-Hoods: Revealing the Meaning in Hagar's Narrative." *Black Theology* 10, no. 1 (2012) 77–92.

Mußner, Franz. *Der Galaterbrief*. HThKNT. Freiburg: Herder, 1974.

———. *Theologie der Freiheit nach Paulus*. Quaestiones disputatae 75. Freiburg: Herder, 1976.

Myers, Alicia D. "'For It Has Been Written': Paul's Use of Isa 54:1 in Gal 4:27 in Light of Gal 3:1–5:1." *PRSt* 37, no. 3 (2010) 295–308.

Myers, Jacob M. *I and II Esdras*. AB 42. Garden City, NY: Doubleday, 1974.

Nanos, Mark D. *The Irony of Galatians: Paul's Letter in First-Century Context*. Minneapolis: Fortress, 2002.

Newsom, Carol A. *Daniel*. OTL. Louisville: Westminster John Knox, 2014.

Nickelsburg, George W. E. "Enoch, First Book Of." In *ABD*, edited by David Noel Freedman. New York: Doubleday, 1992.

———. *1 Enoch 1: Chapters 1–36, 81–108*. Hermeneia. Minneapolis: Fortress, 2001.

Nickelsburg, George W. E., and James C. VanderKam. *1 Enoch 2: Chapters 37–82*. Hermeneia. Minneapolis: Fortress, 2012.

Nikaido, S. "Hagar and Ishmael as Literary Figures: An Intertextual Study." *VT* 51, no. 2 (2001) 219–42.

Nogalski, James. "Jerusalem, Samaria and Bethel in the Book of the Twelve." In *Die Stadt im Zwölfprophetenbuch*, edited by Aaron Schart and Jutta Krispenz, 251–68. BZAW 428. Berlin: De Gruyter, 2012.

Oakes, Peter. *Galatians*. Paideia. Grand Rapids: Baker Academic, 2015.

Oepke, Albrecht. *Der Brief des Paulus an die Galater*. THKNT. Berlin: Evangelische, 1973.

O'Neal, G. Michael. *Interpreting Habakkuk as Scripture: An Application of the Canonical Approach of Brevard S. Childs*. StBibLit 9. New York: Peter Lang, 2007.

O'Neill, J. C. *The Recovery of Paul's Letter to the Galatians*. London: SPCK, 1972.

Oosting, Reinoud. *The Role of Zion/Jerusalem in Isaiah 40–55: A Corpus-Linguistic Approach*. SSN 59. Leiden: Brill, 2013.

Ortlund, Dane C. "Phinehan Zeal: A Consideration of James Dunn's Proposal." *JSP* 20, no. 4 (2011) 299–315.

———. *Zeal without Knowledge: The Concept of Zeal in Romans 10, Galatians 1, and Philippians 3*. LNTS 472. London: T. & T. Clark, 2012.

Oswalt, John N. *The Bible among the Myths: Unique Revelation or Just Ancient Literature?* Grand Rapids: Zondervan, 2009.

———. *The Book of Isaiah: Chapters 1–39*. NICOT. Grand Rapids: Eerdmans, 1986.
———. *The Book of Isaiah: Chapters 40–66*. NICOT. Grand Rapids: Eerdmans, 1998.
———. "Myth of the Dragon and Old Testament Faith." *EvQ* 49 (1977) 163–72.
———. "Recent Studies in Old Testament Eschatology and Apocalyptic." *JETS* 24, no. 4 (1981) 289–301.
Pagels, Elaine H. "The Social History of Satan, the 'Intimate Enemy': A Preliminary Sketch." *HTR* 84, no. 2 (1991) 105–28.
Parsons, Mikeal C. *Acts*. Paideia. Grand Rapids: Baker Academic, 2008.
Perriman, Andrew C. "The Rhetorical Strategy of Galatians 4:21–5:1." *EvQ* 65 (1993) 27–42.
Petersen, David L. "A Book of the Twelve?" In *Reading and Hearing the Book of the Twelve*, edited by James Nogalski and Marvin A. Sweeney, 3–10. SymS 15. Atlanta: SBL, 2000.
———. "Genesis and Family Values." *JBL* 124, no. 1 (2005) 5–23.
Peterson, David. *The Acts of the Apostles*. PNTC. Grand Rapids: Eerdmans, 2009.
Pfeiffer, Robert H. *History of New Testament Times: With an Introduction to the Apocrypha*. New York: Harper, 1949.
Philolenko, Marc. "La doctrine qoumrânienne des deux Espirits: Ses origines iraniennes et ses prolongements deans le judaïsme essénien et le christianism antique." In *Apocalyptique Iranienne et dualisme Qoumrânien*, edited by Geo Widengren et al., 163–211. Recherches Intertestamentaires 2. Paris: Adrien Maisonneuve, 1995.
Pierce, Ronald W. "Spiritual Failure, Postponement, and Daniel 9." *TJ* 10, no. 2 (1989) 211–22.
Plöger, Otto. *Theocracy and Eschatology*. Oxford: Blackwell, 1968.
Plummer, Robert L. *Paul's Understanding of the Church's Mission: Did the Apostle Paul Expect the Early Christian Communities to Evangelize?* Paternoster Biblical Monographs. Milton Keynes, UK: Paternoster, 2006.
———. "The Role of Suffering in the Mission of Paul and the Mission of the Church." *SBJT* 17, no. 4 (2014) 6–19.
Pobee, John S. *Persecution and Martyrdom in the Theology of Paul*. JSNTSup 6. Sheffield: JSOT 1985.
Porath, Renatus. "Die 'Stadt der Blutschuld'—eine lateinamerikanische Perspektive." In *Die Stadt im Zwölfprophetenbuch*, edited by Aaron Schart and Jutta Krispenz, 327–38. BZAW 428. Berlin: De Gruyter, 2012.
Prokhorov, Alexander V. "Taking the Jews Out of the Equation: Galatians 6.12–17 as a Summons to Cease Evading Persecution." *JSNT* 36, no. 2 (2013) 172–88.
Proudfoot, Merrill. *Suffering: A Christian Understanding*. Philadelphia: Westminster, 1964.
Ramsay, William Mitchell. *St. Paul the Traveller and the Roman Citizen*. London: Hodder & Stoughton, 1910.
Redditt, Paul L. "The Formation of the Book of the Twelve: A Review of Research." In *Thematic Threads in the Book of the Twelve*, edited by Paul L. Redditt and Aaron Schart, 1–26. BZAW 325. Berlin: De Gruyter, 2003.
Reed, Annette Yoshiko. "Enochic and Mosaic Traditions in Jubilees: The Evidence of Angelology and Demonology." In *Enoch and the Mosaic Torah: The Evidence of Jubilees*, edited by Gabriele Boccaccini and Giovanni Ibba, 353–68. Grand Rapids: Eerdmans, 2009.

———. *Fallen Angels and the History of Judaism and Christianity: The Reception of Enochic Literature*. Cambridge: Cambridge University Press, 2005.

Reif, Stefan C. "The Damascus Document from the Cairo Genizah: Its Discovery, Early Study and Historical Significance." In *The Damascus Document: A Centennial of Discovery*, edited by Joseph M. Baumgarten et al., 109–31. STDJ 34. Leiden: Brill, 2000.

Rendtorff, Rolf. "How to Read the Book of the Twelve as a Theological Unity." In *Reading and Hearing the Book of the Twelve*, edited by James Nogalski and Marvin A. Sweeney, 75–87. SymS 15. Atlanta: SBL, 2000.

Riesner, Rainer. *Paul's Early Period: Chronology, Mission Strategy, Theology*. Grand Rapids: Eerdmans, 1998.

Ringgren, H. "Jüdische Apokalyptik." *RGG* 3 (1912) 464–66.

Rives, J. B. "The Decree of Decius and the Religion of Empire." *JRS* 89 (1999) 135–54.

Roberts, J. J. M. *Nahum, Habakkuk, and Zephaniah*. OTL. Louisville: Westminster John Knox, 1991.

Robertson, A. T. *A Grammar of the Greek New Testament in the Light of Historical Research*. London: Hodder & Stoughton, 1919.

Robertson, O. Palmer. *The Books of Nahum, Habakkuk, and Zephaniah*. NICOT. Grand Rapids: Eerdmans, 1990.

Robinson, Bernard P. "Characterization in the Hagar and Ishmael Narratives." *SJOT* 27, no. 2 (2013) 198–215.

Robinson, H. Wheeler. *Corporate Personality in Ancient Israel*. Philadelphia: Fortress, 1980.

Robinson, O. F. *The Criminal Law of Ancient Rome*. Baltimore: Johns Hopkins University Press, 1996.

Rosner, Brian S. *Paul and the Law: Keeping the Commandments of God*. NSBT. Downers Grove, IL: IVP Academic, 2013.

Routledge, Robin. "Is There a Narrative Substructure Underlying the Book of Isaiah?" *TynBul* 55, no. 2 (2004) 183–204.

Ruiten, Jaques T. A. G. M. van. *Abraham in the Book of Jubilees: The Rewriting of Genesis 11:26—25:10 in the Book of Jubilees 11:14—23:8*. JSJSup 161. Leiden: Brill, 2012.

———. *Primaeval History Interpreted: The Rewriting of Genesis 1–11 in the Book of Jubilees*. JSJSup 66. Leiden: Brill, 2000.

Ruprecht, Eberhard. "Der Traditionsgeschichtliche Hintergrund der Einzelnen Elemente von Genesis XII 2–3." *VT* 29, no. 4 (1979) 444–64.

———. "Vorgegebene Tradition und Theologische Gestaltung in Genesis XII 1–3." *VT* 29, no. 2 (1979) 171–88.

Rusam, Dietrich. "Neue Belege zu den Στοιχεῖα Τοῦ Κόσμου (Gal 4,3.9; Kol 2,8.20)." *ZNW* 83 (1992) 119–25.

Russell, Walter Bo. "Does the Christian Have 'Flesh' in Gal 5:13–26." *JETS* 36, no. 2 (1993) 179–87.

———. *The Flesh/Spirit Conflict in Galatians*. Lanham, MD: University Press of America, 1997.

Sailhamer, John. "Creation, Genesis 1–11, and the Canon." *BBR* 10, no. 1 (2000) 89–106.

Sanders, E. P. *Paul and Palestinian Judaism: A Comparison of Patterns of Religion*. Philadelphia: Fortress, 1977.

Sandnes, Karl Olav. *Paul, One of the Prophets? A Contribution to the Apostle's Self-Understanding*. WUNT 2.43. Tübingen: Mohr Siebeck, 1991.

Sänger, Dieter. "Ἰουδαϊσμός—ἰουδαΐζειν—ἰουδαϊκῶς: Sprachliche und semantische Überlegungen im Blick auf Gal 1,13 f. und 2,14." *ZNW* 108, no. 1 (2017) 150–85.
Sarna, Nahum M. *Genesis*. The JPS Torah Commentary. Philadelphia: Jewish Publication Society, 1989.
Schart, Aaron. *Die Entstehung des Zwölfprophetenbuchs: Neubearbeitungen von Amos im Rahmen schriftenübergreifender Redaktionsprozesse*. BZAW 260. Berlin: De Gruyter, 1998.
Schechter, Solomon. *Fragments of a Zadokite Work*. Documents of the Jewish Secretaries 1. Cambridge: Cambridge University Press, 1910.
Scheuer, Blaženka. *The Return of YHWH: The Tension between Deliverance and Repentance in Isaiah 40–55*. BZAW 377. Berlin: De Gruyter, 2008.
Schlier, Heinrich. *Der Brief an die Galater*. KEK. Göttingen: Vandenhoeck & Ruprecht, 1951.
Schnabel, Eckhard J. *Acts*. ZECNT. Grand Rapids: Zondervan, 2012.
———. "Divine Tyranny and Public Humiliation: A Suggestion for the Interpretation of the Lydian and Phrygian Confession Inscriptions." *NovT* 45, no. 2 (2003) 160–88.
Schomer, Justus Christoph. *Exegesis in Omnes Epistolas S. Pauli Minores, Ad Galatas, Ad Ephesios, Ad Philippenses, Ad Colossenses, Utramque Ad Thessalonicenses, Utramque Ad Timotheum, Ad Titum & Ad Philemonem*. Rostock, Germ.: Weppling, 1706.
Schreiner, Josef. *Das 4. Buch Esra*. Jüdische Schriften aus hellenistisch-römischer Zeit 5/4. Gütersloh: Mohn, 1981.
Schreiner, Thomas R. *Galatians*. ZECNT. Grand Rapids: Zondervan, 2010.
———. *New Testament Theology: Magnifying God in Christ*. Grand Rapids: Baker Academic, 2008.
———. *Paul, Apostle of God's Glory in Christ: A Pauline Theology*. Downers Grove, IL: IVP Academic, 2001.
Schultz, Brian. *Conquering the World: The War Scroll (1QM) Reconsidered*. STDJ 76. Leiden: Brill, 2009.
———. "The Kittim of Assyria." *RevQ* 23, no. 1 (2007) 63–77.
Schultz, Richard L. "The Origins and Basic Arguments of the Multi-Author View of the Composition of Isaiah: Where Are We Now and How Did We Get Here?" In *Bind Up the Testimony: Explorations in the Genesis of the Book of Isaiah*, edited by Daniel I. Block and Richard L. Schultz, 7–32. Peabody, MA: Hendrickson, 2015.
Schwartz, Daniel R. *2 Maccabees*. CEJL. Berlin: De Gruyter, 2008.
Schwartz, Joshua. "Ishmael at Play: On Exegesis and Jewish Society." *HUCA* 66 (1995) 203–21.
Schweitzer, Albert. *The Quest of the Historical Jesus: A Critical Study of Its Progress from Reimarus to Wrede*. Translated by W. Montgomery. New York: Macmillan, 1968.
Schweizer, Eduard. "Slaves of the Elements and Worshipers of Angels: Gal 4:3, 9 and Col 2:8, 18, 20." *JBL* 107 (1988) 455–68.
Scobie, Charles H. H. *The Ways of Our God: An Approach to Biblical Theology*. Grand Rapids: Eerdmans, 2003.
Scott, Ian W. *Paul's Way of Knowing: Story, Experience, and the Spirit*. Grand Rapids: Baker Academic, 2008.
Scott, James M. *On Earth as in Heaven: The Restoration of Sacred Time and Sacred Space in the Book of Jubilees*. JSJSup 91. Leiden: Brill, 2005.

Segal, Alan F. *Paul the Convert: The Apostolate and Apostasy of Saul the Pharisee*. New Haven: Yale University Press, 1990.

Segal, Michael. *The Book of Jubilees: Rewritten Bible, Redaction, Ideology and Theology*. JSJSup 117. Leiden: Brill, 2007.

Seifrid, Mark A. "Paul, Luther, and Justification in Gal 2:15–21." *WTJ* 65, no. 2 (2003) 215–30.

———. *The Second Letter to the Corinthians*. PNTC. Grand Rapids: Eerdmans, 2014.

Seitz, Christopher R. *Figured Out: Typology and Providence in Christian Scripture*. Louisville: Westminster John Knox, 2001.

Sequeira, Aubrey, and Samuel C. Emadi. "Biblical-Theological Exegesis and the Nature of Typology." *SBJT* 21, no. 1 (2017) 11–34.

Seybold, Klaus, et al., eds. "Der Psalter und seine Redaktionsgeschichte." In *Neue Wege der Psalmenforschung*, 243–77. HBS 1. Freiburg: Herder, 1994.

Shaked, Shaul. "Qumran and Iran: Further Considerations." *IOS* 2 (1972) 433–46.

Sherwin-White, A. N. "Why Were the Early Christians Persecuted?—An Amendment." *Past and Present* 27 (1964) 23–27.

Sigmon, Brian O. "Between Eden and Egypt: Echoes of the Garden Narrative in the Story of Joseph and His Brothers." PhD diss., Marquette University, 2013.

Silva, Moisés. "Eschatological Structures in Galatians." In *To Tell the Mystery: Essays on New Testament Eschatology in Honor of Robert H. Gundry*, edited by Thomas E. Schmidt and Moisés Silva, 140–62. JSNTSup 100. Sheffield: JSOT 1994.

———. "The Truth of the Gospel: Paul's Mission according to Galatians." In *The Gospel to the Nations: Perspectives on Paul's Mission*, edited by Peter Bolt and Mark Thompson, 51–61. Downers Grove, IL: InterVarsity, 2000.

Smith, Barry D. *Paul's Seven Explanations of the Suffering of the Righteous*. StBibLit 47. New York: Lang, 2002.

Smith, Christopher C. "Ἐκκλεῖσαι in Galatians 4:17: The Motif of the Excluded Lover as a Metaphor of Manipulation." *CBQ* 58, no. 3 (1996) 480–99.

Smith, Mark S. "The Concept of the 'City' ('Town') in Ugarit." In *Die Stadt im Zwölfprophetenbuch*, edited by Aaron Schart and Jutta Krispenz, 107–46. BZAW 428. Berlin: De Gruyter, 2012.

———. "The Problem of the God and His Manifestations: The Case of the Baals at Ugarit, with Implications for Yahweh of Various Locales." In *Die Stadt im Zwölfprophetenbuch*, edited by Aaron Schart and Jutta Krispenz, 205–50. BZAW 428. Berlin: De Gruyter, 2012.

Smith, Ralph L. *Micah–Malachi*. WBC. Waco, TX: Word, 1984.

Sollamo, Raija. "War and Violence in the Ideology of the Qumran Community." In *Verbum et Calamus: Semitic and Related Studies in Honour of the Sixtieth Birthday of Professor Tapani Harviainen*, edited by Hannu Juusola et al., 341–52. StudOr. Helsinki: Finish Oriental Society, 2004.

Speiser, E. A. *Genesis*. AB 1. Garden City, NY: Doubleday, 1964.

Starling, David. "Justifying Allegory: Scripture, Rhetoric, and Reason in Galatians 4:21—5:1." *JTI* 9, no. 2 (2015) 227–45.

Ste. Croix, G. E. M. de. "Why Were the Early Christians Persecuted?—A Rejoinder." *Past and Present* 27 (1964) 28–33.

———. "Why Were the Early Christians Persecuted?" *Past and Present* 26 (1963) 6–38.

Steinmann, Andrew E. *Daniel*. Concordia Commentary. St. Louis: Concordia, 2008.

———. "The Shape of Things to Come: The Genre of the Historical Apocalypse in Ancient Jewish and Christian Literature." PhD diss., University of Michigan, 1990.

Steinmetz, Devora. *From Father to Son: Kinship, Conflict, and Continuity in Genesis*. Literary Currents in Biblical Interpretation. Louisville: Westminster John Knox, 1991.
Stendahl, Krister. *Paul among Jews and Gentiles and Other Essays*. Philadelphia: Fortress, 1976.
Stern, Philip D. "The 'Blind Servant' Imagery of Deutero-Isaiah and Its Implications." *Biblica* 75, no. 2 (1994) 224–32.
Stewart, Alexander E. "Narrative World, Rhetorical Logic, and the Voice of the Author in 4 Ezra." *JBL* 132, no. 2 (2013) 373–91.
Stone, Michael E. *Fourth Ezra*. Hermeneia. Minneapolis: Fortress, 1990.
Stuckenbruck, Loren T. "The Book of Jubilees and the Origin of Evil." In *Enoch and the Mosaic Torah: The Evidence of Jubilees*, edited by Gabriele Boccaccini and Giovanni Ibba, 294–308. Grand Rapids: Eerdmans, 2009.
———. *1 Enoch 91–108*. CEJL. Berlin: De Gruyter, 2007.
Sulzbach, Carla. "The Fate of Jerusalem in 2 Baruch and 4 Ezra: From Earth to Heaven and Back?" In *Interpreting 4 Ezra and 2 Baruch: International Studies*, edited by Gabriele Boccaccini and Jason M. Zurawski, 138–52. LSTS 87. London: T. & T. Clark, 2014.
Sweeney, Marvin A. "Structure, Genre, and Intent in the Book of Habakkuk." *VT* 41, no. 1 (1991) 63–83.
Tannehill, Robert C. *Dying and Rising with Christ: A Study in Pauline Theology*. BZNW 32. Berlin: Töpelmann, 1967.
Thielman, Frank. *From Plight to Solution: A Jewish Framework for Understanding Paul's View of the Law in Galatians and Romans*. Supplements to NovT 61. Leiden: Brill, 1989.
———. *Theology of the New Testament: A Canonical and Synthetic Approach*. Grand Rapids: Zondervan, 2005.
Tiemeyer, Lena-Sofia. *For the Comfort of Zion: The Geographical and Theological Location of Isaiah 40–55*. VTSup 139. Leiden: Brill, 2011.
Tilly, Michael. *1 Makkabäer*. HThKAT. Freiburg: Herder, 2015.
Tov, Emanuel, and John Strugnell, eds. *Discoveries in the Judaean Desert*. 40 vols. Oxford: Clarendon, 1955–2009.
Treier, Daniel J. "Typology." In *Dictionary for the Theological Interpretation of the Bible*, edited by Kevin J. Vanhoozer. Grand Rapids: Baker Academic, 2005.
VanderKam, James C. *The Book of Jubilees: A Critical Text*. CSCO 510. Leuven, Belg.: Peeters, 1989.
———. *The Book of Jubilees*. Guides to Apocrypha and Pseudepigrapha. Sheffield: Sheffield Academic Press, 2001.
———. *Calendars in the Dead Sea Scrolls: Measuring Time*. Literature of the Dead Sea Scrolls. London: Routledge, 1998.
———. "Daniel 7 in the Similitudes of Enoch (1 Enoch 37–71)." In *Biblical Traditions in Transmission: Essays in Honour of Michael A. Knibb*, edited by Charlotte Hempel and Judith M. Lieu, 291–307. JSJSup 111. Leiden: Brill, 2006.
Van Deventer, Hans J. M. "The End of the End, or, What Is the Deuteronomist (Still) Doing in Daniel?" In *Past, Present, Future: The Deuteronomistic History and the Prophets*, edited by Johannes C. de Moor and Harry F. van Rooy, 62–75. OtSt 44. Leiden: Brill, 2000.
Vanhoye, Albert. "La Définition de l' "autre Évangile" En Ga 1,6–7." *Biblica* 83, no. 3 (2002) 392–98.

———. "Médiateur des anges en Ga 3:19-20." *Biblica* 59, no. 3 (1978) 403-11.

Van Voorst, Robert E. "Why Is There No Thanksgiving Period in Galatians? An Assessment of an Exegetical Commonplace." *JBL* 129, no. 1 (2010) 153-72.

Vermes, Geza. *The Complete Dead Sea Scrolls in English*. London: Penguin, 2011.

Von Rad, Gerhard. *Genesis*. OTL. Philadelphia: Westminster, 1972.

———. *Old Testament Theology*. Vol. 2, *The Theology of Israel's Prophetic Traditions*. Translated by D. M. G. Stalker. OTL. Louisville: Westminster John Knox, 1965.

———. *Wisdom in Israel*. Translated by J. Martin. Nashville: Abingdon, 1972.

Wacholder, Ben Zion. *The New Damascus Document: The Midrash on the Eschatological Torah of the Dead Sea Scrolls: Reconstruction, Translation and Commentary*. STDJ 56. Leiden: Brill, 2007.

———. "The Teacher of Righteousness Is Alive, Awaiting the Messiah: האסף in CD as Allusion to the Sinaitic and Damascene Covenants." *HUCA* 70/71 (1999) 75-92.

Wallace, Daniel B. *Greek Grammar Beyond the Basics: An Exegetical Syntax of the New Testament*. Grand Rapids: Zondervan, 1996.

Walter, Nikolaus. "Paul and the Opponents of the Christ-Gospel in Galatia." In *The Galatians Debate: Contemporary Issues in Rhetorical and Historical Interpretation*, edited by Mark D. Nanos, 362-66. Peabody, MA: Hendrickson, 2002.

Waltke, Bruce K. "A Canonical Process Approach to the Psalms." In *Tradition and Testament: Essays in Honor of Charles Lee Feinberg*, edited by John S. Feinberg and Paul D. Feinberg, 3-18. Chicago: Moody, 1981.

———. *Genesis: A Commentary*. Grand Rapids: Zondervan, 2001.

Walton, John H. "Psalms: A Cantata about the Davidic Covenant." *JETS* 34, no. 1 (1991) 21-31.

Warfield, B. B. *The Inspiration and Authority of the Bible*. Philadelphia: Presbyterian & Reformed, 1948.

Watson, Francis. *Paul, Judaism, and the Gentiles: A Sociological Approach*. Cambridge: Cambridge University Press, 1986.

———. *Paul, Judaism, and the Gentiles: A Sociological Approach*. Grand Rapids: Eerdmans, 2007.

Watts, John D. W. *Isaiah 34-66*. WBC. Waco, TX: Word, 1987.

Weima, Jeffrey A. D. "Gal 6.11-18: A Hermeneutical Key to the Galatian Letter." *CTJ* 28 (1993) 90-107.

Weiser, Artur. *The Psalms*. OTL. London: SCM, 1962.

Weitzman, Steven. "Warring against Terror: The War Scroll and the Mobilization of Emotion." *JSJ* 40, no. 2 (2009) 213-41.

Wellhausen, Julius. *Prolegomena to the History of Ancient Israel*. Translated by J. Sutherland Black and Allan Menzies. Edinburgh: Black, 1885.

Wenham, Gordon J. *Genesis 1-15*. WBC. Waco, TX: Word, 1987.

———. *Genesis 16-50*. WBC. Dallas: Word, 1994.

———. *Psalms as Torah: Reading Biblical Song Ethically*. Grand Rapids: Baker Academic, 2012.

———. "Towards a Canonical Reading of the Psalms." In *Canon and Biblical Interpretation*, edited by Craig G. Bartholomew et al., 333-51. Scripture and Hermeneutics 7. Grand Rapids: Zondervan, 2006.

Wénin, André. "La fraternité, 'projet éthique' dans les récits de la Genèse." *FoiVie* 104, no. 4 (2005) 24-35.

———. "Ismaël et Isaac, ou la fraternité contrariée dans le récit de la Genèse." *ETR* 90, no. 4 (2015) 489–502.
Westerholm, Stephen. *Justification Reconsidered: Rethinking a Pauline Theme*. Grand Rapids: Eerdmans, 2013.
———. *Perspectives Old and New on Paul: The "Lutheran" Paul and His Critics*. Grand Rapids: Eerdmans, 2004.
Westermann, Claus. *Genesis 1–11*. Translated by John J. Scullion. Minneapolis: Augsburg, 1984.
———. *Isaiah 40–66*. OTL. Philadelphia: Westminster, 1969.
———. *Praise and Lament in the Psalms*. Translated by Keith R. Crim and Richard N. Soulen. Atlanta: John Knox, 1981.
Whitehead, Philip. "Habakkuk and the Problem of Suffering: Theodicy Deferred." *JTI* 10, no. 2 (2016) 265–81.
Wilken, Robert Louis. "In Defense of Allegory." *ModTh* 14, no. 2 (1998) 197–212.
Wilk, Florian. *Die Bedeutung des Jesajabuches für Paulus*. FRLANT 179. Göttingen: Vandenhoeck & Ruprecht, 1998.
Willett, Tom W. *Eschatology in the Theodicies of 2 Baruch and 4 Ezra*. JSPSup 4. Sheffield: Sheffield Academic Press, 1989.
Williams, Jarvis J. *Christ Died for Our Sins: Representation and Substitution in Romans and Their Jewish Martyrological Background*. Eugene, OR: Pickwick, 2015.
———. *One New Man: The Cross and Racial Reconciliation in Pauline Theology*. Nashville: B&H Academic, 2010.
Williams, Sam K. *Galatians*. ANTC. Nashville: Abingdon, 1997.
Willitts, Joel. "Isa 54,1 in Gal 4,24b–27: Reading Genesis in Light of Isaiah." *ZNW* 96 (2005) 188–210.
Wilshire, Leland E. "The Servant-City: A New Interpretation of the Servant of the Lord in the Servant Songs of Deutero-Isaiah." *JBL* 94, no. 3 (1975) 356–67.
Wilson, Gerald H. *The Editing of the Hebrew Psalter*. SBLDS 76. Chico, CA: Scholars, 1985.
———. "Evidence of Editorial Division in the Hebrew Psalter." *VT* 34, no. 3 (1984) 336–52.
———. "The Shape of the Book of Psalms." *Int* 46, no. 2 (1992) 129–42.
———. "Shaping the Psalter: A Consideration of Editorial Linkage in the Book of Psalms." In *The Shape and Shaping of the Psalter*, edited by J. Clinton McCann, 72–82. JSOTSup 159. Sheffield: JSOT 1993.
Wilson, Todd A. *The Curse of the Law and the Crisis in Galatia: Reassessing the Purpose of Galatians*. WUNT 2.225. Tübingen: Mohr Siebeck, 2007.
Winter, Bruce W. *Divine Honours for the Caesars: The First Christians' Responses*. Grand Rapids: Eerdmans, 2015.
———. *Seek the Welfare of the City: Christians as Benefactors and Citizens*. First Century Christians in the Graeco-Roman World. Grand Rapids: Eerdmans, 1994.
Wischmeyer, Oda. "ΦΥΣΙΣ und ΚΤΙΣΙΣ bei Paulus: Die paulinische Rede von Schöpfung und Natur." *ZTK* 93, no. 3 (1996) 352–75.
Witherington, Ben, III. *Grace in Galatia: A Commentary on St. Paul's Letter to the Galatians*. Grand Rapids: Eerdmans, 1998.
———. *Isaiah Old and New: Exegesis, Intertextuality, and Hermeneutics*. Minneapolis: Fortress, 2017.

Witulski, Thomas. *Die Adressaten des Galaterbriefes: Untersuchungen zur Gemeinde von Antiochia ad Pisidiam*. FRLANT 193. Göttingen: Vandenhoeck & Ruprecht, 2000.

Woude, Adam S. van der. "Wicked Priest or Wicked Priests? Reflections on the Identification of the Wicked Priest in the Habakkuk Commentary." *JJS* 33, no. 1–2 (1982) 349–59.

Woyke, Johannes. "Nochmals zu den 'schwachen und unfähigen Elementen' (Gal 4.9) Paulus, Philo und die στοιχεῖα τοῦ κόσμου." *NTS* 54, no. 2 (2008) 221–34.

Wright, N. T. *The Climax of the Covenant: Christ and the Law in Pauline Theology*. Edinburgh: T. & T. Clark, 1991.

———. *Justification: God's Plan and Paul's Vision*. Downers Grove, IL: IVP Academic, 2009.

———. *Paul and His Recent Interpreters*. Minneapolis: Fortress, 2015.

———. *Paul and the Faithfulness of God*. 2 vols. Origins and the Question of God. Minneapolis: Fortress, 2013.

Yadin, Yigael. *The Scroll of the War of the Sons of Light against the Sons of Darkness*. Translated by Batya Rabin and Chaim Rabin. Oxford: Oxford University Press, 1962.

Yates, John W. *The Spirit and Creation in Paul*. WUNT 2.251. Tübingen: Mohr Siebeck, 2008.

Yoder Neufeld, Thomas R. *Put on the Armour of God: The Divine Warrior from Isaiah to Ephesians*. JSNTSup 140. Sheffield: Sheffield Academic Press, 1997.

Young, Edward J. *The Book of Isaiah*. 3 vols. NICOT. Grand Rapids: Eerdmans, 1972.

Zaehner, Robert Charles. *Zurvan: A Zoroastrian Dilemma*. New York: Biblo and Tannen, 1955.

Zakai, Avihu, and David Weinstein. "Erich Auerbach and His 'Figura': An Apology for the Old Testament in an Age of Aryan Philology." *Religions* 3 (2012) 320–38.

Zakovitch, Yair. "On the Ordering of Psalms as Demonstrated by Psalms 136–150." In *The Oxford Handbook of the Psalms*, edited by William P. Brown, 214–28. Oxford: Oxford University Press, 2014.

Zenger, Erich. "The Composition and Theology of the Fifth Book of Psalms, Psalms 107–145." *JSOT* 23, no. 80 (1998) 77–102.

Zerbe, Gordon Mark. *Non-Retaliation in Early Jewish and New Testament Texts: Ethical Themes in Social Contexts*. JSPSup 13. Sheffield: Sheffield Academic Press, 1993.

Zucker, David J. "Isaac: A Life of Bitter Laughter." *JBQ* 40, no. 2 (2012) 105–10.

———. "What Sarah Saw: Envisioning Genesis 21:9–10." *JBQ* 36, no. 1 (2008) 54–62.

Ancient Documents Index

OLD TESTAMENT

Genesis

1:1	36n35, 58, 161
1:3	58n21
1:26–30	58
1:28	58
1:31	59
2:4	57
3:1–13	59
3:15	15, 59, 76n126, 161–65, 174
3:17–19	59
3:24	166
4:1–16	59, 164
4:16	166
5:1	57
6:1–4	85, 94
6:9	57
6:17	58
9:1	58
9:7	58
9:18–28	162
10:1	57
10:9–10	75n120
11:1–9	70n89
11:2	82n8
11:4	75n120
11:8–9	58
11:10	57
11:27	57
12:1–2	60, 161
12:3	57–58, 161
12:10–20	59n30, 60
12:15	161
12:17	57
13:15	57
14	60–61
15	61
15:6	56
16	61
16:1–12	164
16:1–4	59n30
16:14	164n93
16:21	164
17:7–14	132, 141
17:7	57
17:17	157, 165
17:18–21	164
18:12	157, 165
18:13	157
18:15	157, 165
18:18	57
19:4–11	59n30
19:14	157
19:30–38	59n30, 162
20	61
20:1–18	59n30
21:3	165
21:6	157, 165
21:9	4, 143–75
21:10	57, 144n5, 149–50, 166
21:12	165–66
21:21	166
22:18	57

Genesis (continued)

24:7	57
24:62	164n93
25:11	164n93
25:12	57
25:19	57
25:26	89
26:4	57
26:6–11	59n30
26:8	157–58
27:41	163
28:6–9	164n93
28:14	57
29:30	59n30
30:5	59n30
30:9	59n30
32:13	33n20
34:1–4	59n30
34:17	159–60
34:25–29	162
35:2–4	162
35:22	59n30, 162
36:1	57
36:9	57
37:2	57
37:5–11	163
37:12–36	162
37:19–22	163
38:1–30	59n30, 162
39:7–20	59n30
39:14	157
39:17	157
41:57	58, 61, 161
47:10	61
49:1	61

Exodus

3:7	21
15	55
15:1–21	71
32:4	158n66
32:6	157–58, 160

Leviticus

19:28	119–20

Numbers

25:10–18	96, 116

Deuteronomy

4:26	37n35
17:14–20	63
23:2–9	168n106
33:2	76n124

Judges

5	55, 71
5:4	76n124
16:25	157–58
16:27	157

1 Samuel

18:7	157
17:37	33n20

2 Samuel

2:14	157–58
6:5	157–58
6:21	157–58
19:9	102n113
22	71

2 Kings

6:17	97n88, 99
7:6	97n88
7:8	99
19:35	97n88
23:28–30	75n117

1 Chronicles

13:8	157–58
15:29	157–58
16:31	37n35

2 Chronicles

30:10	157
32:20–21	97n88
35:20–27	75n117

Esther

9:26	133

Job

5:22	157
8:21	157
12:4	157
29:24	157
30:1	157
39:7	157
39:18	157
39:22	157
40:20	157
40:29	157–58
41:21	157

Psalms

1	61–64, 66–67
2	61–64, 66–67
2:4	157
3–7	63n57
3	63–64, 67
6	62
10	61n43
22	62
37	62
37:14	157
44	61n43
52:8	157
57:8–12	66n68
58:2	33n20
59:9	157
60:7–14	66n68
68	55, 71
87:5	61
104:26	157
107–150	65–67
108	66
110:4	148n23
118–119	66
118	65n64
119	65n66
125:5	61
126:2	157
128:6	61
143:2	45, 61
144	66–67
145	67
146–150	67
146:16	37n35
150	64

Proverbs

1:26	157
8:30	157
8:31	157
10:23	157
14:3	157
26:19	157–58, 160
29:9	157
31:25	157

Ecclesiastes

2:2	157
3:4	157
7:3	157
7:6	157
10:19	157

Isaiah

3:16	158
7–12	97
7:9	69
13:6–8	123n62
14:32	69
19:23–25	69n89
37:19	67
37:36	97n88
39	97
39:1–8	68
40–66	36, 67–73
40–55	37, 68–70
40	69
40:3	103
43:8	37n43
43:18–19	36
45:7	102n113
45:10	123n62
48:1–8	36
49–54	22–24
49:1–6	22
49:1	67

Isaiah (continued)

49:16	90
51:2	146
52:13–53:12	161n79
53	24n164
53:5	8
53:5–6	22
53:10	8, 22
53:12	22
54:1	67, 123, 146–47
56–66	70–73
59	71
60–62	72
63	71
64:10	147
65–66	37, 71–72, 147
65:7	36
65:17	37n43
65:17–18	36
66:22	36

Jeremiah

2:24	164n91
6:24	123n62
15:17	157–58
20:7	157
30:19	157
31:4	157
31:31	105
37:19	158
38:4	158
48:26–27	157
48:39	157

Lamentations

1:7	157
3:14	157

Ezekiel

23:32	157

Daniel

1–6	82–83, 109
1:1–2	82
2	83
3	8, 83
6	8
7	83–84, 92, 109
7:13–14	87
7:24	84
8–12	84
8:14	84
8:23	8
9:2	84
9:3–19	109
9:24–26	84
9:24	8
10	108
11:20	97n88
11:35	8
11:40–45	106n130
12	84

Hosea

8:9	164n91

Joel

1:15	73n110
2:1	73n110
2:11	73n110
3:4	73n110
4:14	73n110

Amos

5:18	73n110
5:20	73n110
6:6	133

Obadiah

15	73n110

Micah

4:10	123n62

Habakkuk

1	74–75
1:2–4	74n117
1:10	157
2	75–76

ANCIENT DOCUMENTS INDEX

2:4	73, 77
3	55, 76
3:16–19	76

Zephaniah

1:7	73n110
1:14	73n110

Zechariah

8:5	157–58
11:5	133
14	55

Malachi

3:23	73n110

NEW TESTAMENT

Matthew

5:11	113n7
12:40	145
13:40	145
16:21	133
23:35	167n101
24:27	145–46
24:37	145–46

Luke

11:51	167n101
14:27	120
17:24	145–46
23:2	131n112

John

2:17	116
5:21	145–46
5:26	145–46
19:12–16	131n112
19:17	120

Acts

3:18	133
4:35	115n12
4:37	115n12
5:2	115n12
5:17	116
7:10	33n20
7:34	33n20
7:52	113n7
7:58	115
8:1	115
8:3	115
9:1–2	115
9:13–14	115n14
9:21	115n14
13:13–14:23	124, 126, 130–31, 139, 141
13:14–52	117
13:45	116
13:50	134
14:1–23	117
14:5	134
14:8–20	121
14:19	134
14:22	134
17:5–9	134
17:5	116n20
17:6–8	131n112
17:13	140
18:17	134
22:3–4	116
23:2–9	131n112
23:27	33n20
26:9–12	115
26:17	33n20

Romans

1:20	36
1:25	36
5:12	145
5:19	145
5:21	145–46
6:4	145–46
6:19	145–46
8:15	114n8
8:19–22	36
8:39	36

Romans (continued)

10:2	135
12:2	31, 32n18
12:14	113n7
13:13	116n20

1 Corinthians

1:20–28	33
1:20	31–32
2:6–8	31–32
2:6	33
2:13	33
3:18–19	33
3:18	31–32
3:22	33
4:9	33, 113n7
4:12	113n7
4:13	33
5:10	33
6:2	33
7:31	33
7:33–34	33
8:4	33
10:7	158n66
10:11	31, 148
11:12	145
11:32	33
12:26	133
12:31	135
13:14	116n20
14:1	135
14:10	33
14:12	116n20
14:39	135
15:2	170n121
15:9	113n7, 115
15:22	145–46
16:1	145

2 Corinthians

1:6	133
2:14–3:3	122
4:4	31–32
4:6	37
4:10	120
4:14	180
5:15	38
5:17	36, 37
5:18–19	38
7:7	135
11:2	135
11:23–33	121

Galatians

1:3	22, 173
1:4–5	31
1:4	3, 9, 30, 32, 39–40, 47, 52, 79, 123, 172, 177
1:6–9	41, 178
1:6	134, 141
1:7	140
1:8–9	114n8, 141
1:10–24	42–43
1:10	22, 172–73
1:13–14	10, 18, 125, 135, 167–69
1:13	113–16, 140–41, 168, 171n122, 179
1:14	116, 135
1:15–16	22
1:15	67
1:16	110, 123, 180
1:22	124–25
1:23	113–17, 140–41, 167–69, 179
2:1–3:29	51
2:2–21	43–45
2:4–5	41
2:4	18, 131, 141, 173
2:7–10	110
2:12	125, 136
2:14	41
2:16	61, 128
2:19–21	6, 35, 114n8, 118–19, 173n131
2:20–21	40
2:20	22
2:21	139n147, 172n127
3:1–14	17, 45–46
3:1–5	119n33
3:1	40, 114, 118–19, 124, 140–41

… ANCIENT DOCUMENTS INDEX   217

Reference	Pages
3:2	134
3:3–4	9
3:4	21, 22, 114, 132–35, 139–41, 169–70
3:6–4:11	141, 148
3:6	56
3:7–9	110
3:8	56
3:10–14	114n8
3:10	45, 56
3:11	73
3:13	56
3:15–29	46–47
3:16	57, 172
3:21	139n147
3:22	47, 56
3:23–25	35
3:28	180
3:29	146, 172–73
4	47–48
4:3–7	172
4:3–5	3, 34
4:3	33, 39, 172
4:4–7	40, 173
4:6–7	22
4:6	21, 114n8
4:7	148, 150
4:8–11	3, 39
4:8	67
4:9	34, 140–41, 150
4:10	35, 127
4:11	170n121
4:12–5:1	22
4:12–15	9, 119n33
4:13	114, 120–22, 124
4:14	121n51
4:15	142
4:16–20	137
4:16	41, 142
4:17–19	114
4:17–18	135–37, 141
4:17	139, 141
4:19	123–24, 137, 142
4:21–5:1	57, 137–38, 144–49
4:21–22	154
4:21	56, 148
4:22	56
4:24	147–48
4:25–31	124
4:25–26	123
4:26	39, 61, 148
4:27	56, 67, 123, 154
4:28	145–46, 150
4:29	4, 16, 22–24, 51, 113–14, 132, 137–41, 143–75, 178–79
4:30	21, 56–57, 144n5, 149, 154, 167
4:31	146
5:1	48, 79, 123, 140–41, 150, 172–73, 180
5:4	20, 136, 141, 150
5:5	29, 38–39
5:6	38
5:7	141
5:9	167
5:10	140
5:11	40, 113–14, 117–18, 122, 124, 135, 141, 171–72, 178
5:12	20, 140
5:13–6:10	17, 49–51
5:13–26	114n8
5:16	142
5:17	3, 167
5:21	29, 38–39
5:22–23	38
5:24–25	6
6:8	29, 31, 38–39
6:11–17	18, 20, 22
6:12–13	120, 136–37, 141, 171
6:12	113–14, 122, 124–32, 135, 139–41, 170–72, 178–79
6:14–15	3, 6, 30, 35, 39, 118
6:14	33, 40
6:15	36, 38
6:16	29, 38, 61

Galatians (continued)

6:17	9, 114, 119–20, 122, 124, 141, 172–74

Ephesians

1:21	31
2:2	31
2:7	31
3:9	31

Philippians

1:29	133
3:6	113n7, 115

Colossians

1:15	33
1:23	33
1:24–29	119
1:26	31

1 Thessalonians

1:4–6	134
2:1–12	119
2:14	133
3:1–5	180
3:3–5	121
4:1	134

2 Thessalonians

1:5	133
1:12	133

1 Timothy

1:13	115
1:17	31
6:17	31–32

2 Timothy

1:9	31
3:12	179
4:10	31–32

Titus

1:2	31
2:12	31–32
2:14	116n20

Hebrews

5:8	133
11:4	167n101
11:10	48n94
11:16	48n94
11:19	148
12:22	48n94
12:24	167n101
12:26	146
13:14	48n94

James

2:26	145n10
4:2	116n20

1 Peter

2:19	133
3:13	116n20
3:14	140
5:13	70n89

2 Peter

3:6–7	146
3:10	34n23
3:12	34n23
3:13	36n33

Revelation

2:10	133
3:12	48n94
12:13	113n7
17–18	70n89
21:1	36n33
21:2	48n94
21:10–21	48n94

APOCRYPHA

Additions to Daniel 82n7

1 Esdras

5:3	158

1 Maccabees

1:10–15	96
1:33–40	96
1:56–57	96
1:63–64	96
2:24–28	96, 116
2:26	114n9
2:49–50	96
2:50–60	116
2:54	96
3:1–9	96
3:21–22	97, 109
3:59–60	96
4:9–11	96–97
4:24–25	96–97
4:30–33	96–97
5:33	96–97
7:36–38	96–97
7:40–42	96–97
8	97
9:13	96n83
9:46	96–97
9:54–57	96n83
12:1–23	97

2 Maccabees

1:11	97n89
1:17	97n89
1:24–29	97n89
2:17–18	97n89
3:22–34	97
3:39	97
5:2–4	98, 109
6:10–33	98
6:10–17	109
6:12–16	8
6:31	109
7:1–42	98, 99n97
7:9	109
8:2–4	97
8:18	98
8:19	97n88
8:23	98
8:29	97
9:5–12	98
10:4	97
10:16	97
10:27	97
10:29–31	98, 108
10:38	97
11:8–14	98
12:6	97
12:15–16	97
12:28	97
12:36	97
12:41–42	97
13:15	98
14:34–36	97
14:46	97
15:16	98
15:21–24	97
15:22	97n88
15:27	97

4 Maccabees

1:7	99
1:13–35	99
1:18	100
4:10–12	97
5:22–24	100
6:9–10	100
6:28–29	100
6:31–35	99
7:3	98n96, 109
7:19	98n96
9:8	98n96, 100, 109
9:24	100
12:19	100n103
13:1–18	99
13:17	98n96
14:1	100
14:11–17:6	100

4 Maccabees (continued)

15:13	100
15:29	99–100
16:14	100
17:1	100n103
17:7–16	99
17:21–22	100
17:22	8
18:10–19	100

Sirach

32:12	158
47:3	158

Tobit

13:16–17	48n94

Wisdom of Solomon

7:17	34n23
7:17–19	35n25
13:1–2	35n25
19:18	34n23
19:18–20	35n25

∼

OLD TESTAMENT PSEUDEPIGRAPHA

Ascension of Isaiah   8

2 Baruch   13

1:5	91, 109
4:1	91
4:2–6	48n94, 90
12:2–4	92n56
22:4	90
23:4	91
23:7	90
29–30	90
32:1	91
36–39	90
39:7	91, 109
42:2	91
44	91
44:12	37n35
48:18	91
48:22	91
48:42	91, 108
48:46	91
51:7	91
53–74	90
54:5	91
54:15–16	91
54:19	91
54:21	91
56:5	91
56:6	123n62
59:2	91
72:6	91–92, 109
75:2–8	91
76:2–3	111
77:11	91
77:16	91
78:3–5	91
78:5–7	19
78:6–7	92
79:3	91
82:2	90
84:8	19
84:11	91
85:10	90
85:14–15	19

1 Enoch

1–36	13, 85–86
1:2–4	85, 92, 109
1:5–9	86
6–8	108
6–7	86
8	108
10:1–8	86
15:8–16:3	86
19:1	86
37–71	86–87
46	87
51:1–5	87
51:4	109
55:4	86
56:1	86

62:4	123n62
69:3	87
69:7	87
69:11	87
72–82	85
72:1	37n35
91–108	85, 87
93:1–17	87

4 Ezra

	13
3:7–8	88, 108
3:28–35	88, 109
4:2	88
4:26–27	89
4:30–32	88
4:42	123n62
5:50–55	89
6:8–10	89
6:20	89
6:54	88
7:11–12	88
7:20	90
7:26	48n94, 89, 109
7:48	88–90
7:51	90
7:76–87	89
7:113	89
7:118	89
8:1	90
8:3	90
8:52	89
9:1–2	89
9:18–22	90
12:31–34	89
13:8–45	89, 92, 109
14:10–12	89
14:13–18	89
14:17	89

Jubilees

1:1–2:1	93
1:11	94
1:13–18	95, 109
1:20	95
1:29	37n35, 93, 95, 109
2:2	94
3	93
4:1	93
4:21–22	94, 108
4:26	37n35, 95
5:1	94
5:9	94
6:36–37	94n68
7:21–25	94
8:1–4	94
10:1–6	94, 108
10:7–9	94
11:4–5	94
11:9–22	94
12:1–27	94
15:31–33	95, 109, 111
17:4	160
17:16	94
18:12	94
19:28	95
22:17	94
23:11–21	95
23:22–32	95
48	95
49:2	95

Letter of Aristeas

214	133n119

DEAD SEA SCROLLS

Pesher Habakkuk

VIII, 8–9	104

War Scroll

I, 1	106–7
I, 4–5	106
I, 5	109
I, 10	106
I, 14	106–7
II, 6–14	106, 111
II, 8	106n133
III–IV	107
XI, 1–5	107

War Scroll (continued)

XI, 8	107
XI, 9–10	107, 109
XII, 7–9	107
XIII	106

Community Rule

I, 9–10	101
I, 18	102
II, 19	102
III, 17–25	101–2
III, 18	103
III, 20–23	108
III, 25	108
IV, 2–14	102
IV, 15–26	102
VIII, 13–16	102–3
IX, 11	102–3
X, 21	102

Damascus Document

I, 5–18	104
III, 1–11	104
III, 20	105
IV, 13–18	105
V, 18–19	104–5, 109
VI, 4–21	105
VII, 20–VIII, 3	105
IX–XVI	105
XX, 15	105

Temple Scroll

| II | 107n139 |

~

PHILO

De aeternitate mundi

| 107 | 34n23 |

De vita contemplativa

| 1.3 | 35n25 |

~

JOSEPHUS

Jewish Antiquities

| 1.215 | 151n36, 160n75 |
| 3.312 | 133n119 |

~

RABBINIC TEXTS

Tosefta Soṭah

| 6.6 | 151n36, 159n69 |

Targum Onqelos

| Gen 21:9 | 151n36, 160n72 |

Targum Pseudo-Jonathan

| Gen 21:9–11 | 151n36, 160n71 |

Targum Jonathan

| Gen 21:9 | 160n71 |

Pesiqta Rabbati

| 48.2 | 151n36, 160n73 |

Pirqe Rabbi Eliezer

| 30 | 151n36 |

Genesis Rabbah

| 53.11 | 159–60 |

Exodus Rabbah

| 1.1 | 160n71 |

ANCIENT NEAR EASTERN TEXTS

Enuma Elish

4 — 71n96

Yasna

30–31 — 102n112

CLASSICAL TEXTS

Aristophanes, *Birds*

660 — 159

Herodotus, *Histories*

1.114 — 159

Homeric Hymns

3.204–6 — 159

Plato, *Symposium*

174e — 133n119

Pliny the Younger, *Epistulae*

10.96–97 — 129

Plutarch, *De Iside et Osiride*

46–47 — 102n112

Suetonius, *Divus Claudius*

25 — 129

Valerius Maximus

9.2.1 — 116n13